# Trusting Toddlers

# Trusting Toddlers
## Planning for One- to Three-Year-Olds in Child Care Centers

Anne Stonehouse

Editor

Original edition published by:
Australian Early Childhood Association Inc.

North American edition published by:
Redleaf Press
a division of Resources for Child Caring

# Dedication

To my friend, Jennifer Brickmayer, who first taught me to be sensitive to and to appreciate toddlers in general;

And to Daniel and Eric, who have taught me more than anyone else about toddlers and other things, and who continue to teach me.

Published by:   Redleaf Press
                formerly Toys 'n Things Press
                a division of Resources for Child Caring
                450 North Syndicate  Suite 5
                St. Paul, Minnesota  55104-4125

Distributed by: Gryphon House
                PO Box 275
                Mt. Rainier, Maryland  20712

ISBN: 0-934140-71-5

**Library of Congress Cataloging-in-Publication Data**

Trusting toddlers : planning for one- to three-year-olds in child
    care centers / Anne Stonehouse, editor. – North American ed.
        p.   cm.
    Includes bibliographical references.
    1. Day care centers–Planning. 2. Day care centers–
Australia–Planning. 3. Toddlers–Care. 4. Toddlers–Care–
Australia.
I. Stonehouse, Anne.
HV851.T78  1990                         90-23388

# Contents

# Foreword to North American Edition

Toddlers are a special, wonderful class of people. Like pre-adolescents of junior high age, they don't fit into tidy definitions. Neither dependent infants nor self-reliant preschoolers, toddlers are furiously becoming mobile, verbal, autonomous, social, and truly thoughtful. Yet they are still babies, in almost every sense of the word. Over the last ten years, toddlers have steadily marched, or more accurately wobbled, into organized child care. For the most part, they have not been well served.

More than any other age, toddlers are situationally disadvantaged in child care. Defined by their past and future, they are usually treated either like old babies —inconveniently mobile—or like young imitation preschoolers—regretfully limited in their powers to function in a group. They find themselves too often in "one size fits all" programs, and the size is not geared to their development. They commonly suffer too many restrictions, too much waiting, too many no's, too little privacy and quiet, and too much or too little stimulation. They are made to march to a group drum beat rather than to their own unique and changing rhythms. Toddlers deserve programs of their own, environments of their own, teachers trained specifically in their care, and books of their own. *Trusting Toddlers* is a book that celebrates toddlers and their care, and it belongs only to them and the people who care for them.

The great pleasure in reading and using *Trusting Toddlers* is that here is a book by professionals who have acquired the taste for toddlers—they genuinely appreciate and enjoy toddlers for what they are, not simply what they will become (walking, talking, "teachable" beings). They delight in toddlerhood without flinching from the reality that toddlers can be incredibly annoying: "Toddlers' zest for life, their tireless curiosity and zeal to find out, their total involvement in the here and now makes them exhausting, demanding, and wonderful at the same time." (Stonehouse) The authors' respect and liking for this fascinating period of development comes through on every page and makes this book especially valuable.

What makes *Trusting Toddlers* enormously useful is that the experiences of the authors are in the very real world of child care. They have obviously struggled with making programs work for toddlers and the teachers who care for them. The authors understand child care; that curriculum or "programming" should incorporate every aspect of the day and "includes both *how* and *why* caregivers decide to do what they do with toddlers, as well as *what* they do." (Stonehouse)

Realism tempers all the analysis in *Trusting Toddlers* and the advice offered is down to earth and practical. Although well informed by research and knowledge of the literature, it is not a book of academic prescriptions of "shoulds," or suggestions based on model programs. Nor is it a description of the "best ways to do things." Throughout, the authors recognize that there is often no "best" way, no "right" set of practices or techniques. In a thorough and sensitive chapter on discipline filled with concrete suggestions, Faye McKay ends with a realistic "Unfortunately, there are no magic or foolproof answers. Every situation has to be handled individually and immediately. Children cannot be expected to wait for discipline to happen, while a caregiver considers the options." Pam Schurch's chapter on utilizing a multicultural perspective in toddler programs is filled with imaginative suggestions, and outlines an approach rarely tried (at least in the United States) that has children experience "multiculturalism as a way of life and (be) accepted, even by under threes, as variation in the expression of human existence." There are two valuable discussions of the work life of caregivers in child care, raising issues of the work, stress, and recognition, and looking at working conditions that can improve the lives of child care staff.

This is an Australian book, but that presents no problem to an American audience. Australian toddlers and their programs are quite similar to their American counterparts. The uniqueness of toddler care is shared by both settings and each gains a powerful advantage by examining the solutions of the other. *Trusting Toddlers* is a book for all caregivers, directors, trainers and students who care passionately about toddlers. Every chapter leaves one with a better sense of what toddlers and their care is all about.

*Jim Greenman*

# Foreword to Original Edition

It is with pleasure that I introduce this book, the most recent AECA publication on quality issues in day care. The editor, an eminent writer on children's services, has brought together Australian experts in the field to provide a comprehensive discussion of care for toddlers.

Two features stand out from my reading of the book. The first of these is the importance of respect for children, of regarding and treating children as full human beings. Additionally, Anne Stonehouse and other contributors emphasize the particular needs of toddlers, the need to recognize toddlerhood as a special stage of being with unique needs and demands.

Related to this is the second outstanding feature of the book; its consistent emphasis on the importance of high quality day care for toddlers. At a time when public debate is predominantly on the number of services available at the expense of considerations of quality, this book serves as a cogent reminder of the paramount importance of quality service delivery.

I recommend the book to all involved in care for toddlers and congratulate its authors on a fine contribution to the promotion of high quality care for toddlers.

*Anne Murray, OAM*
*National President, AECA*

# Introduction

The title of this book was chosen carefully. *Trusting Toddlers* reflects the two main themes of the book. These are firstly that one to three year olds are vulnerable human beings in a stage of their development where feeling secure and confident about and comfortable with the adults who are part of their lives is of prime importance. Toddlers trust the adults who care for them, they believe what they are told and absorb from the experiences provided for them messages that stay with them throughout their lives and have a major influence on their development, most particularly their self concept. In short, toddlers are trusting.

Hence one of the most important characteristics of a program of high quality for one to three year olds is the presence of sufficient numbers of warm caring staff that the children can rely on. Staff:child ratios must be high, to permit loving attention and care.

Caregivers must be present for a substantial amount of time, and there must be as few of them totally as possible. How can a toddler come to trust someone who is present only a small amount of time? Similarly, how can a toddler come to trust anyone if the care of that child is shared by large numbers of people? Centers would be advised to monitor carefully the total number of staff involved in the care of one to three year olds, and to be very cautious about using part-time staff or instigating a system of rotating staff through different groups in the center. While there may be some advantages to adults, there are likely to be disadvantageous effects on toddlers' feelings of security.

The second theme of the book is that those who would care well for toddlers must trust them. They must in a sense let the toddlers be the teachers and learn from them. Caring well, interacting effectively, responding sensibly and sensitively, and generally doing the right thing by one to three year olds is the result of watching them and listening to them with an open mind. In other words, programs of high quality happen when staff allow the children they care for to be themselves, and build the program around that. Good caregivers say in their words and interactions with toddlers, "I like you; I accept you as you are; I trust you with your drive to grow and become; I trust myself to be able to meet all of the challenges that will come my way while you are in my care; therefore I can give you room, freedom to become. I trust you to guide me in how to help you".

As with most things, that is easier said than done, particularly when one considers the special challenges this age group presents because of their developmental characteristics. Some people might feel that a further interpretation of the title of the book is that one can trust toddlers trust them to test, to get into things, to defy, to be messy, to be on the go all the time. The lack of highly qualified people with particular expertise and experience with this age group, and the low status and poor working conditions that most staff have to contend with contribute also to the challenge of providing an excellent experience in child care for this age group.

The pages that follow contain the collective wisdom on toddlers in day care of a number of early childhood professionals working in Australia. Consequently, the book contains a number of different perspectives on the topic of providing a program of high quality to children in the second and third years of life. That is both its strength and its weakness. A book with a cast of thousands, such as this one has, cannot achieve a totally cohesive treatment of the topic in the way that a book written by a single author can. Readers will notice some duplication of information in various chapters. However, it is significant that so many authorities, with such diverse backgrounds and experiences of toddlers, have similar priorities when it comes to what is important in programming for this age group.

The scope of the book is limited, as there are some areas not covered at all and others only alluded to briefly. For example, there is no attention to nutritional concerns, family day care settings for this age group, integrating children with special needs, and only brief mention of health concerns. While the importance of these topics and others is acknowledged, as well as the need for resource materials in these areas, the scope of the book could have been broadened only at the expense of the depth of coverage of topics. Given that some authors in the current book complained that they were only able to scratch the surface of their assigned topic with the number of pages they were allowed to use, to have included other topics as well would have resulted in a very superficial treatment of any of them.

The book has been written for practitioners as well as students in early childhood or child care courses, with a deliberate effort to balance a realistic approach to caring for toddlers with clear statements of ideals and what should be worked toward. Hopefully it will reinforce and support many of the practices currently implemented, provide a rationale and a context for others, as well as inform and give new ideas.

*Anne Stonehouse*

# Contributors

**Cynthia a' Beckett** is currently a Senior Tutor in the School of Early Childhood Studies, Brisbane College of Advanced Education. Prior to taking up her current position, she worked for eleven years in preschool, day care, and family support programs in Melbourne, and as a preschool advisor with the Creche and Kindergarten Association in Brisbane.

**Margaret Clyde** is the Principal Lecturer in Early Childhood at Melbourne College of Advanced Education Institute of Early Childhood Development. She is Editor of the Australian Journal of Early Childhood; her interest in toddlers was enhanced by participation in a "First Three Years of Life" Summer School with Burton White in 1976.

**Lyn Fasoli** is a Lecturer in Early Childhood and Child Care at the Darwin Institute of Technology. She has had many years of experience working in a variety of early childhood positions. In 1987 she obtained her Master's Degree from Wheelock College in Boston, Massachusetts.

**Faye McKay** has been a Lecturer in the Child Care Studies Department of Prahran College of TAFE in Melbourne for the past ten years. Her practical experience includes teaching in city and country kindergartens, working for two years as Coordinator of Inservice and Parent Programs at the Melbourne Lady Gowrie Child Centre and rearing her own children.

**Barbara Nielsen** is currently Principal of Lindisfarne Anglican Parish School in Adelaide. In 1985 she was Coordinator of the C Nursery Team at the Adelaide Lady Gowrie Child Centre and Coordinator of Inservice Programs. Prior to that she worked in primary schools in South Australia.

**Bev Olsson** is currently Director of the child care center at Griffith University in Brisbane. Prior to that she was Coordinator of the Day Care Unit at the Brisbane Lady Gowrie Child Centre and contributed to inservice programs for child care staff throughout Queensland. She has had extensive teaching experience in both community kindergartens and long day care.

**Pat Patterson** was for many years Coordinator of Parent and Inservice Programs at the Brisbane Lady Gowrie Child Centre. She has been involved in many aspects of the Centre's work, including research, teaching, writing and video production.

**Marcelle Psaltis** is currently a Lecturer in the Associate Diploma in Social Science (Child Care) at the Perth Community College. She was previously employed at the Darwin Institute of Technology as a Lecturer in Child Care and prior to that at the Perth Lady Gowrie Child Centre where she worked in a variety of positions, the most recent of which was Resource and Development Coordinator.

**Penny Ryan** until recently was Coordinator of Community Child Care in New South Wales. For many years she was involved as a researcher on women's issues in health, education, and the labor movement. She has written widely on these topics. She is also the mother of two children.

**Pam Schurch** is Assistant Director of the Lady Gowrie Child Centre in Sydney. The particular emphasis of her work has been on the education and care of under three year olds, and resource development.

**Patricia Sebastian** is Family and Children's Services Coordinator for the Hawthorn City Council in Melbourne. Prior to that, she was a Lecturer at the Melbourne College of Advanced Education Institute of Early Childhood Development. She is the author of a number of publications, including Handle with Care (AE Press, 1986).

**Anne Stonehouse** is currently Principal Lecturer in Child Care at the Darwin Institute of Technology. She has been Coordinator of Child Care and Parent Programs at the Melbourne Lady Gowrie Child Centre, a Lecturer in the Child Care Course at Prahran College in Melbourne, and worked in infant and toddler programs at Cornell University in the U.S. She has written a number of publications.

# Chapter 1

# Characteristics of Toddlers

## Anne Stonehouse

*This is the "stage setting" chapter, in as much as any interaction with or experience or environment planned for toddlers should be based on their characteristics and needs. Those people who program for toddlers sometimes separate out those characteristics that relate directly to so-called play and learning activities. However, attention in programming must be paid to other characteristics, particularly those in the areas of social and emotional development, the need for a few close relationships with caring adults, and considerable help in getting along with other children. The remaining chapters of this book follow on from this description of toddlers.*

The task of relating sensitively to toddlers and offering an appropriate program is made more difficult when caregivers think of them as being "in between" babies and preschoolers. Toddlerhood is a state of being, with its own developmental characteristics and needs. Gonzalez-Mena (1986) asserts that many descriptions of toddlers come from comparing them with older children and the result is a negative view of toddlers' behavior, a deficit model that emphasizes what toddlers lack. She says that "when teachers or parents think of toddlers as miniature preschoolers, we invite problems because our expectations are not appropriate" (p. 47).

This view of toddlers as being in between is often reflected in child care programs for the age group. Some centers place toddlers in an environment that is more appropriate for babies and is therefore unstimulating and often boring to toddlers. In other centers, the physical environment, the experiences and activities, and even the adults' interactions and communication with toddlers can best be described as a diluted preschool program. This latter type of program often embodies expectations that are too high, resulting in frustration for the caregivers as well as the children.

Admittedly, caring well for any age group involves knowing where they have been and where they are going. Good planning, however, relies most strongly on understanding *where the children are now*, and basing the materials and experiences on that understanding. It is often suggested that one of the outstanding characteristics of toddlers is their fluctuation between two states. Their behavior is at times "babyish", as they appear to want the closeness, the care, the dependency that they had as babies, they sometimes adopt a stance of helplessness, and they demonstrate at times a lack of control that is characteristic of a younger age group. At other times, they surprise their caregivers with

1

their maturity, their wisdom, their self sufficiency. The fact that they can move from one state to the other many times a day and for no apparent reason is one of the factors that makes caring for this age group a particular challenge. This characteristic of toddlers is known in some circles as the "Dr. Jekyll - Mr. Hyde phenomenon".

Toddlers are still a somewhat misunderstood and maligned segment of the population, in that there is, among the community in general, inordinate emphasis placed on their negative or less desirable characteristics. Labels such as "terrible twos" abound, and portrayals of parenting or caregiving for this age group often involve exaggerated accounts of their unpleasant aspects, with the implicit or explicit assumption that the adult's survival is the ultimate aim. In child care this negative view of toddlers is reflected in some centers in a lower standard of program being offered to this age group than to older or younger children. Similarly, caregivers and aspiring caregivers in college training courses often express a preference for older children because "you can do so much with them you can teach them things". In other words, the positive side of toddlers, their strengths, the reasons that some people choose toddlers as their favourite age group to work with, is often overlooked.

Professionals have gone overboard in describing and analyzing the "terrible twos" and highlighting every possible difficulty that may arise with toddlers. One wonders to what extent enhanced awareness of the terrible possibilities contributes to a self-fulfilling prophecy. That is, perhaps part of the reason some toddlers become "terrible twos" is that they are expected to. Most parents and child care workers, especially those who read books, know about biting, possessiveness, egocentrism, lack of self control, defiance, uncooperativeness, "pigheadedness", eating and sleeping problems, volatile emotions, and temper tantrums long before they occur. Knowledge of these is so widespread that toddlers who do not demonstrate all of these qualities are sometimes thought to be abnormal'. It has been said of one very popular book on toddlers that having people read it before becoming parents would be an effective way to lower the birth rate; that is, that readers would be so put off by the description of the trials and traumas of living with

toddlers that they would decide to remain childless! Toddlerhood can be a difficult time for the child and the adults who are caregivers, but for every negative characteristic that is attributed to one to three year olds, there is a positive one.

Toddlers are delightful for many reasons. Their unbridled excitement and enthusiasm for anything that captures their interest—pouring water from one container to another, catching dust particles in a sunbeam, eating spaghetti, making a light come on, for example, brings adults back in touch with the joy of living. Many people admit that one of the best things about working with very young children is that it affords them an acceptable excuse for doing "childish" things—blowing bubbles, building sand castles, chasing balloons. Secondly, the sheer determination of toddlers to master and control far exceeds that of adults. Watch a young toddler, or "wobbler" more accurately, trying to stay upright while traversing a small hill, or observe a two year old who wants to put her shoes on ("Do it myself", she says adamantly, annoyed by your offer of help). There is no doubt that toddlers try longer and harder than most people. The speed and eagerness with which new skills are accomplished, new understandings digested and used, new knowledge sought and applied by toddlers sets a very high standard, and is exhilarating though exhausting to share. Fourthly, expanding ability to communicate in words is perhaps the most universally acknowledged "positive" about toddlers.

The list could go on and on. Toddlers' zest for life, their tireless curiosity and zeal to find out, their total involvement in the here and now makes them exhausting, demanding, and wonderful at the same time. The following pages hopefully convey a realistic picture of working with one to three year olds, but one in which the strengths and delights of toddlers are seen to outweigh the stress, the problems, the negatives.

What follows is not a comprehensive list of characteristics, but rather those that have major implications for providing care of high quality to this age group.

## Person Creating

Many terms are used to describe the phenomenon that Brazelton (1974) calls "person creating". It is referred to also as becoming separate, establishing autonomy, learning assertiveness and becoming independent. Escalona (1974) labels it "the emerging sense of self as an active, motivated, and effective agent" (p. 34). Brazelton and many other experts assert that establishing oneself as a separate human being is the biggest task of toddlerhood. Further, as was stated previously, toddlers are constantly trying to achieve a balance between wanting to be separate and independent, on the one hand, and wanting the security that comes with the closeness and dependence, the "oneness" with the caregiver, that they experienced as babies. This dilemma of wanting two incompatible states of being accounts for much of the turbulence of toddler-hood. Person creating entails the following:

- Being able to make some decisions
- Becoming more self-sufficient
- Resisting coercion and directives from authority figures (in other words, doing exactly the opposite of what the person in charge wants)
- Learning that ones actions have consequences and beginning to take some responsibility for those actions
- Coping with some freedom and choices
- Learning how to influence, to persuade other people.

It is easy to see that this can be an overwhelming task at times for a very young person.

It is interesting to note that person

creating, or defining oneself in relation to other people, happens for the first time in the second or third year of life, but reoccurs throughout life, most typically at adolescence, at the beginning of a marriage or a long term relationship with another adult, with the birth of children, when children grow up and leave home, and when a partner is lost through death, separation, or divorce. All of these life events require reassessment of ones separateness, ones need for independence against the need to care for and be cared for by others (Brazelton, 1974).

Many of the negative labels applied to toddlers, such as aggressive, stubborn, selfish, and naughty, relate to person creating, as do a number of the characteristics which follow.

## Unevenness and Unpredictability

The "Dr. Jekyll and Mr. Hyde" nature of toddlers has been referred to previously. Caregivers of toddlers are often struck by their volatile emotions and dramatic mood swings. They say they do not know what to expect from toddlers from day to day, or even from moment to moment. Toddlers sometimes display understanding, patience, maturity, cooperativeness, independence, a long concentration span, and then instantaneously become just the opposite, and for no apparent reason.

This ability to change makes it easy to expect too much of them. Caregivers may find themselves thinking:

He made it through lunch yesterday without flinging his food, so he should be able to do it today and forever after;

She allowed another child to play with her pile of blocks earlier this morning; therefore she knows to share;

He did not cry last week when his mother left him; he's just screaming to get attention;

She didn't bite anyone this morning; I know she can stop herself.

Unfortunately for those who care for them, the nature of toddlers is to fluctuate between relative maturity and immaturity. That is, doing something once does not mean a toddler is always capable of doing it.

## Fondness for Mobility

One of the most obvious characteristics of toddlers is their fondness for and constant use of their mobility. Toddlers are "on the go" most of the time. In fact, the toddler who has just become mobile has been compared to an adolescent who has just received a driver's licence. Both want to cruise, to move around in space because it feels so good to finally be able to do that independently, without assistance from anyone. Mobility is closely related to person creating for the toddler (and perhaps for the adolescent as well).

Being able to walk gives children a means to try out in a literal sense being separate, moving away, exercising some control over where they are and what they have access to. Programs of high quality should offer toddlers opportunities to use their mobility to broaden their horizons. In fact, provision for moving around is an important part of a "curriculum" for toddlers, as they love large motor activities such as stair climbing, bouncing, jumping, running, pushing things around, and hauling objects.

## Assertiveness

Assertiveness is not the same thing as aggressiveness, although these terms are sometimes confused. Assertiveness is a desirable, positive characteristic, having to do with balancing ones own needs, rights, and wishes against those of other people. Toddlers typically spend a lot of time asserting themselves, and because they are immature and inexperienced, they often do it badly. They test power and limits, sometimes through overt defiance or doing exactly the opposite of what they are told to do. The more the adult asks them to hurry, for example, the slower they go. Or the toddler stares directly at the caregiver, grins broadly, and stands up in the chair or takes a toy from an innocent victim. Older toddlers are masters at teasing or taunting the adult by coming as close as possible to doing something forbidden without quite overstepping the boundaries. For example, a toddler may drop spoonfuls of food off the spoon onto the plate in a very deliberate fashion after having been told not to throw or play with food.

A second manifestation of assertiveness is insistence on "I do it myself" and great pride in accomplishments. Unfortunately, however, toddlers sometimes have an unrealistic sense of omnipotence and think they can do things that they are not capable of. Most caregivers feel powerless when faced with toddlers who insist on doing things they are not capable of, refuse help, but become increasingly frustrated with their ineptitude.

Toddlers are notorious for saying no, perhaps, as has often been suggested, in part because they hear it so frequently. Sometimes indicating a genuine unwillingness to cooperate, "no" may also be a toddler's way of marking a situation in which a choice can be made to go along with the directive or request or to refuse to (Brazelton, 1974). Toddlers sometimes say no to something they actually want. It is as though the need to assert themselves gets in the way. A toddler with bare feet standing on an uncomfortably hot pavement may refuse the adult's directive to put on shoes. A child who has been asking to go outside may resist doing so when the opportunity is offered.

Toddlers, like adults, seem to have a need to communicate to adults that they are doing something because they have chosen to and not because the adult has suggested it or ordered it. The author recalls observing a two and a half year old at a playgroup. As she was uninvolved and wandering aimlessly, the adult in charge, a very skilled preschool teacher tried to get the child to go over to an attractively set up climbing apparatus. In spite of the adult's enthusiasm and skill in communicating with children, and the child's previous enjoyment of climbing activities, she did not show even a glimmer of interest. However, as soon as the adult gave up and moved on to another child, she dashed over to the climbing equipment and played happily for a long time. It was as though she was saying, "I don't want to give you the satisfaction of thinking I am doing this because you suggested it".

Assertiveness sometimes takes the form of refusal to cooperate in routines. All of a sudden having ones face wiped, putting on a sweater to go outside, having a diaper changed, or other routine events that have been part of daily life appear to become unbearable.

Toddlers are notorious for changing their minds. They may ask for an apple and then fling it on the floor in disgust when it is given to them. Sometimes this mind changing may be genuine, as it is difficult to cope with freedom and choices, but sometimes no doubt it represents an attempt to have some power over the adults in charge. Whether the adult allows toddlers to change their minds depends at least in part on the situation and the adult's level of tolerance at the moment, but just as some mind changing is tolerated in adults, so it should be in toddlers when it causes no great inconvenience.

Assertiveness is not a characteristic to be discouraged in toddlers, but rather to be channelled appropriately. Because they are immature and inexperienced, toddlers have little sense of decorum, of their own inadequacies of judgment, and therefore they do not have the ability to discern which are situations when they need to defer to the greater wisdom of adults. Caregivers need to help toddlers become appropriately assertive, to feel that they have choices, some freedom, some power and control over other people and over aspects of their daily experience. This means that sometimes they need to have their way, to win, to persuade others successfully, to negotiate compromises successfully. In order to have those experiences in child care settings, they obviously need adults who are on their side, who are more interested in working with them than having power over them.

## Ritualistic, Set in Their Ways

Some toddlers become set in their ways, and may be compulsive about aspects of their daily routine. They may insist on the same color cup or plate

each day, insist on a ritual at sleep time, protest vigourously if the room is rearranged, refuse carrots that are cut in circles and devour them hungrily if they are in strips, or become very distressed if a female caregiver has a new hairstyle or a male shaves off his beard. It is thought that this characteristic comes from the toddler's need to control and predict daily life to a degree. That is, there are so many aspects of a toddler's life that seem unpredictable, make little sense, or are beyond the child's control, that some toddlers respond by holding dearly to those things that are predictable and secure. One of the challenges for caregivers is to provide an appropriate balance of sameness and novelty in the daily life of a toddler.

## Impulsive, Lacking Self Control

One of the most difficult challenges for the toddler is developing some self control. Comparison of a young baby and a toddler shows the enormous strides that are made in the first three years of life. Babies have no self control. When babies want something they will do anything to get it, and they want it now if not five minutes ago. That is a dramatic contrast to three year olds (on a good day), who have some ability to wait, to do without something they want, to be patient, to stop themselves from doing something they know they should not do. The process of achieving that degree of self control is a difficult one, and full of setbacks.

One of the most difficult characteristics of toddlers for caregivers to be sympathetic toward is their lack of self control. So many times caregivers think or say, "I know Sue knows better, but she does it anyway." Young children will sometimes indicate that they know that what they are doing is not allowed. Picture a toddler standing in front of the video recorder pressing buttons and turning dials and muttering all the while,

"No, no, no". Picture the toddler who comes in and announces solemnly that the book is going for a swim in the toilet. Or a toddler may look at the caregiver with a very knowing look before tipping a cup of juice out on the table.

It must be remembered that knowing what one should do can be a very different matter from having the will power to do it. Talk to smokers who want to stop smoking, or overweight people who would like to be slim. Chances are they can tell you all the reasons why they should stop smoking or overeating, but that does not necessarily mean that they have the will power to do it. The lights and the dials on the video recorder may be so inviting that a toddler may not be able to resist touching them. The biscuits may taste so good that a two year old may not be able to cope with having only one. The ribbon of liquid cascading to the floor may be so interesting that it is impossible not to spill ones milk. Playing in the sandpit may be so much fun that one is incapable of tearing oneself away, even for lunch.

Lack of self control is responsible for one of the most unpleasant phenomena of toddlerhood for both toddlers and the adults who care for them—namely, temper tantrums. There are undoubtedly a variety of explanations for temper tantrums, but the reason that they are just bids for attention, and should therefore be ignored is over used. No doubt temper tantrums are sometimes bids for attention, but often in toddlers they are a way of saying, "I've had it—I can't cope—I'm going to pieces" (Keister, 1972). Someone has said that a temper tantrum is a momentary nervous breakdown. The feelings that cause a toddler to collapse in an incontrollable screaming heap are not very different to those that adults may have at the end of a day when everything has gone wrong. The adult responds by having a few drinks, being short-tempered, or working it out on the squash court. A toddler's ego is fairly fragile and easily shattered by fatigue, frustration, or excitement.

Toddlers often need a gentle but firm adult to help them when they cannot help themselves because of lack of self control, but they need someone who will do it without shaming them or making them feel guilty. They need the security of knowing that someone will help them when they cannot help themselves. Even though they may continue to resist and protest, toddlers can be frightened when they are out of control. They need the security of knowing that they will not be allowed to hurt themselves or other people or the things around them.

## May Develop Fears

It is not uncommon for toddlers to develop fears, the origins of which may be unexplained. They may suddenly become afraid of something that has been part of their environment, such as the vacuum cleaner or the sound of water going down the plug hole in the bath. This characteristic, along with several others, contributes to the feeling that toddlers are unpredictable and somewhat of a mystery. Many of these fears undoubtedly are attributable to the rapid changes in their intellectual growth at this age, which causes them to alter their perspective towards many things.

## Limited Ability to Communicate

In the second and third years of life toddlers make a dramatic increase in their ability to communicate through language. However, they are still limited in their ability to get important messages across clearly to other toddlers and even to adults. Being constantly misunderstood and misinterpreted increases the frustration of being a toddler. Adults who have had the experience of being in a foreign country where they spoke little or none of the language will have no trouble identifying with the dilemma of toddlers.

It is important to remember that toddlers have very strong feelings, such as jealously, rage, anger, frustration, and annoyance, and when they do not have the capacity to express these feelings through language, they will express them in their behavior. For example, it is quite common for toddlers to express boredom or to bid for attention by doing things that they know are not allowed. People who work with toddlers often note a decline in such undesirable behaviors as biting, hitting, temper tantrums, and snatching when the children become more facile verbally.

## Process Orientation, Immersion in the Here and Now

Toddlers have a wonderful capacity to wring out of the most ordinary everyday events and objects something interesting and engrossing. Their zest for learning, exploring, and discovering makes them a joy to be with, but it presents its own frustrations for the caregiver. It may take a toddler an amazingly long time to get from one side of the room to the other, simply because there are so many interesting distractions along the way. Hand washing in preparation for lunch becomes a form of water play, and the object of the exercise is completely forgotten. Young toddlers attempting to seat themselves in a chair may become so absorbed in the act of backing up to it that they continue on past the chair. Pouring requires such concentration that the toddler may forget to stop when the level of the liquid reaches the top of the cup. Toddlers are often totally immersed in the here and now, and consequently are not very good at planning ahead.

They are also process oriented, as some of the examples above illustrate. This implies that it is the doing of the activity that interests them rather than the product at the end. When they play with blocks, for instance, it is the stacking of them or lining them up side by side that captures their attention, not the configuration they have created at the end. Process orientation is most obvious in their use of creative materials. If toddlers are interested in painting, they may very well stay with the activity until all of the paint in the pot has been applied to the paper. Or similarly, toddlers given a pasting activity may not get beyond mounding the paste onto the piece of card. They may not yet be ready to view paste as a medium to make other materials adhere to the card. When the process is complete, interest is lost. In other words, toddlers may not concern themselves with the product or outcome. Young toddlers enjoy moving objects from one place to another. If the adult will allow it, a toddler may push every chair across the room, or take each block off the shelf one at a time and carefully deposit it somewhere else. There is not likely to be an aim to this activity; rather it is done for the sake of doing it.

## Unpredictable Attention Span

Toddlers are frequently said to have a short attention span. Perhaps it is more accurate to say that they have an unpredictable attention span. That is, it is difficult even for adults who know toddlers well to predict with accuracy what is going to engage their interest. Often it is not the thoughtfully chosen supposedly developmentally appropriate play materials or the carefully planned meticulously set out activities which occupy them the longest or the most wholeheartedly, and adults find this disconcerting. Picture a toddler attempting to pick up peas with a fork and get them in to the mouth, or a young toddler who has decided it is time to tackle stair climbing, or a two year old filling containers in the sand pit or pouring at the water table. It is no doubt possible to come up with as many examples of toddlers showing surprisingly long attention spans as showing a more expected lack of concentration.

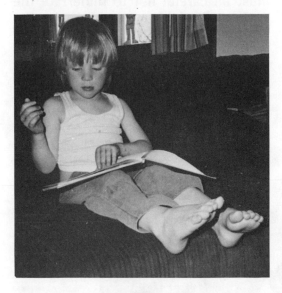

## Busyness, Curiosity, Drive to Explore

Most toddlers are tireless explorers discoverers, and scientists. They spend most of their waking time investigating the world around them. Someone has said that toddlers think with their hands and feet, as well as with their heads. In other words, they learn most effectively through first-hand experience, through their own self-initiated hands-on experiences, rather than by being shown or instructed. One of the most tiring characteristics of toddlers, but at the same time the most rewarding, is their enthusiasm for learning.

## Lack of Understanding

While toddlers make tremendous gains in their understanding of how the social and physical worlds work in the second and third years of life, there is still much that they do not understand. It would be very beneficial for toddlers and the adults who work with them if those adults could see the world the way a toddler sees it. There must be so much

that is confusing for them. For example, it may not be obvious to a two year old why it is acceptable to throw a ball outside but not inside. What is the difference between putting toys in the pool and putting them in the toilet? Why do adults smile when marks are made on the paper on the table, but they frown and speak sternly when the same kind of marks are made in a book in the book corner? After all, adults write in books sometimes. Which are the foods that it is okay to eat with fingers, and which ones need to be eaten with a fork or spoon?

As a result of their confusion or lack of understanding, toddlers often do terrible things with good or at least innocent intentions. For example, a toddler who "helps" to mop up a spill usually makes the mess worse. In fact, it is probably safe to say that any attempt by a toddler to help usually makes the job take longer. When a toddler shows affection to a baby, the baby typically ends up begging for mercy and some help from an adult. It is important for adults to praise toddlers for their good intentions, and help them to execute them more appropriately.

## Increasing Though Limited Social Skills

Toddlers have a great deal of interest in and liking for other children, but unfortunately their skill in getting along does not match their interest. Many of the characteristics mentioned previously work against getting along with others. Toddlers are in a stage of "I-ness and me-ness", of defining themselves as individuals. This requires them to be possessive and to focus on their own needs and wants. They are not capable of worrying too much about the needs and wants of other children.

Consequently, toddlers are not very good at sharing, if by sharing is meant giving up something one wants for oneself. Toddlers do distribute; that is, they go around handing out things to adults and other children. This, unfortunately, is sometimes labeled mistakenly by adults as sharing, and the adult expects the child to be able to share forever after. Distributing is a form of play that differs significantly from sharing. The objects that are distributed are not wanted by the distributor, at least at the time of distribution. If they are desired, the toddler will then begin collecting!

each other. Toddlers who are helped to do so certainly engage in truly social interactions and cooperative play. Adults must be careful not to underrate the social skills of this age group, but at the same time not to have inappropriately high expectations. Individual toddlers will differ enormously. Caregivers should expect to have to provide lots of help and guidance to toddlers in their interactions with other children.

There is considerable debate about the extent to which toddlers are capable of showing sympathy or concern for other children or of taking the perspective of others. Some people argue that the traditional view of toddlers as egocentric is an overrated and outdated one. Anyone who works with toddlers will confirm the inaccuracy of older child development texts which described toddlers as playing alone, with an adult, or along side each other, but not with

## Imitators

Fortunately and unfortunately, toddlers are great imitators. It is unfortunate in that they pick up undesirable behaviors very readily from the people around them. It is fortunate for the adults who work with them because it means that the most effective way to teach toddlers is to be a good model. This approach suggests, for example, that the best way to ensure that toddlers will eventually be good at sharing is to give to them. The most effective way to nourish social skills and an attitude of concern, or willingness to compromise of tolerance for differences, and many other attributes that most caregivers would want to promote in the children they care for, is to demonstrate those characteristics in interacting with the children.

Acceptance of and liking for toddlers is the first step toward providing a good experience for them. Gonzalez-Mena (1986) states the challenge clearly:

When we see toddlerhood as a special and distinct stage of development with its own set of tasks and behaviors, toddler's [sic] behavior becomes more understandable and manageable. Then we are not tempted to impose watered down (or worse yet full-blown) preschool activities upon them. When we stop comparing toddlers with older children, and appreciate them for what they are, toddlers become very likable individuals. They will feel better about themselves because the adults who care for them respect them for what they should be—toddlers. (p. 51)

It is interesting to contemplate to what extent the challenge of offering care of high quality to this age group is due to the fact that so many of the workers, as well as the people who educated those workers, have had more experience with three to five years olds and therefore speak about toddlers from a knowledge base that is primarily about older children. Perhaps caregivers of toddlers need to adopt one of the characteristics of toddlers themselves, and become more oriented to the present, the here and now of toddlers.

## THEREFORE, REQUIRED CHARACTERISTICS OF CAREGIVERS

There is universal agreement that the most critical determinant of the quality of a child care program is the staff. Much of this book embodies implicitly or explicitly a description of an excellent caregiver for this age group. However, there are a few characteristics that should be highlighted. The number of people who are excellent caregivers for this age group is undoubtedly smaller than the number who can care well for over threes. It takes a special skill and sensitivity to relate well to toddlers and to feel challenged in a positive way by their characteristics. The list that follows is a very selective one.

### Appropriate Involvement

A special sensitivity is required to be involved appropriately with toddlers' activities. Knowing when to help, when to leave a child alone, and how to help without taking over the activity, is difficult. It is so much easier to put the puzzle piece in than to help the child to do it. Knowing precisely how to encourage a child to keep trying and to ensure success and have it honestly be the child's success, are rare skills. Because toddlers are so easily distracted from their pursuits, it is important that caregivers assist them in their work rather than detracting from it.

### Tuned In

Excellent caregivers of toddlers seem to have a sixth sense about the meaning of toddlers' behavior and language. Both are more subtle, and consequently more difficult to interpret, than the more obvious behavior and clearer speech of older children. In other words, an adult has to try harder to make sense of the behavior and language of this age group.

## Natural Conversors

Some people feel awkward talking to toddlers, because the feedback may not be direct or may be very subtle. These adults appear to be unconvinced that toddlers understand so much more than they can express in words. The ability to talk in a meaningful but natural way to this age group is a necessary prerequisite for being an excellent caregiver. Some adults say very little, while others simplify their speech in an artificial way, sometimes lapsing into the telegraphic speech that is characteristic of toddlers themselves! "Johnny want biscuit?" "Throw ball", "Look, bird in sky" are all examples of unnecessarily simplified speech. Another unfortunate tactic that some adults resort to as a way of talking to toddlers could be labelled as "the interrogation" or "third degree", that is, barraging toddlers with contrived questions.

Programs of high quality for this age group are characterized by the easy flow of conversation between children and adults, not a constant onslaught of didactic and artificial "verbal stimulation" from adults. Adults are tuned in to toddlers' talk, and respond to the meaning of what toddlers are saying, regardless of how they say it.

## Acceptance of Need for Security

Good caregivers of toddlers understand their need to retreat sometimes to a state of dependence, to have the security, the physical closeness that is identified by some adults as a more appropriate characteristic of infancy than of toddlerhood. Toddlers need a strong secure base to support their emotional, intellectual, and physical adventuring. Excellent caregivers of toddlers know that toddlers need to form close relationships of attachment with them, that they need to be able to trust that someone who knows them and cares about them and whom they know and care about will be there day after day, week after week. Quality care for toddlers cannot be provided by a large rotating cast of caregivers.

This need for security also implies that in program planning, caregivers must take into account the need to balance the novel, the new, the exciting and the predictable, the secure, the serene and the peaceful.

## Respect for Toddlers

The most important prerequisite for caring well for toddlers is a genuine respect for them, an acknowledgement that they are people, not cute little things to be manipulated and managed and exploited because of their inexperience, their naivete, their vulnerability, their trust in those who have responsibility for them. Those people who are responsible for hiring caregivers should look very critically at people who say that they like toddlers because they are "cute" or because of their dependence or because they are so affectionate. Often these people relate to toddlers as objects to be managed and manipulated, and they are often people who rely heavily on power tactics, manipulation, and gimmicks in their interactions with this age group.

In a book called *Caring*, Rita Warren (1977) writes about the necessity of accepting children as the beginning of caring well for them. Some excerpts from that book follow, as they state clearly and pointedly what respect for children involves.

My own choice is to eliminate all tricks, including distraction, manipulation, happy face signs, clean plate clubs, and other such gimmicks which, from my point of view, only insult children's intelligence and integrity... Essential to every approach is the acceptance of children.

Acceptance does not mean a kind of passive toleration, but rather an active affirmation of the value of each human individual, not in terms of the person's achievements or behavior but simply in terms of his or her existence. It means looking through and beyond the superficial barriers which may arise out of the differences between us.

The barriers between adults and young children include those of time and distance from early childhood experiences and the normal repression of memories of the primitive drives which move children. When we see a three-year-old hit a one-year-old over the head with a block, we are horrified because we can no longer remember when we had so little control over anger and so little understanding of consequences. To be in touch with young children's feelings requires effort and the willingness to revive in ourselves some of the troubling and terrifying conflicts young children experience.

Acceptance of a child does not happen automatically; it is a goal and not a given. It is hard to trust people who say that they "love children" as though children were a breed apart and it was possible to love or hate them in toto. Those same people often talk in a special voice to children, talk about children's "own special little world" and in many ways consign them to it or leave them in it out of the adult's incapacity to bridge the gap.

Each child's birthright, it seems to me, is to be accepted without reservation.

When we think clearly about what we want for children, our own and other people's, it is obvious that we want them to grow up to be our peers. If we could keep that fact in the forefront of our attitudes toward children, we might avoid many of the fruitless battles and instead serve as guides, welcomers, and protectors as children make their valiant efforts to grow up and join us.

(Warren, 1977; pp. 2, 3, 6)

**REFERENCES**

Brazelton, T.B. (1974). *Toddlers and Parents*. New York: Delacorte Press.

Escalona, S.K. (1974). "Developmental Issues in the Second Year of Life: Their Implications for Day Care Practices." In P.B. Neubauer (Ed.). *Early Child Day Care*. New York: Jason Aronson.

Gonzalez-Mena, J. (1986). "Toddlers: What to Expect." *Young Children*, November, 47-51.

Keister, M.E. (1972). *Discipline: The Secret Heart of Child Care*. Greensboro, N.C.: University of North Carolina at Greensboro.

Warren, R. (1977). *Caring*. Washington, D.C.: National Association for the Education of Young Children.

*Photographs:* Lady Gowrie Child Center, Brisbane; Bev Olsson; Lady Gowrie Child Center, Hobart; Pam Schurch.

# Chapter 2

# One Perspective on Programming for Toddlers

## Anne Stonehouse

*People who work with young children are often searching for the 'right" way to program, a system that will work flawlessly. The following chapter does not contain such a system, as the author believes that, just as there is no one right way to rear children, neither is there a right way to program for toddlers. Each individual has to experiment and work out a way that feels comfortable, and undoubtedly this will change with time. The discussion that follows provides a general framework, a rational, for program planning. It embodies a comprehensive, holistic approach to programming, encouraging people to look at the total experience they are offering to children.*

Programming for toddlers is a popular topic for in-service education activities for child care workers. The concept inevitably elicits a variety of comments, including the following:

> I always feel as though we're not doing enough with them, that we should be doing more than just letting them play.

> We have a planned program each morning from 9:30 until 11:00, except Fridays when we just let them have free play.

> We offer two or three activities each day; one before morning tea, and a messy one in the afternoon; the rest of the time is just free play.

> We choose a theme each week and base as many of our activities as we can on that theme.

> You can't really program for toddlers.

> You shouldn't program for toddlers. After all, they're only little, and besides, if they do it all now they will be bored when they get into the three to fives group.

Each of those statements represents a common but inappropriate view of programming. For some people, the term programming' conjures up an image of a fairly inflexible structure characterized by adult direction of activities, lack of choice, children spending large amounts of time working in groups, and often a heavy diet of watered-down or not watered down preschool activities. Children who spend time in those types of programs deserve sympathy, but so do the adults who struggle to operate that kind of program with toddlers, for it is such hard work for the adults.

An approach to programming for toddlers which is at the opposite end of the continuum is captured in the following description of a toddler program from a student who completed a field placement: "It's just boring. The staff don't plan anything, they don't change anything. Every day is just the same—the same toys—the same routines. The children are bored, and so are the staff. There must be more to it than that."

The aim of this chapter is to present a different view of programming, a broader view than either of those suggested above, and one that is based on the particular characteristics of the age group. The very nature of toddlers contributes to a feeling of uncertainty about the appropriateness of the programming being done on their behalf. Their capacity to change from somewhat reasonable, rational people to quite the opposite, their mysteriousness emanating from their inability to tell their caregivers exactly what is on their minds, their unevenness of moods and interests make it easy for adults to be uncertain about whether they are doing the right thing.

## SIDETRACKS

Some people get sidetracked with their programming. Some common sidetracks are described briefly below:

**1. The Egg Carton Curriculum.** One "sidetrack" is to base the program on the unusual, the novel, the different. In these programs it appears that children make things and do things because they interest the staff and will impress the parents, and not necessarily because they have meaning or are appropriate for the children. An emphasis on gimmicky art and craft activities (the egg carton curriculum, it might be labeled) for toddlers rather than allowing them to explore creative materials in a fairly unstructured way would be a good example of this approach to programming.

**2. Acceleration.** Other people seem preoccupied with a future orientation toward toddlers, with the way they want them to be and the skills they want them to have in a couple of years, and they devote much time and energy to trying to make them be that way now. This approach to programming is suggested in a comment made by a caregiver in describing her program. She said that the twos to threes spend most of the day with older children but are separated out sometimes "for some *instruction*-things they need to learn like cutting with scissors and sharing". Gonzalez-

Mena (1986) cautions that adults must avoid viewing toddlers as lacking many desirable skills and characteristics that they will have later. Rather, caregivers need to accept the developmental characteristics of the age group and base programming on those characteristics. This will minimize the tendency to offer toddlers a "watered-down" version of a program appropriate for three to five year olds.

It is inappropriate to base programs on the aim of getting toddlers to achieve skills or competencies early, to rush them through their toddlerhood. Some common examples of inappropriate acceleration would be training toddlers to sit quietly in a group, teaching numbers and letters in a formal way, or building in intentionally exercises that require sharing or waiting or taking turns.

**3. Fill-in-the-Blanks.** Undoubtedly the most common approach to programming is inserting a few predictable activities at specific times of the day into a pre-set unchanging timetable in a fairly predictable, unchanging environment. This approach to programming is reinforced by the lack of time many staff working in child care have to plan and prepare for their time with children. Each week the empty slots on the photocopied sheet are filled in with activities such as dough, water play, collage, and drawing on computer paper with crayons. The rationale that is used for selecting the activities is often simply that children enjoy them.

At other times this so-called 'programmed' part of the day is treated as a special 'educational' time, where children are being taught particular skills such as counting or recognition of colors or shapes, or other so-called 'preschool' skills in a fairly structured way. In some centers, this part of the day is referred to as 'kindy time'. This is the attitude toward programming implied when a person says, "The children start arriving at 7.30, but the morning program begins at 9.30".

With this type of programming where the emphasis is on activities, it often happens that the rest of the day, the time not designated as activity time, just happens. The way it happens is often influenced heavily by considerations other than the children's needs, for example, getting the job done quickly, getting the room tidied up and keeping it that way (out comes the video), or managing a lunch break for a staff member.

The problem with this approach to programming is that children do not shut off their interest, energy, and enthusiasm for learning during those times that just happen. They cannot save up learning ability to focus it on activity time. It is a great waste of their time when care and planning does not go into every aspect of their experience in care. Besides, such a large proportion of a toddler's time in care is spent in routine activities. Saying that the program begins two hours after the first child arrives is like saying that children do not begin their education until they start school! The program begins the minute the first child arrives, and finishes when the last child leaves.

**4. Themes.** Some programs for toddlers are built around or contorted into a theme, and an active effort is made to make as much of the week's activities, as well as the food and the physical environment, fit the theme. The attraction of theme planning for the adults is that it gives them a rationale, a framework to 'hang' their work on. There is something satisfying about making everything one does for a week relate somehow to green, or the circus, or foods, or whatever the theme is. It undoubtedly contributes to a feeling of having taught something, and adds an element of integrity and cohesiveness to what can feel like a chaotic, disorganized job.

16

While there are some advantages for staff in programming for toddlers with themes, there are many drawbacks for the children. A major drawback is that while themes may provide some continuity and a rationale for the adults, they just do not make sense to toddlers. Toddlers are not able to put the week's activities into a meaningful whole. Given the nature of some of the themes that are used, one could question whether or not it is possible for anyone to make them meaningful! The author has heard of the following themes being used with toddlers: free activities, emotions, green and square (simultaneously this group had a theme, a color, and a shape for each week), the circus, sounds and cartoon characters. Often the themes that are chosen for this age group involve concepts and experiences that are important, but which must be built in naturally as they relate to something that is meaningful to the child. Themes lend themselves to encouraging the provision of artificial experiences and potentially meaningful experiences out of context, so that they have little meaning to the child. A caregiver talks about emotions when emotions occur, not because it is Tuesday of the week of the Emotions theme!

A more serious concern is that in an effort to make things fit the theme caregivers may overlook experiences that match the children's interests and abilities and provide inappropriate and sometimes meaningless activities instead. Theme planning, when taken seriously, may result in caregivers paying less attention to building on children's interests and may be a disincentive to taking advantage of spontaneously occurring events (Lambert, et al., 1986). An example may assist in reinforcing this point. A pair of caregivers who based their planning on very extensive execution of themes were describing to the author the success of a week's theme on the subject of babies. They said that one of the activities the toddlers had enjoyed most was bathing dolls. They had set up basins of water, wash cloths, towels and soap, and had borrowed the center's entire collection of dolls. They were surprised and pleased at the length of time the children were occupied with the activity, the care they took, and the amount of good conversation that took place in the context of the activity. When the author commented that they probably then followed up with frequent doll bathing and variations on that activity in the days following, the caregivers' response was that they had not been able to offer dolly washing for quite a few weeks after because it did not fit into the theme!

**5. Non-Programming.** As indicated above, some people responsible for programs for toddlers plan very little, their rationale being that it is inappropriate or impossible to plan for this age group. If asked how the children spend their time, they may reply that there is lots of free play.

## A NEW DEFINITION

This discussion of what programming is begins with a list of what programming is not:

It is not just what is done during non-routine times in a child care program.

It is not just a card file of activities.

It is not a set of so-called "educational" activities that happen at tables with expensive materials at particular times of the day. What isn't educational for a toddler, and what is so special about sitting at a table?

It is not limited to how the plan is written down, what sort of framework and format are used.

Programming includes both *how* and *why* caregivers decide to do what they do with toddlers, as well as *what* they do. Programming should incorporate every aspect of the day, including the following:

- The provisions made for greeting children and parents at the beginning of the day, helping them separate from each other, and helping children settle in daily to the center program;
- The extent to which parents are made to feel welcomed, are communicated with, and are involved in decision making;
- The way lunch is served; the general orientation to all routines;
- The way the equipment, materials, and furniture are set up;
- The group size, the age range, the staff:child ratio;
- The timetable itself, and the flexibility with which it is adhered to;
- The extent to which self-directed play, as opposed to structured activities or more formal teaching methods, is valued;
- The play activities and experiences offered, their developmental appropriateness as well as the way in which they are offered;
- The attitude toward 'differences' of all sorts, whether they be related to sex, race, culture, skin color, abilities, level of maturity, developmental achievements, or just individual differences among children and families;
- The pace of the program, and the emphasis placed on giving toddlers time to 'do it themselves', to feel unhurried; in other words, the extent to which the program is run on 'toddler time';
- The flow of the day; efforts made to ease toddlers into sleep or quiet times; to minimize waiting; to give the day a kind of integrity;

- The orientation of staff—whether they see their jobs primarily as managing or supervising the children and overseeing the program operation, or whether they value getting down and actually working *with* the children;
- The caregivers' ability to talk appropriately and naturally to toddlers, to encourage toddlers to talk, to listen sensitively to toddlers' attempts to communicate, and to interpret what they have said;
- The extent to which caregivers place priority on giving toddlers authentic meaningful experiences that relate to "real life" and that acknowledge that toddlers enjoy participating in the meaningful work of people around them. For example, toddlers would prefer and would learn more from tearing lettuce for a salad than from tearing up paper; from helping to fold the diapers than from sitting at a table folding paper;
- Most importantly, the sensitivity and skill the caregivers bring to their interactions with toddlers, the degree to which they are allied with or on the side of the children, working *with* them and respecting them instead of supervising or controlling or "minding" them.

The above list is not a comprehensive one, but it singles out some of the most critical dimensions in assessing the quality of a program for toddlers. It should be noticed that activities, the usual things people program for, constitute only one of several important considerations.

If programming is everything one does as well as the rationale behind it, then it follows that everyone who works with a group of toddlers does programming, even if they do not write anything down. One might say that some programming is unconscious!

## THE ORIGINS OF PROGRAMMING

The way a person programs, even when it is unconscious or unwritten, reflects at least three things which come from experience and/or formal qualifications:

1. Their knowledge and understanding of child development and their resulting ideas about what children need and how they learn and develop (Lambert, *et al.*, 1986).

2. Their goals and objectives for the group, based on general understanding of that age group as well as specific knowledge of the particular group being planned for, as every group of children has its own specific characteristics (Patterson, 1978).

3. Their philosophy, their ideas about how to go about achieving those goals and objectives.

These can be translated easily into actual practices. For example, a person who plans for and expects all toddlers in a group to all do the same thing at the same time is making a statement about the programming philosophy. A child care worker who insists on having a rocking chair or a soft couch in the room is saying something about toddlers' needs. A caregiver who says, "We just want to keep them busy and happy and be sure that most days they've made something to take home because the parents like that" is making a strong statement about goals and objectives. A caregiver who aims for a relaxed lunchtime with a fair bit of conversation and messiness is carrying out a philosophy.

All of these people, some of whom may believe that they do not program, are making a statement about their beliefs about what is best for children and how to go about achieving that. It is useful for all caregivers to stand back periodically, take a look at their own work with toddlers, and ask themselves what it says about their beliefs about what is important in working with children.

### Knowledge of Individual Children

In addition to general knowledge and understanding, goals and objectives, and a philosophy, good programming takes into account the particular group as well as the individual children one is working with. In all programs parents should be used as resources for information about their child. The best planning for individual children incorporates the professional staff members' first-hand knowledge of the child as well as the parents' more extensive knowledge based on their longer experience of the child and their intense involvement.

A way must be found to record information about individual children, to ensure that the needs and interests of each child are being taken into account in the program, and that the fit of the program with individual children is being monitored. One suggestion is that the written plan should always include the names of at least three or four children, ensuring that over time all children are included (Patterson, 1978). Other people go even further and advocate planning for the group as though planning for three or four children in the group, solely on the basis of their needs, and rotating the children focused on in each plan.

Whatever method is used, one of the particular challenges of staff is to combine effectively and naturally overall plans and plans for individual children. As Patterson (1978) says:

Plans for the group as a whole, and the plans for individual children are interlocking, and inevitably one will influence the other. The important thing is that both exist, for neither on its own provides the complete program plan ... Plans for the group as a whole will include much of the actual programme content, whereas plans for individuals may be behaviorally oriented, and include as well experiences based on particular children's needs and interests. (p. 21)

One of the particular challenges for staff in child care is to ensure that they are not just focusing on difficult, disruptive, or 'problem' children in their plans as well as in their actual interactions. While there are a number of checklists available to help caregivers focus on the competencies of individual children, many experts support the value of frequent open-ended observations as a superior way to capture the richness and complexity of children's behavior (Lambert, *et al.*, 1986), or as a supplement to checklists. The use of checklists alone, while viewed by some as certainly better than no way of collecting information on individual children, may restrict the observer's attention to those items that are contained in the checklist. However, some experts (Lambert, *et al.*, 1986) have expressed great concerns with the use of "charts of development sequences, developmental surveys, check lists" (p. 6) and other types of developmental records as a basis for program planning. It is beyond the scope of this chapter to go into detail, but the importance of observing the behavior of individual children cannot be overstated.

Fortunately, there are a number of excellent resource materials to assist early childhood personnel to plan for individuals as well as the group, including suggested techniques. Some of these are listed in the references at the end of this chapter.

## Parents

Ideally, a program of high quality takes into account parents' aims and objectives for their child and incorporates them into programming (Patterson, 1978). This, like most things, is easier to state than to put into practice, even when parents' aims and objectives do not differ significantly from those of staff. The task is infinitely more complicated, however, when parents' aims and objectives are incompatible with those of the program. What do staff do, for example, when a parent expresses a strong desire for her two year old daughter to learn some table manners, or wants the staff to toilet train her 19 month old who is showing no signs of readiness or interest in using the toilet? As Watts and Patterson (1985) indicate, there are not yet adequate procedures worked out to involve parents in program planning.

## Spontaneity, Unexpected Events

The best programs happen when the person in charge is very willing to throw the program away for the moment! Life in a child care center is full of unexpected events, some pleasant, some not so pleasant. Caregivers need to be prepared to adjust their program for a number of reasons. The mood of the children may not fit with what is planned. Why suffer through a story time when everyone is squirming and bursting with energy and wanting to go outside? It is said in another chapter that toddlers have a somewhat unpredictable attention span, and that it is not possible for even a very experienced and skilled caregiver to always predict successfully what is going to capture and hold their interest. Yet it takes a lot of strength for a caregiver who sees that an activity is not going well to put it away, having planned and prepared it carefully in the certainty that it would interest the toddlers for a long time.

Similarly, a program of high quality capitalizes on spontaneous events and the stimulation provided by the children (Patterson, 1978). If Sarah comes in on Monday morning with a bag full of treasures she found at the beach and bubbling enthusiasm for the adventures she had there at the weekend, a competent, confident program planner will adjust the plans for the morning to build on this child's experiences and the interests of the other children in them.

Cataldo (1983) acknowledges the need for a balance between activities which are "planned and arranged" and "those that occur in the natural course of events" (p. 132). She says:

Problems arise with too much or too little planning. The consequence of over planning is that children's experiences can be restricted or forced into adult molds that reduce choice or pleasure. Too little open playtime, for example, can result in fewer opportunities for independent learning, exploration, peer interaction, and other kinds of valuable experiences. On the other hand, a lack of planning can contribute to staff confusion, little variety over the program year, inappropriate expectations, and a general lack of professionalism. (pp. 132, 133)

### 'Wrench in the Works'

In addition to the above, there are a number of factors that influence in a major way the programs that are offered to toddlers in child care centers. All of them contribute to the quality of the program, and in many centers they interfere with quality, as they prevent staff from programming the way they would

like to. Many of them are outside the control of the person in charge of the group, and some are outside the control of the center. As some of these are covered in other chapters in this book, they will only be listed here.

They are:
• Age range in the group
• Number of children in the group
• Staff:child ratio
• Size and arrangement of physical space, both indoors and out
• Equipment available, appropriateness, condition, amount
• Length of the day for children and staff
• Composition of the group—mix of full-time, part-time, and occasional children
• Time available to individual staff members and to staff working in the same group to plan, prepare, discuss
• Access to resources, including people, ideas, and materials, to assist with programming
• Backgrounds, values, and priorities of staff
• Valuing of programming within the center
• General community attitudes toward child care

### Staff Attitudes Toward Toddlers and Toddler Programming

Numbers 8 and 10 above bear some discussion as they are often not acknowledged, and yet they influence programming in a major way. In many centers, there are people working together who have quite different understanding of children's development and needs, incompatible aims and objectives, and varying philosophies from those of their co-workers. These may come from their formal training, their experience, or most likely a mixture of both. Yet they go about their daily work with toddlers under the assumption that they all think similarly, not even acknowledging these differences, much less working through them and resolving them.

As long as discussions are kept at the level of nice general goals for example, promoting a positive self concept accepting individual differences, nourishing an inquisitive, assertive attitude toward the environment, fostering creativity there is no argument. When those nice cliches are translated into actual practices for actual toddlers however, staff may discover that they do not agree. What do they do about those children who show no interest in cleaning up? How should they respond when George bites the next time? Is it okay if Karen does not want to join the music group? What is the value of having everyone make a bunny mask at Easter time, and if it is decided to offer that activity, what happens when Brian wants to make a monster mask instead of a bunny? Does it matter if 2-1/2 year old Toby, who has had a lot of pressure put on him, wants to use his fingers for all food, including soup? At that level, it is not so easy to agree, and yet it is at that level that the children experience their caregivers.

## A DIAGRAMMATIC REPRESENTATION OF PROGRAMMING

The approach to programming being advocated in this book is represented in the diagram on page 23. This diagram is a synthesis of the components of program planning suggested by several experts (Patterson, 1978; Lambert *et al.*, 1986). Understandably, the reaction of many child care workers to this diagram may be, "Amazing! I hardly have time to go to the toilet, and it is being suggested that I must think about all these things. Forget it!" The point is that conscientious, skilled child care workers who do a good job with toddlers *do* go through this process, regardless of what the piece of paper containing their program looks

like. Perhaps a few examples to illustrate the diagram will reassure the skeptical.

### Example 1:

**General knowledge of child development:** Children establish a picture of themselves, a self concept, before the age of three. This self concept influences their attitude toward learning, new experiences, and plays a major role in their social relationships.

**General goals and objectives:** To enhance a positive self concept.

**Philosophy:** Enable children to have many success experiences; ensure that they get positive feedback from adults and other children.

**Implications for programming:** a) Ensure that the range of puzzles we provide allows children to be challenged, but by and large, to be successful; b) Adults should praise children for hard work, for cooperating, for helping other children; c) If a child is struggling with a task that he is unable to accomplish successfully, the adult with try unobtrusively to make it simpler or redirect the child to an easier task.

(There would be literally hundreds of additional concrete ways that staff assist toddlers to develop a positive self concept.)

**Specific knowledge:** Tim, age 2 months, has been very interested in the past few days in trying to dress himself.

**Parents' wisdom:** The caregiver commented on this to his father, who said that this has been happening at home as well, and that at the weekend he had two terrible temper tantrums because he wanted to put his socks and shoes on, could not do it, and refused to let anyone help him.

**Identification of strengths and needs:** Tim's interest in being self-sufficient is a strength; the caregiver has noticed that he is very adept at putting his underpants on; he almost always gets them on

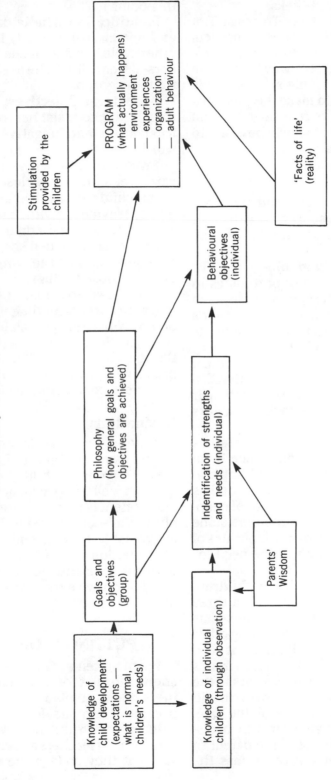

SOURCES OF PROGRAMS

(or how staff end up doing what they do whether they realize it or not!)

PROGRAM
(what actually happens)
— environment
— experiences
— organization
— adult behaviour

Stimulation provided by the children

'Facts of life' (reality)

Behavioural objectives (individual)

Philosophy (how general goals and objectives are achieved)

Identification of strengths and needs (individual)

Goals and objectives (group)

Knowledge of individual children (through observation)

Parents' Wisdom

Knowledge of child development (expectations — what is normal, children's needs)

(Derived in part from Patterson, 1978; Lambert et al., 1986).

the right way; he needs help to be able to cope with shoes and socks.

**Behavioral objective:** To assist Tim in being able to dress himself, particularly to put on shoes and socks.

**Program:** Caregiver always takes time to let Tim undress himself, pulls his socks off his heel to make it easier, suggests to his parents that they buy him some slip-on shoes that will be easier to manage than laces or buckles.

## Example 2:

**General Knowledge:** Toddlers have a great deal of interest in being with other children, but their social skills are limited.

**General goals and objectives:** To provide children with opportunities to have pleasant interactions with each other, to help them enjoy one another's company, to give them a positive attitude toward being with other children.

**General Philosophy:** Protect them from each other, use preventative discipline, be there to help them with their interactions, model the social behaviors you want them to adopt.

**Program:** Spread the play materials around the space to discourage them from 'bunching and clumping' (Greenman, 1982); avoid play materials and activities that require a lot of cooperation; try to give children time alone or in small groups; provide duplicates of favorite toys to minimize the need for sharing.

**Knowledge of individual children:** Joan, age 29 months, has bitten three children in the past two days; she seems not to be able to cope with having other children interfere with her play at all.

**Parents' wisdom:** Her mother has mentioned that there are visitors in the house with a very active two year old who wants to be with Joan all the time. (Note: Caregivers would use their discretion and knowledge of the parent to decide whether or not to discuss the biting specifically with her mother at this point.)

**Identification of individual strengths and needs:** Joan is easily frustrated by other children; she needs help to stop herself from biting; she needs time away from the group.

**Behavioral Objectives:** To stop her from biting; to assist her to express her frustration and negative feelings in words.

**Program:** As much as is possible a caregiver should stay close to her when other children are nearby to prevent biting; provide her with time on her own; let her accompany adults doing tasks out of the room; when she is frustrated or angry, tell her the words to say to express those feelings.

These two examples hopefully will reassure caregivers that although they do not consciously think in the categories specified in the diagram, and although they may not undertake the process implied in it, they do incorporate these considerations in their plan.

## Evaluation

A good program is one in which mechanisms are built in for evaluating the effectiveness of both the overall program as well as specific activities. This assessment is then used for future planning. While assessments by outsiders are valuable, by far the most useful form of evaluation comes from staff who are willing to look critically at what they are doing and revise their program accordingly (Patterson, 1978).

## PUTTING IT ON PAPER

People often seek the "right" answer about a format for programming. While there are a number of resources that prescribe formats for planning, individuals have to find their own way. Most experienced teachers and caregivers will say that they change the way they go about programming every few years, that they have not discovered the "perfect" way. Whatever the format, however, the process should include the following:

- A mechanism for recording information about individual children and using that information to plan;
- A means of evaluating individual activities and experiences as well as the overall plan;
- Opportunities to look critically at the daily routines with the aim of making them as child centered as possible;
- Examination of the "troublesome" times of the day;
- Appraisal of the timetable itself;
- Consideration of the physical environment;
- Recognition of the need for flexibility and the desirability of a balance between sticking to a plan and spontaneity.

Watts and Patterson (1985) stress the necessity of linking goals, objectives, and philosophy to what actually happens on a day-to-day basis if quality is to be maintained. Their criteria for effective programming are as follows:

- Clear links to be established between the entire range of goals and the proposed program of activities;
- The establishment of short-term and long-term goals (for the group and for individuals) that take cognizance of the pattern of child development and the expected sequences in children's development of understandings, skills, and competencies;
- The programming of activities that are specifically planned to lead children further in their progress toward short-term and, hence the long-term goals;
- The provision in planning for flexible response to situations and to child needs (so critical with these young children);
- The recording of individual children's progress;
- The reappraisal of both goals and procedures in the light of outcomes. (p. 172)

It is easy in the rush of doing everything that must be done in a program for toddlers to lose sight of the reasons for doing what is done, and for caregivers to lapse into a rather mindless non-critical approach to programming that hardly goes beyond filling up the time and getting through the day. That approach is not satisfying to children, but neither is it very stimulating for staff. Strategies and supports need to be put in place to assist the very busy people who work with toddlers not to get sidetracked.

Sometimes the comment is made that a formal process of programming is necessary only for inexperienced staff. Watts and Patterson (1985) stress that it is essential that even highly experienced staff engage in program planning in order to ensure that they are meeting the needs of all the children they care for.

While this chapter has not been prescriptive, and may therefore be disappointing to some readers, it has established a broad context for programming into which the remaining chapters of the book fit. Patterson (1978) has summed up programming as follows:

Take a quantity of accessible broad educational goals, mix with some specific goals, and blend together with a working knowledge of child development. Add careful observation, considerable thought, and some writing, and blend with a large degree of common sense and a genuine interest in and concern for children. The method of presentation needs to be flexible. (pp. 26, 27)

## REFERENCES

Cataldo, C.Z. (1983). *Infant and Toddler Programs*. Reading, Mass.: Addison-Wesley Publishing Company.

Gonzalez-Mena, J. (1986). Toddlers: *What to Expect*. Young Children, November, 47-51.

Greenman, J. (1982). Designing Infant/Toddler Environments. In R. Lurie and R. Neugebauer, (Eds.). *Caring for Infants and Toddlers: What Works, What Doesn't*, Vol. 2. Redmond, Washington: Child Care Information Exchanges.

Lambert, B., Clyde, M. and Reeves, K. (1986). *Planning for Individual Needs in Early Childhood Services, Parts I and II*. Australian Early Childhood Resource Booklets. No. 1, March and No. 2, May.

Patterson, P. (1978). *Planning Early Childhood Programmes*. Canberra: Australian Early Childhood Association.

Watts, B.H. and Patterson, P. (1985). *In Search of Quality*. Brisbane: Lady Gowrie Child Centre.

---

*Photographs:* Lady Gowrie Child Centre, Brisbane

# Chapter 3

# Principles of Group Care

## Pam Schurch

*Some important assumptions or principles lie behind programs of high quality for toddlers. Often they are implicit, taken for granted by staff. It helps to articulate them, not only to help staff keep them in mind, but as a basis for discussion of policies and practices of the center. More importantly, a statement of principles will assist parents who use the program to appreciate and understand the care their children are receiving. The principles described in the chapter by Schurch, which follows, are woven throughout the rest of the book.*

The basic needs of all children are the same, whatever age they may be. But perhaps it is fair to say that the younger the children, and the longer they spend in day care, the greater their need to be gently and lovingly accommodated in conditions closest to what most would consider a good, natural, home environment, with the same goals as those wanted by most parents for their children. How can the two environments, home and day care, be blended, or at least brought closer to each other, to give to under threes this sort of group care?

Staff can:
- soften the environment,
- interact with the children closely and lovingly,
- individualize the program, introducing many home-style activities,
- include, involve and share with parents.

### "Softening" the Environment

How should the center look and feel to the small children who spend many of their waking hours in it? What changes to its physical appearance and its atmosphere, both indoors and out, will give it that comfortable, home-like quality? Young children, and adults too, who spend such long hours in a day care center need to be in a relaxed and welcoming environment, where the atmosphere is one of home, and the feeling of being in an institution is minimized.

Most centers do not start off "soft", but this need not be expensive or difficult to achieve, although it may be slow! Eventually there should be curtains at the windows, bright coverings and pot plants on the tables, carpet and soft rugs on the floor, and abundant cushions, bean-bags and wall hangings, to brighten and soften the surroundings and lift the spirits. Two valuable and much-used additions might be a rocking chair, comforter of so many small, tired bodies,

27

relaxed on a lap, or a soft but firm pillow, a challenge, but not a threat, to young toddlers learning to climb, roll, and tumble. A soft center has a wonderfully calming, comforting and positive effect on all its users. It feels good, it welcomes children and visitors, it does not intimidate parents. Adults working with young children are assisted by such surroundings to treat children in a natural manner.

Toddlers need quiet spaces, and places to withdraw into for privacy and escape from noise and busy activity, bookshelves and room dividers which break up large areas into cozier, more personal, and more manageable (to a small child) spaces; places for just being, just looking, perhaps with the sound of soft music nearby. Some centers even have a bed in which a child can curl up, with a bottle or a book, and perhaps fall asleep.

Even under-threes in day care can be encouraged to feel proud of and help to maintain their visually attractive, inviting surroundings, watering pot plants and the garden, plumping up cushions, sweeping and dusting.

## What About the Garden?

The garden is not just the back yard, but an important extension of indoor play space, and the "feel" of it, its structure and management, can strongly influence, either positively or negatively, the behavior, attitudes, and sense of security of the small children who use it. "Soft" areas, a "soft" atmosphere, and careful planning of garden layout can encourage small children to pause, take time in discovery and exploration, interact with each other in a positive way, and share relaxed, unhurried time with loved adults.

How can one soften a garden? With rugs, bean-bags, cushions, and play materials to be used quietly under a tree or a garden umbrella; with a hammock which can hold an adult and a child (or two); with Turkish baby hammocks strung between trees or equipment; with additional greenery, in flower beds, pots, or hanging; with pleasant variations of color and texture in the garden's natural materials. A deck alongside the sandpit; a low, fixed table with fixed log seats; part of the lawn allowed to grow into long, lush green grass. Such garden areas encourage the enjoyment of small group interaction, just as the instincts for socialization and co-operation start to emerge in the going-on-threes.

## Interacting Closely and Lovingly with Children

Loving adults are the key to what under threes learn and how they respond to experiences. They model themselves on their caregivers, absorbing and internalizing their attitudes, values and behavior, and reflecting them in their own. This is "silent teaching", and it can nourish such qualities as generosity, curiosity, sympathy, consideration, a sense of right and wrong.

Especially during the long hours of day care, the most important thing that an adult can do is to give complete attention to a child, and to provide much unhurried time for one-child to one-adult contact and conversation. It is just so easy for the caregivers to talk with each other, for perhaps more time than they realize, with the resultant loss of so many valuable "teachable" moments and opportunities for closeness with children. Research indicates that the participation, interest and guidance of adults in children's activities has a very strong positive effect on the quality of the learning which takes place during play.

When attempting to evaluate the quality of caregiver relationships with under threes, it is good to ask questions such as these:

- Do staff maintain easy and comfortable dialogue with small children, thus providing a natural, ongoing educational component to the day?
- Do staff make time often during the day for cuddling, relaxing, laughing, singing with children and general enjoyment of each other?
- Do staff keep as close to the physical level of the children as possible, sitting on the floor with them, on low chairs or bean-bags, or having them on laps?
- Is the program set up to provide frequent contact with a small number of adults, giving importance to verbal skills, with children and caregivers as partners in language play?
- Do staff facilitate and encourage exploration and experimentation the way in which under threes learn best?
- Is self-esteem in the children built through activities at which they will, for the most part, succeed, and are staff generous with praise and recognition of their efforts?
- Are there many opportunities for the learning of life skills, such as independence and self-discipline, at appropriate levels to meet the developmental capabilities of under threes?
- Do caregivers give tender, loving support (which is NOT "spoiling") to a small child in a needy developmental phase, realizing how quickly, given support, the need will pass?

Above all, and it bears repeating, the most important contribution adults can make to children is to provide them with warm, loving interest and ongoing dialogue, in an environment which is relaxed, unhurried, flexible, and geared to each child's individual needs.

## Individualizing the Program

How can the day's program be tailored so that it offers satisfaction and fulfillment and a degree of comfortable familiarity to under threes? Each hungry two year old needs to eat, and then to sleep, when an inner clock says so, and not when plans for the group dictate. A child needing to be held and rocked on someone's lap needs it now, not later. Opportunities for being alone, for having precious time with just one adult, for doing nothing, or for being deeply involved—such flexibility should be woven into the pattern of the day for all children, but particularly for those under three.

It is necessary to remember that children arriving early at the center, with parents who are on their way to work, may have just been through a stressful period of "getting ready for school" and are in extra need of a pressure-free, calm and gentle unwinding period, and perhaps a lap to sit on, soft relaxing music, or a story. At the day's end too, pressures build in tired children who watch the arrival of other children's parents, but not theirs, often with increasing dismay. At that time there is a need for special, absorbing occupations, perhaps kept always for this particular time slot, a welcoming lap or happy music on the tape recorder.

Treasures and especially loved objects from home may restore balance in the day of a child who is upset and lonely. Ones own blanket or sleeping toy on the bed makes the world of difference to how sleep-time is viewed. Flexibility such as this recognizes a child's emotional needs and individuality. It has succeeded in narrowing the gap between home and day care, to some degree blending the two environments.

What are the activities and occupations small children would be having if they were at home all day, and which also tie in with the developmental interests of under threes? The most satisfying of all "play" activities for toddlers often consist of tasks carried out with cared-for adults—real work! This can be:

- In the kitchen, helping to wash up, hand the tea-towel, dry a dish (non-breakable), fold a towel, turn a tap on and off, get a pot, or help unpack the dishwasher.

- Fetching and carrying the letters or newspapers, diapers, pins, powder for the baby, the adult's basket, keys or purse.
- On wash day, carrying the clothes to the laundry, handing them for hanging out on the clothes line, carrying clean clothes to cupboards.
- At clean-up time, sweeping, dusting, wiping down tables.

In all these occupations wonderful opportunities exist for the extension of knowledge, the development of language and the learning of concepts.

The same opportunities can exist in the day care center and provide another way of blending the two environments and narrowing the gap. Going to the shops, walking around the block, visiting each other's homes, having visitors in to share the day—the inclusion of these home-style activities and those discussed above allows the under threes an extension to already familiar experiences, which are challenging, stimulating, and developmentally appropriate.

## What About Parents?

Mutual trust and acceptance in the relationship between parents and caregivers and strong communication between them will directly affect the feeling of contentment and acceptance the young child develops towards the care experience.

What feelings do staff want parents to have as they go off to work in the mornings and when they return in the evenings? They want feelings of confidence:

- that the caregivers of their children will be open and responsive to parental needs, as well as to those of the children.
- that staff will be listeners, encouraging and supporting parents in their role, and also caring conveyors of information.
- that staff will always take time to give verbal feedback about their child's

day, providing written feedback in the form of newsletters, a daily newsboard, and lunch/sleep information.

- that caregivers view themselves as partners with parents in the care and education of their children.
- that they will always be welcome to pause between work and home, to share activities with their children; talk to other parents; have a cup of tea and talk with the caregivers; just relax, as many do, in the rocking chair, recharging batteries.

## In Conclusion

The principles discussed in this chapter can be translated into a list of aims for children. It would be appropriate to share such a list as the one that follows with parents and new staff, and to ensure that the experiences offered are consistent with these aims.

## General Aims for Toddlers in Care

- To provide a secure, flexible, *caring, "home-like" environment* in which they will feel confident and protected.
- To ensure that their *first* separation from parents is *gradual and free of anxiety* (for parents too), with parents and staff working closely together.
- To build *high self-esteem* through positive expectations, encouragement and approval.
- To plan the environment so that the children are *mostly successful* in what they attempt, and thus eager to ac-

quire and master the skills they need for independence.

- To encourage the development of attitudes of *caring and concern for others*; of awareness of needs; of wonder and excitement and curiosity about the world they live in.
- To encourage the *beginning of self-control and self-discipline* in their relationships with other children and adults, through sharing tasks, waiting, having turns, respecting the rights and property of others, being part of a group.
- To develop in them a recognition and acceptance of *limits set on behavior*— few and reasonable limits, relating to health, safety and other people's rights.
- To plan the day so that there is a natural *pattern* and rhythm of quiet and active occupations, providing a secure base for development, unrushed, simple and relaxed.
- To provide activities which *match the developmental needs* of the children and allow for exploration and experimentation with the materials, with no emphasis on the "finished product".
- To develop in the children *awareness and acceptance of other cultures*.
- *To offer them a richly happy time* of growth in living and learning... through doing.

If staff believe strongly in the validity of the ideas put forward here, and work steadily and enthusiastically towards their realization, group care for the under threes should be a joyful and positive experience for both families and caregivers.

# REFERENCES

Irvine, J. (1984). Play in Day Care. In *Handbook for Day Care*. Canberra: Australian Early Childhood Association Inc.

Kellett, 5. (1984). Under 3s in Day Care—Their Special Needs. In *Handbook for Day Care*. Canberra: Australian Early Childhood Association Inc.

Miles, A. (1984). Settling In New Families. In *Handbook for Day Care*, Canberra: Australian Early Childhood Association Inc.

Patterson, P. (1984). Quality Care. In *Handbook for Day Care*. Canberra: Australian Early Childhood Association Inc.

Simons, J. (1984). The Indoor Environment: A Soft Option. In *Handbook for Day Care*, Canberra: Australian Early Childhood Association Inc.

Staff, West Tamworth Children's Centre (1984). West Tamworth Children's Centre (Long Day Care): A Case Study. In *Handbook for Day Care*. Canberra: Australian Early Childhood Association Inc.

---

*Photographs:* Lady Gowrie Child Centre, Brisbane

# Chapter 4

# Toddler Environments: Planning to Meet their Needs

## Patricia Sebastian

*In keeping with the broad view of programming set out in Chapter 2, the following chapter on toddler environments should be viewed as a chapter about programming. Sebastian gives convincing evidence that the effectiveness of the total experience offered to toddlers depends so much on the care taken with the physical environment. It is not that the environment provides the context in which programming happens. The environment in a toddler care program is a critically important component of the program. Those people in charge of programs for one to three year olds would be well advised to look carefully at their physical environment to see whether it is supporting good programming or being an impediment to it.*

Toddlers have particular needs, especially when they are in group care situations, and yet there is often little thought given to what their particular needs are, and how these can best be accommodated within the group care environment. Because there has been little emphasis on planning to meet the developmental needs of this age group, toddlers have tended to become something of a "no man's land", and hence they have either been included in the infant environment or expected to adjust to the challenges of a setting for over threes.

The gradual recognition, however, of the toddler age group as one which has specific characteristics and needs, has led to more attention being given, not only to what their needs are, but also to how the physical environment can best be developed to support them. The environment and how it is arranged will have a major impact on whether these needs can be met within the toddler program or not.

Most people have had experiences where feelings and behavior have altered in response to the environment, such as upon entering a library or a cathedral, or being in the midst of the congestion of a department store sale. Consider also the overwhelming feelings of depression experienced when walking into a cold, dingy and oppressive house, particularly one where young children are cared for.

If the atmosphere created by the environment has such an impact on adults, then its influence on children in group care situations is particularly powerful, as young children experience the world more physically than do the adults around them (Greenman, 1982). This chapter focuses on how the environment can be developed to be supportive of both toddlers and adults in the program.

What influences the decisions made about the environment? When shaping ideas for planning the environment it is

33

worth stopping to consider what really influences the decisions that are made. Decisions will usually be influenced by:
- the values held
- knowledge of toddlers' needs and development
- the material resources available to operate with
- the adults' creativity and resourcefulness.

## VALUES AND PLANNING ENVIRONMENTS

"An infant-toddler program, including its physical arrangement, is determined by and reflects the teacher's preferences and values".

(Weiser, 1982, p. 274)

Feeney (1979) highlights the importance of understanding the role that values play in the decisions made about how to guide children's development. She identifies two extreme value positions based on the assumptions one may make about people as learners. She states that teachers (or caregivers) who feel:

"that the world demands people who are self-directed, caring, creative, and capable of adapting to rapid change tend to believe that people are motivated by an innate desire to learn and grow. Those who hold this view believe in encouraging the growth of the whole child with equal emphasis in all areas of development. They see their role as providing a structured environment rich in resources, in which they help children formulate questions about their experiences and express their ideas.

"On the other hand, teachers who feel that people need to conform to the requirements of a society through mastering a body of existing knowledge tend to see people as basically receptive and molded by their environment. Those who hold this view

act as the providers of knowledge and major sources of wisdom and authority in the lives of children." (pp. 35, 36.)

The above quote, although seemingly more appropriate for an older age group, does help demonstrate the different values that may influence planning for toddlers. For example, if caregivers do value individuals who are self-directed, then the environments they plan for toddlers should provide opportunities for them to learn through developing their own initiative, exploring and discovering.

Furthermore, if caregivers value people who are able to act independently, make choices and solve problems, then environments for toddlers should be structured in such a way as to promote opportunities for them:
- to be independent, for example to be able to reach the materials and equipment available;
- to make choices about what to do from the variety of experiences provided; and
- to solve problems, by being given appropriate challenges and time to meet them.

On the other hand, an environment and atmosphere which demands conformity, total control and little opportunity for independent thought and action, is likely to restrict the learning opportunities for toddlers. Such action may result in children who lack initiative and creativity and who are unmotivated and dependent on others to initiate their learning.

When caregivers take time to clarify their own values, not only are they more likely to evaluate the way in which they structure the environment for toddlers, but they are also more likely to be consistent in their approach to meeting toddlers' needs and fostering their development.

## TODDLERS' NEEDS AND DEVELOPMENT

### Safety and Health

A toddler environment must be one that provides opportunities to test out developing skills. It should be planned in such a way that it promotes maximum levels of safety and health care, while at the same time ensuring that there is minimal interruption to the amount of stimulation, challenge and comfort provided.

Toddlers spend much of their day in extensive exploration of and experimentation on the world around them. In particular, they are likely to be in constant motion, testing out their newly developing physical skills. Careful attention to the safety and health aspects of the environment will help to promote feelings of trust and encourage the exploratory behavior and curiosity of toddlers.

Eliminating hazards in the initial stages of planning will play a major part in establishing a safe environment. The potential problems created within the toddler area by essential services such as electricity, heaters and plumbing need to be considered. For example, power outlets should be placed out of reach or covered with child-proof covers, and there should be enough outlets in the room to eliminate the need for leads. Heaters must be protected by childproof safety guards, and child-proof gates, locks and fences around the playground will not only make the supervision of toddlers less stressful, but will encourage staff to interact with toddlers in a more relaxed way.

Because toddlers are highly susceptible to communicable diseases, and infections spread rapidly within a group care environment, careful attention needs to be given to how the environment is planned to support adults in the maintenance of sound hygienic prac-

tices. For example, the careful placement of diaper changing and toileting areas and hand washing facilities will help staff keep cross infection to a minimum.

Falls are a major cause of injury and subsequent hospital admission in the toddler age group. The need toddlers have to test out their physical abilities, particularly climbing, often results in falls, and adults need to plan to accommodate these newly emerging skills. An environment planned to support the safety and health of toddlers would ensure that there are:

- places to climb, both indoors and out, which are protected with appropriate impact-absorbing surfaces and which act as a cushion to falls.
- child-proof railings and bannisters placed around elevated areas and stairs both indoors and out, reducing the incidence of falls.
- non-skid surfacing, particularly in areas where surfaces are likely to get wet (for example, bathrooms and

transition zones between indoors and out).
- approved safety glass in all low windows, doors and mirrors.
- child-proof locks and cupboards for the storage of dangerous materials.

## An Emotionally Warm and Supportive Environment

As toddlers extend the horizon of their world, their gradual push for separateness and independence will involve a great deal of practice, risk-taking and inevitable mishaps. In a new and challenging environment it is possible for toddlers to feel overwhelmed, pressured and even "out of control".

However, when environments are planned carefully for toddlers and they actively promote feelings of trust, security and warmth, it is more likely that the toddlers will develop feelings of mastery, power and competence in dealing with their world. An emotionally warm and supportive environment would include:
- *The creation of an aesthetically pleasing and harmonious atmosphere.* This can be facilitated by the careful use of appropriate color schemes. Although

responses to color are highly individual, the use of soft neutral and unobtrusive colors on walls and floor surfacing is more appropriate to provide a warm and relaxed backdrop against which the more colorful displays of toddlers' play materials, equipment and creative work are set.
- *One which promotes a feeling of softness, warmth and comfort.* This can be achieved by encouraging soft elements which are as "home-like" as possible, such as soft chairs and cushions, furnishings and textured natural materials which add warmth and feeling. Carpet or other soft and warm floor covering will allow toddlers to spend much of their time using the floor as their playing surface or walking around with bare feet.
- *Private places where toddlers can withdraw and be alone and be secluded from others.* "To be able to withdraw and be alone, and to experience a sense of privacy, intimacy and solitude is essential for one's identity" (Sebastian 1986, p. 96). Intimate spaces where adults can cuddle a child or read a story to one child should also be a feature of the toddler environment. Private places can be easily

created by screening off areas with couches or cupboards, placing a large box with soft pillows scattered inside for toddlers and even adults to sit in, or draping a large piece of soft material over an area for toddlers to sit inside.

- *Secure bases to return to and ones that are consistent and predictable.* Toddlers' ability to move and extend their explorations is directly related to the degree of security and stability felt. Toddlers need to develop a sense of belonging, and this can be achieved best by creating clearly defined home bases for them to return to, with their own personal areas for sleeping and storage of belongings, individualized attention to toddlers' variations in sleep patterns will be accommodated to best by ensuring that there are separate quiet areas adjacent to, and easily supervised by, adults.
- *An environment which supports toddlers will reflect the need to reduce frustration levels by ensuring adequate space is available for toddlers to move around in comfortably.* Because most of the toddlers' exploratory play is related to motor activity such as pushing, pulling, and climbing, there is likely to be a great deal of motion in the toddler area. Toddlers need space to move, but more importantly enough space to manipulate equipment and indeed their own bodies within that space, without undue restrictions or collisions with furniture or other toddlers.
- *Careful attention to the number of people who will share the space in the toddler area.* Research has demonstrated that group size and adult:child ratios are inextricably linked to quality care, and where toddlers are concerned, the maximum size of the group should be no more than 6 to 10 (Abt Associates 1979). When overcrowding occurs, particularly in the toddler area, there is likely to be an increase

in negative, aggressive, or idle behavior. Crowding violates individuals' personal space, and the younger the child the more personal space they require.

## An Environment Which Offers Stimulating Learning Experiences

Toddlers are budding scientists (Honig, 1983). They spend much of their time exploring and manipulating their environment, they are curious, and they test the limits of the environment, including often the adults within it.

Toddlers need a stimulating and challenging environment. However, it should be planned carefully to match the toddlers' level of functioning, whilst at the same time offering new challenges. Toddlers are vulnerable to extremes in stimulation (Cataldo, 1982). Too much can become overwhelming and confusing, and toddlers who are too excited are apt to make themselves and everyone else miserable, while too little stimulation can depress motivation and learning. Therefore consideration must be given to the following:

- the need for an environment which encourages child initiated and self-directed experiences, and which encourages adventurous exploration, experimentation and manipulation with a variety of objects. It should also provide opportunities for children to make independent choices that are appropriate for this age group, and the freedom to act creatively. The feelings of personal accomplishment and autonomy which are generated when toddlers master a skill or task they have initiated is an important foundation block for building competence and confidence.
- providing opportunities which help foster a feeling of competence and power over the environment. This can be facilitated by designing an environment in which toddlers can make de-

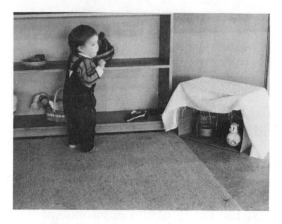

cisions independently and be in control of the equipment and facilities within it. For example, bathroom facilities should be designed to encourage toddlers to develop independence in their personal needs, such as toileting and hand washing, while receiving only minimal help from adults. Additionally, appropriately planned environments should enable toddlers to:

- reach hooks to hang up coats or towels;
- select their own equipment from orderly displays on shelves which are at their height;
- accept some responsibility for cleaning up, because adults have carefully planned the storage units which make it easy for toddlers to identify where things "live", and they have provided sinks low enough for toddlers to help wash brushes and other equipment.

## An Environment Which Supports Their Developing Social Skills

Toddlers are beginning to establish and enjoy personal relationships with others outside their immediate family, but respect for the rights of others does not come easily. Sharing personal belongings, toys, equipment, and even space can be very hard for the toddler.

Therefore it is important that there are enough favorite materials so that there is less need for constant sharing.

Whilst it is typical for toddlers to play alone or alongside others, and their curiosity regarding other children is marked, they are sometimes resentful if the other children intrude on their play (Leavitt, 1985). Therefore they need enough space so that they can move freely without having to compete with others for use of the space. Similarly, spaces need to be developed which will support both individual as well as small group activities.

Planning activity centers which encourage small groups of children (preferably no more than four) to use them at any one time, and keeping them well spaced in relation to one another, will help to reduce the confusion between "mine" and "yours" when they are using materials which may look alike, such as dough, paste, or puzzles (Biddle, 1984).

Additionally toddlers find it difficult to wait for turns on equipment, to use the wash basin or toilet or to have their meals served. Their behavior will demonstrate clearly to their caregivers when expectations are not age appropriate, and it will probably be necessary to change the environment, both physical and human, to reduce conditions which lead to undesirable behavior.

## Material Resources and Adults' Creativity and Resourcefulness

Creating an environment will of necessity be constrained by the floor space and design available. Further constraints may occur as a result of the limited money required to purchase even the most basic equipment.

Fortunately, toddlers do not need expensive or exacting replicas of particular items (for example, home corner furniture) and so it is important that adults who work with toddlers are able to call upon their own creativity and resourcefulness to acquire the much needed equipment or materials with which to create a responsive learning environment. For example, large cardboard boxes and cylinders, which so often end up as junk waste material, can provide unlimited possibilities in a toddler room, whereas lengths of material either donated or purchased cheaply from "seconds" shops will help to provide some of the softness needed.

When staff and parents are resourceful, creative and have the time to execute their ideas, then it is possible to create a rich environment for toddlers inexpensively.

## STRUCTURING SPACE FOR LEARNING

A carefully designed toddler area will support adults in their work, and will help to facilitate a more responsive environment, whereas a poorly designed one will place time-consuming burdens on both staff and children (Weiser, 1982). In order to achieve this there are a number of important features that need to be considered.

### Acoustics

Control over the noise levels within the toddler area is an important aspect in planning. High noise levels can be distracting and fatiguing and indeed quite stressful for both the toddler and staff. High noise levels can also make verbal communication with others difficult and can affect auditory discrimination (Cohen, 1973). Noise levels can be minimized by the use of sound absorbent materials such as carpets, curtains, fabric wall hangings and upholstered chairs. In some cases acoustic tile ceilings may need to be installed. Control over noise levels can also be assisted by separating the noisy activities from the quieter ones.

### Accessibility

The space and equipment need to be arranged in such a way as to enable accessibility for both the toddler and adult without too many restrictions:

- Bathrooms should be situated where toddlers and staff can gain direct access from both indoors and out. As some toddlers may still require diaper changes, clear visual connections between the play areas and the bathroom need to be provided.
- Storage facilities for children should be located at child height so that toddlers can see and select the materials they wish to play with.
- Other storage areas should also be easily accessible to facilitate the need for staff to change materials and modify the environment according to the needs of individuals and the group during the day.

### Flexibility

An environment which can be changed around easily with a minimum of fuss is more likely to be able to respond to individual needs, changes in the developmental needs of toddlers, and the "very human wish for novelty" (Prescott, 1984, p. 49). Although there will be some aspects of the environment that cannot be changed, with careful planning it is possible to rearrange the setting if the equipment has been selected with this

39

prospect in mind. For example, cupboards with lockable castors and room dividers will enable spaces to be recreated, whereas the use of lino overlays may enable messy areas to be relocated.

- appropriate visual and physical connections between various activity areas,
- transition areas where interactions with older and younger children can occur naturally, and

## Extending Horizons

Toddlers in full day programs can easily be isolated from the mainstream of daily life, and as Prescott (1972) remarks, "they may have no contact with the kitchen, the street or anyone coming in the front door. This results in monotony which must be as deadly for adults as well as for children" (p. 55). In homes toddlers can hover around watching adults go about their daily chores; they can observe what happens in the kitchen or laundry, or poke around the exciting contents of cupboards which are being sorted and cleaned out. The kinds of experiences that a toddler builds up in the home are not always easy to offer within the walls of a playroom. As toddlers engage in much observational learning and imitation it is essential that the environment should promote:

- observation spaces where toddlers can view the daily happenings within the center, and indeed the outside world.

## Spatial Arrangement

The quality of life for toddlers in day care will be reflected by the way in which the space is organized. As Moore et al. (1979) state:

Modified open space allows for more child initiative, variety of opportunities, freedom for exploration, opportunities for the child to control the environment, opportunities for autonomy and initiative, sensory stimulation and environmental responsiveness. Yet it is also a way to control noise, to zone activities into different areas, and to provide close adult supervision. (pp. 904, 905)

Toddler spaces should be zoned

into activity areas which are partially enclosed or defined by low screens, shelving, or perhaps a change in floor surfacing or level. Areas which are defined and developed around intended usage will convey to toddlers strong messages and will support appropriate behaviors (Sebastian, 1986). By zoning spaces into defined areas, it is possible for toddlers to move independently, discover activities, make choices about what they will do, and attend to learning tasks.

Each activity area can be created to project or suggest the intent of the area. For example there will need to be spaces for:

- physical activity and exploration indoors. Toddlers will also need opportunities to climb and push and pull objects when indoors. Typical of most toddler behavior is their drive to practice both fine and gross motor skills. Toddlers will engage in much gathering and rearranging of materials (Sponseller, 1974). They will fill and dump containers and stack and knock down buildings. If adults want to avoid the need for restrictive controls over toddlers, then the space and equipment and its arrangement will take into account the need to practice these skills.
- a manipulative area, where puzzles, construction equipment, and busy boxes are housed.
- secluded spaces, perhaps created by the use of a large, sturdy cardboard box.
- quiet areas, which encourage relaxation, and a feeling of comfort. Quiet areas need to be rich in a variety of soft textures.
- areas for messy play where toddlers can experience sensory activities such as sand, water, finger paint, and washing up.
- a home corner/dramatic play area, where toddlers can engage in imitation and pretend play.

- a curiosity corner where interesting exhibits that can be touched, manipulated and explored are arranged.
- storage. Ample storage spaces need to be included in the toddler environment. There need to be spaces for storage of children's belongings and "treasures", storage for toddlers' bedding that is easily accessible to adults, storage for equipment when not in use, and spaces where toddlers' materials and equipment are displayed and available for selection by them.

Toddlers' needs change frequently during the day, and a responsive environment will ensure that adults have quick and easy access to materials so that they can change them without fuss during an activity period if individual or group needs suggest this. The more difficult adults find it to set up or put equipment away, the less likely they are to respond to individual needs by introducing the appropriate materials.

## Creating a Sense of Order

Toddlers try to assert themselves, particularly as they are developing a feeling of independence. Not only do they want to do things for themselves, but they want to try to do it their way. As a consequence, toddler areas are prone to chaos and disorder, as the tendency is towards messiness, tipping, pouring (both solids and liquids) and even hurling or kicking things across the room. Structuring the environment to reduce the chaos and disorder can be achieved by:

- planning the room arrangement carefully so that it can be easily restored to order. Aspects such as the proximity of storage and washing facilities adjacent to working or play spaces will be of prime consideration and will reduce unnecessary movement between areas. Attention to how materials are displayed for selection

by toddlers will have implications for the ease with which they can be returned to the shelf or storage facility.

- encouraging toddlers and adults to keep the equipment they have chosen to play with in its designated area or to return it when they have finished with it. As toddlers are encouraged to learn that there is a special place for everything their sense of order in the environment develops.

- creating clearly defined pathways between activity areas so that toddlers can move freely around the area with a minimum of interference and interruptions from each other, also reducing the need for discipline. As Greenman (1982) observes:

> "Space that structures the flow of children through natural barriers and encourages natural dispersion into corners and alcoves reduces the amount of time caregivers perform as traffic and crowd control police. Entrance to and exits from spaces that require motor decisions, such as a step up or down, opening a gate or crawling through a hole, reduce wandering." (p. 35)

## Creating the Sleeping Environment

The sleep patterns of a group of toddlers will vary considerably, not only between individuals, but also an individual's pattern may change according to changing daily circumstances. For example, the toddler may have had little sleep the night before and may have woken up particularly tired and grumpy, or it is possible that in the early stages of an illness the toddler will be tired.

It is particularly difficult to meet individual needs of toddlers if separate sleeping or quiet areas are not provided within the day care setting. The area should be acoustically although not visually separated from the mainstream activities, with adjustable controls over lighting, heating and cooling, and it should promote the feelings of warmth, softness and comfort usually found in a home environment.

Each toddler should have his or her own bedding, and it should always be located in a regular place to help toddlers gain a feeling of personal space and security.

## A Bathroom Designed For Toddlers

Accomplishing independence in toileting is a major task for toddlers. As they develop the skills and independence needed to take care of their bodily functions, they are likely to spend a considerable amount of time in the bathroom area. Therefore the area needs to be planned to be as pleasant and as

42

trouble free as possible.

Bathrooms should be located where toddlers are free to come and go according to their individual needs. Where possible, provision for direct access to both the indoor and outdoor area is desirable. They should also be designed to provide a clear view from the playroom so that adults are able to monitor toddlers' behavior. Washbasins and toilets should be able to be controlled independently by toddlers and water needs to be thermostatically controlled to prevent scalds from water.

Some toddlers will still be in diapers, and it will be important that the changing bench is designed to promote safety and easy attention to hygienic practices to reduce the risks of cross infection. Adult hand washing facilities should be located adjacent to the change bench, preferably with elbow controls fitted to the taps.

Storage facilities for both clean and dirty diapers should be within easy reach of the change bench, to avoid the need for staff to move away from a child while he or she is on the bench.

As some toddlers are likely to be quite heavy, consideration may also need to be given to the need to provide steps up to the change bench. This would help reduce the possibility of back injury occurring to staff who are constantly having to lift and carry children.

Overall, the bathroom needs to be aesthetically pleasing, as children learning to use the toilet will spend time "sitting" at regular intervals, and hence efforts should be made to create a pleasant and interesting area. Natural light, particularly sunlight, the use of color and hanging baskets of plants can help to create an interesting and relaxing area.

## Adult Areas

Parents are the most significant adults in the toddlers' life, and staff in day care programs must make every effort to develop and sustain their relationship with parents. Providing a warm and welcoming entry area will make the transition from home to center a more comfortable experience for both parents and child. The most important aspect in fostering relationships however, is the warmth of the acknowledgement the child and parent receive from staff each day as they enter their area.

Staff also need places to relax. If they are to remain responsive and sensitive to toddlers' demands then they must have uninterrupted time away from children to rest and relax and recoup their flagging energy. As with all other areas in the center, the staff area should be aesthetically pleasing and furnished with comfortable lounging chairs.

When the environment is planned with developmental needs in mind, then it is likely to be responsive and supportive of toddlers' endless energy for exploring both the physical as well as the interpersonal dimensions of the environment.

## REFERENCES

Abt Associates (1979). *Children at the Centre: Final Report of the National Day Care Study.* Cambridge, Mass.: Abt Associates.

Biddle, J. (1984). Programming for the One to Three Year Olds. *Handbook for Day Care.* Canberra: Australian Early Childhood Association Inc.

Cataldo, c. (1982). Very Early Childhood Education for Infants and Toddlers. *Childhood Education*, Jan./Feb., 149-154.

Cohen, S; Glass, D; and Singer, J. Apartment Noise, Auditory Discrimination & Reading Ability in Children. *Journal of Experimental Social Psychology*, Vol. 9, 402-422.

Feeney, S. and Christensen, D. (1979). *Who am I in the Lives of Children.* Columbus, Ohio: Charles E. Merrill Publishers.

Greenman, J. (1982). Designing Infant/Toddler Environments. In R. Lurie and R. Neugebauer (Eds.). *Caring for Infants and Toddlers: What Works, What Doesn't.* Vol. 2. Redmond, Washington: Child Care Information Exchange.

Honig, A. (1983). *Meeting the Needs of Infants. Dimensions*, January, 4-7.

Leavitt, R and Eheart, B. (1985). *Toddler Day Care.* Lexington, Ma., Lexington Books.

Moore, G., Lane, T. Hill, A. Cohen, U. and McGinty, T. (1979). *Recommendations for Child Care Centre.* Milwaukee: University of Milwaukee/Wisconsin Centre for Architecture and Urban Planning Research Report.

Prescott, E. (1972). *Day Care as a Child Rearing Environment.* Washington, DC.: National Association for the Education of Young Children.

Prescott, E. (1984). The Physical Setting in Day Care. In J. Greenman and R. Fuqua (Eds.). *Making Day Care Better.* New York: Teachers College Press.

Sebastian, P. (1986). *Handle with Care: A Guide to Early Childhood Administration.* Melbourne: AE Press.

Sponseller, D. (1974). Designing a Play Environment for Toddlers. In D. Sponseller (Ed.). *Play as a Learning Medium.* Washington DC.: National Association for the Education of Young Children.

Weiser, M. (1982). *Group Care and Education of Infants and Toddlers.* St. Louis, Missouri: C.V. Mosby Company.

---

*Photographs:* Lady Gowrie Child Centre, Melbourne

# Chapter 5

# A Multicultural Perspective on Programming for Toddlers

## Pam Schurch

*Multiculturalism is a topic of great interest in many aspects of contemporary Australian society, including programs for children. Multicultural activities and experiences are not something to be tacked on to a program or offered at specific times, but rather an attitude that permeates every aspect of the program. It is not something that must be considered only if there are children in the program from "different" cultures, or a problem to be solved, but rather an approach that benefits and enriches the experiences of all children.*

*The following chapter argues convincingly that it is not only possible but very important to begin with programs for babies and toddlers to incorporate a multicultural perspective. The chapter revolves around a colorful, detailed, and sensitive description of one center, the lady Gowrie Child Centre in Sydney, in its efforts to provide for all toddlers in the program a truly multicultural experience. From this account readers will be able to extract the principles important to apply to the operation of other programs.*

A truly multicultural education begins at birth. Parental attitudes of openness and receptivity are learned and absorbed by even very young children. Families need to value the fact that people and lifestyles are different, to view this as a positive, non-threatening aspect of life, and to find exciting and fulfilling the opportunities which occur to share in these cultural variations. As well, parents and caregivers need to emphasize the similarities among people, so that young children come to realize that although people may look, speak and act very differently, they share the same needs and feelings. We all have joy and sadness in our lives, we all need to experience success, recognition, praise and respect for our language and culture, and we all need a positive self concept.

Effective teachers (and that includes parents) can become skilled at incorporating awareness of the immediate and broader social world into a child's life. A comment (or a touch) on a child's beautifully wiry, curly hair; an Indian visitor eating with the fingers of the right hand; a baby being carried strapped to its mother's back—these are a few of those moments which lend themselves to the incidental teaching which can take place nearly every minute of the day, at the hands of sensitive adults.

These are "teachable moments". A two year old can learn from these, when language is simple and accompanied by gestures.

What are the basic qualities necessary for the development of good interpersonal relationships within ones own immediate social environment? They are:

- Awareness of others, their viewpoints and perspectives.
- The ability to communicate, to talk

things over, to listen to others, to accept a different view.
- Willingness and the ability to cooperate, adapt and be flexible.
- A sense of social responsibility.

These too are the qualities and skills necessary for harmonious living in a multicultural society. Can children learn them, to some extent, at a very early age? Such skills are just beginning to emerge in very young children, who can be motivated to practice and expand them as they mature and develop.

ourselves, people we enjoy, with interesting lifestyles that are good to share.

Very young children learn through concrete experiences and the everyday, basic living activities which have strong meaning for them. Under threes absorb the concept of multiculturalism almost through the pores of their skin if exposed to it through day-to-day living with adults who naturally and spontaneously communicate with them through their own language, who introduce aspects of their own lifestyle into normal

At a children's center where there are staff of different nationalities who present their way of life in a natural, continuous manner, weaving their language and customs into the fabric of the day, the children in their care soon associate what they hear, see and experience with those loved adults.

"Going-on-threes" may not express themselves quite like this:
"We made Turkish biscuits and drank Turkish tea from a samovar"...
but more like this:
"We made Berra's biscuits, and had tea from Berra's teapot"...
but the message has been received: people are different, speak differently, do things differently, but are people like

daily events, and who themselves have a deep and genuine desire to know more about other people.

To illustrate some aspects of the multicultural perspective in an under threes program, let us follow a two-year-old African boy on a day early in his attendance at a center...

As Sipho and his mother come through the door, the atmosphere is one of welcome and relaxation. Sipho's mother feels cheered at the sight of a poster which says "we cuddle" in several languages, including her own. Music with a lovely beat (Greek dancing music) is playing, and Sipho at once stamps and claps to the rhythm. He is welcomed with a hug and his own language greeting, "Molo wena!" The room is bright and inviting. There are wall hangings and decorative panels showing intricate traditional Maori and Tongan patterns. There is a cosy retreat space near the books, with a canopy overhead (a bit like an Eastern tent), and a grass New Guinean mat on the floor. There are enlarged photographs low on the wall. They are of the local community where Sipho now lives. There is the train station, there is the shop. Sipho feels good.

He joins two children in the home corner. The table is very low with cushions around it (Greek and Turkish style) and on the table are Turkish teacups, a samovar, and a bowl and spoon made of hollowed gourds, from Africa. Sipho feels at home. The dolls are brown-skinned, sallow-skinned, pink-skinned and one has on a shirt made from traditional African cloth.

Sipho puts a Thai cap on his head, wooden clogs on his feet, and pushes the brown doll outside in the stroller. There are clothes commonly worn by people of other cultures hanging on a rack, but Sipho prefers hats and shoes, as many under threes do.

Outside, hammocks are up for the baby population of Sipho's room. Turkish hammocks made from lengths of material folded between two parallel ropes and suspended from trees. One, made in Bangladesh, is woven from jute. It hangs from a branch and contains a most contented sleeping baby. Four babies in a row sleep peacefully, gently rocking, in the Turkish hammocks.

The low table is outside now, the cushions around it, ready for a "Greek breakfast" of fresh bread, olives, feta cheese, and milk. Sipho is becoming accustomed to the taste of olives and feta cheese—in fact he quite likes them.

He goes to wash his hands. In the bathroom, the Turkish teacher is changing Susan. Susan can say "Bir... Iki... Ooch" (1, 2, 3 in Turkish), and can point to ears, eyes, mouth and nose when she hears the words in Turkish. Outside some children have not yet settled down around the table. "Otur!" says the Turkish teacher ("sit down"), and because they understand the familiar word, the children sit.

Some of the children have walked up the street with their teachers to visit Bridget's home. She is Chinese. Bridget's mother has a big "Welcome" sign on the front door, in Cantonese! Bridget is so pleased and proud to

show her toys to all her friends, and to share them too. She shows them her bed and her back yard. They all have Chinese cookies baked by Bridget's mother and then sing Bridget's favorite songs... "Mary had a little lamb" in Cantonese, and "Humpty Dumpty" in English. Bridget's teacher takes photographs. Maybe one will be good enough to blow up, mount, and turn into a simple three-piece puzzle. Bridget will be so pleased! Her mother will be so proud, will feel so much a part of the Center.

At the Center, Sipho and the other children are having music. There are Spanish, Greek and Turkish songs and very simple games. One that Sipho loves is Greek. Another is a Turkish lullaby when dolls (and some *real* babies!) rest comfortably on cushions placed on outstretched legs, and are gently rocked to the words of the song. Now it is nearly lunch time.

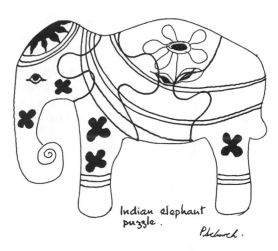

Indian elephant puzzle.

Sipho sits on a grass mat outside with the Indian teacher, as she shows him how to do the simple wooden elephant puzzle from India and then sings a sweet, lilting song about an elephant. It is a strange sound. Sipho listens carefully.

Sipho sits at the table for lunch. Bridget says "sig fan" ("eat" in Cantonese). At home, being the youngest at the table, Bridget must say "sig fan" to her elders before she may start her meal. Sometimes she does so at the center too. Today it is Thai soup for lunch. It looks strange, but tastes delicious! Sipho has Thai soup all over his face and hands.

The Turkish teacher has warm, rolled up wash cloths next to each child's place, as *her* grandmother in Turkey used to do, when she was young.

Now Sipho is tired. His bed is ready, his own special home-blanket on it. Beside his bed on the wall is a picture of an African baby, strapped on his mother's back, asleep. Sipho loves this picture; he often looks at it; it makes him feel good. He falls asleep to the soft, gentle music on the tape recorder. Sipho must sleep long and well today, for tonight with his parents he will return to the Center after dark. It is the night when Greek Independence Day will be celebrated and families will cook Greek food and share it in a wonderful Greek "feast", before the musicians come with Bazouki and a Cretan lyre to play for the dancers. Sipho will dance too, along with all the other children.

From this description, then, it can be seen that multiculturalism can be experienced as a way of life and accepted, even by under threes, as variation in the expression of human existence. There are three important areas which lend themselves to promoting and encouraging acceptance and understanding of, and positive enthusiasm for, cultural diversity. These are:
• the physical environment,
• language and language-related experiences,
• attitudes.

48

## The Physical Environment

Looking at the under threes' area in a multicultural program we see:

*On the Walls:*
- Posters depicting other countries and lifestyles;
  Life in a traditional Chinese family; A father bathing and feeding the baby; Grandparents as carers;
  A family in a high-rise apartment block.
- Soft wall hangings, and a velvety Indian wall carpet which lends itself to stroking!
- Photographs of the local neighborhood; of the children who attend the center; of their houses; of the multicultural toys and instruments in the room.
  Some of these are enlarged to use on the walls, others have been used to make simple three and four piece puzzles or matching card games. All boost the good feelings of self-worth children need to experience.
- Patterns and designs drawn from various cultures (Maori, Tongan, Middle Eastern) used to expose the children to the colors, forms and textures enjoyed by groups other than their own. There are many ways of expressing beauty.
- Words to other-language songs often sung, written phonetically for easy reading by the adults.

*In the Home Corner:*
- The velvety Indian wall carpet, a woven grass mat on the floor, cushions with distinctive Thai and Indian covers, and over it all, a canopy made from a gold and green shimmery bedspread. Here, in this retreat from the busy room, children relax and look at books or have a story read to them, or enjoy a small, intimate singing group.
- Books. These have simple "here and now' content; some are photograph books of the room's happenings and all can easily be "read" in two languages.

*On Shelves Around the Room*
- Toys from various countries to be used in small groups, so that there can be maximum use made of language and discussion opportunities.
- Tapes of music from all over the world, with words and rhythm unfamiliar and stimulating to children.
- Musical instruments from Asia, Africa, Greece, Turkey, South America, India—all chosen for their simplicity, cultural distinctiveness and variety of tone and sound.

*On the Floors:*
- Woven grass mats from Island countries in constant practical use, inside or in the garden.
- A beautifully patterned and coloured Numdah Indian rug, a welcome at the entrance door.

*Out in the Garden:*
- Hammocks used daily to lull babies and young toddlers to sleep to the sound of birds and rustling leaves. (So far we have collected four different hammock styles—Turkish, Icelandic, Bangladesh and the normal European kind, but wide and deep enough to hold an adult and three or four children!)
- Again, Islander woven grass mats used instead of rugs or blankets, for story or singing groups or quiet activities in the garden.

*Hanging from the Ceiling:*
- Three Chinese sunshades over the home corner.
- Chinese "fish" mobiles.
- A wire ball of Australian dried flowers.
  These objects, the experiences they offer, and feelings they evoke speak to the children, though not in words, of differences yet similarities, of variations in familiar things.

chinese fish mobile.

home corner.

hanging flowerball - Australian dried flowers.

## Language

The acceptance of the validity of languages other than English is essential in the center.

*Why is it important to maintain the first language?*
- For communication at home with parents and other family members.
- For self esteem and to avoid the feeling that the language is inferior and unacceptable.
- So that the center may demonstrate respect for a child's first language English may be dominant, but that doesn't make it "best".
- As a link with the family's own culture.
- A second language is learned best if the first language is well established.
- Cognitive and affective areas develop more fully if the first language is used as the child learns English.

*How to help.*
- Learn basic phrases of welcome, endearment, expression of need.
- Accept children communicating with each other in their own language.
- Learn songs, rhymes, games of other languages.
- Employ bilingual ethnic workers to use children's first language with them.

## Language-Related Activities

Most important of all is the inclusion on the staff of people who speak another language and have the ability to share aspects of their culture with children and parents in a spontaneous, natural, enthusiastic manner. Children of 18 months are not too young to understand some of what is said to them regularly, daily, in another language, relating to meaningful activities. Simple directions, terms of endearment and praise, naming of body parts, some counting, simple songs and rhymes—very small children continually surprise us with their understanding of these, in Greek, Turkish and Persian.

Parents often ask, "What is the song my child is singing at home? It sounds…different". It turns out to be the song or rhyme the child especially loves, and hears, at music time—the Persian song about magpies flying, which ends with the child in your lap and gentle tickling; or the Greek rollicking game "Koonya bella", with a child rocked and swung on the linked arms of two adults. Just-walking children, when they hear this game beginning, almost form a queue, so eager are they for their turn! Stories, songs, games, conversation—opportunities can be made throughout the day for exposure to the beauty and delight of another language, for children to begin to understand that "Greek is an Australian language, Turkish is an Australian language."

## Parents

All this having been said, it remains of great importance for the involvement, enthusiasm and commitment of parents (both Anglo-Australian and those from other lands) that attitudes of welcome and acceptance are apparent in the physical environment. Ways of indicating interest and respect to parents include:

- A message of welcome or greeting, in various languages, on the door. Parents will willingly add their language when they know it would be welcome! Communication between center and families is the cornerstone of multicultural progress.
- In the hallway, a display of posters and pictures reflecting the multicultural mix of Australia, with captions in several languages. (Parents are happy to see some languages represented, not necessarily always theirs. They willingly help with translations, and thus another bond is forged.)
- Names of teachers, details of the program, an explanation of how the program works, and how parents can participate, in relevant languages.
- Enrollment forms and information booklets in as many languages as possible. When this does not meet a specific need, make use of the bilingual resources of the neighborhood (local school, health service interpreters etc,).
- Labels on pictures of familiar objects ("house", "baby", "car", "horse") in the languages represented in the room; again a request gladly fulfilled by parents.
- To say 'hello' to Dimitri we say 'Kalemera'. To say 'goodbye' we say 'Yasou'. Dimitri is from Greece. A sign like this on the wall in the playroom for each child of a non-English speaking family teaches staff and other families those words of greeting and farewell which should be habitually in use. Parents again will write the words and teach the pronunciation.
- A photograph book of the daily life in the playroom, with simple, translated text, gives new families of all nationalities a clear idea of aims, objectives and attitudes.
- Translate information into other languages.
- Involve other same-language parents for bridging and support to new families.
- Provide the opportunity to communicate by way of own language to parents.
- Get parents to read or tell stories in their own language.

- Teach basic concepts—color, shape, for example, in both languages.

The fabric of Australian society is in a state of change as impact is made on it by the influx of other cultural groups.

If staff in children's services are serious about the value of a multicultural society then the character of our children's services must change to reflect this.

Staff must expect to change as they listen to, learn from, reflect on, and question messages from parents. Attitudes will be challenged and they will be given a new and sometimes uncomfortable perspective on their work. Some accepted practices will have to change. Accessibility, receptivity, flexibility and warmth of feeling will ensure an ability to meet these changes in a positive way.

## Attitudes

Goals for most centers would include making consistent efforts to:
- Expand children's awareness of others.

- Expand their capacity to communicate.
- Expand their willingness and ability to co-operate.
- Expand their sense of social responsibility.

These qualities are so necessary for living in a multicultural society.

But can they be encouraged in such very young children as those not yet three? Some ways might be:
- By encouraging social interaction, and non-violent ways of solving conflict, and by offering praise and recognition whenever sharing or other cooperative behavior occurs.
- By consistently calling children's attention to other points of view.
- By encouraging children to listen to the simple explanations given of why things should and should not be.
- By encouraging children's involvement in shared tasks and chores. "Justwalkers" love to move and drag chairs, wipe tables, pick up, push dinner carts,

"fold" the diapers.

- By the careful arrangement of equipment and space, so that cooperative small group play is encouraged.
- By gathering small groups together for stories, singing, just talking, and by encouraging quiet, hesitant children to join in with confidence, to feel relaxed and open to learning, to feel positive towards each other.

## Conclusion

From a very young age then, in ways appropriate to their developmental ability, through "real life" experiences, and through seizing the teachable moments which occur throughout the day, it is possible to guide and influence even very young children towards acceptance and understanding. By weaving the concept of shared human experience and cultural diversity into all aspects of the daily program, child care workers can enrich and extend the lives of all the families with whom they work.

---

*Photographs and illustrations:* Pam Schurch.

# Chapter 6

# Nurturing Creativity

## Lyn Fasoli

*The concept of creativity, as presented in the following chapter by Fasoli, is broad in scope, and encompasses all aspects of a program for toddlers. Whereas treatments of creativity often focus exclusively on areas of expressive and creative arts (art and craft and music and movement), Fasoli reminds readers of the value of verbal creativity and, more importantly, the critical role that a creative approach plays in encouraging problem solving and general thinking ability. She begins with positive acceptance of toddlers, and links many of their characteristics to creativity. She reminds the reader that toddlers are naturally very creative, and that in fact the caregiver's role is to protect and preserve many of the characteristics that toddlers have.*

The word *creativity* tends to bring to mind images of certain kinds of people, people who are considered to be creative, gifted, artistic. Creativity is not typically associated with plumbing or nursing or automotive mechanics. A parent defusing a temper tantrum in a two year old is not likely to be labeled as creative. However, imagine the following situation. At the checkout of a supermarket a two year old is determined to have a box of candy that sits no more than 20 centimeters away on the "temptation rack" strategically located at the point of exit. This creative parent anticipates the scene that is about to occur and breaks into a jolly rendition of that old favorite, "Bananas in Pyjamas". The child pauses, stares in amazement and pleasure, and distracted for that critical moment, manages to get through the checkout. Scene avoided! This is a creative response to a situation that usually elicits a monotonously predictable set of behaviors in most parents. The conventional response, threats of smacks, ferociously whispered through clenched teeth, is seen all too often despite the fact that it is usually an ineffective as well as unpleasant technique.

The words "predictable" and "conventional" were used above to describe a non-creative approach to life and tantrums. This assumes that creativity is doing something unpredictable and somewhat unconventional. However, using silly songs is quite a normal, conventional and predictable thing for parents of young children to do. The difference is that this parent chose to use that particular silly song in that particular circumstance. That is what made it a creative response. A known, familiar thing, the song, was used in a novel way.

Children are always doing this sort of thing, probably because they are so little acquainted with adult conventions. They make associations quite naturally between things they already know in order to arrive at outcomes that are new and different, associations that perhaps adults do not make because they are older and more logical. An example of this association process is an episode that happened with a small friend of the author, Martin, a just three year old with a very healthy imagination. He came upstairs wearing a Superman cape and confronted his mother and a friend with the astounding fact that he could not fly!

Martin: Why can't I fly?
Mum: Because you haven't got any wings Marty.
Martin: Superman hasn't got any wings.
Mum: Oh, that's just t.v. They use wires to keep him up.
Martin: Can we get some wires?
Mum: No, they'd cut your tummy. It would hurt!
Martin: (Thinking intensely for 10 seconds) I know! We'll put them on the cape.
Mum: What? Oh, the wires. No that wouldn't work because the cape would rip.

Martin chattered on, half to himself, half to the adults. Then he refocused on the adults and, reaching behind him, held out his cape. "I want to fly like this", he said determinedly. The adults finally caught on to what he was thinking and realized that the primary aspect of this flying thing was to have the cape streaming in the wind. "Ah!" his mother reacted enthusiastically, "Why don't you ride your bike!" Martin exited quickly and was soon seen hurtling dangerously down the driveway on his tricycle, head reversed, admiring his fluttering cape.

The way Martin was thinking was entirely logical by his standards and, by persevering, the adults were able to tune in to the association he had made between flying and a fluttering cape. Martin's response to his need to fly was creative. His logic did not consider the real characteristics of materials and was therefore faulty by adult standards. Yet he did solve the problem; with his persistence, with his ability to keep thinking of alternative solutions, and with his trust that the two distracted but basically willing and interested adults would stay with him until the problem was solved.

Piaget (in Duckworth, 1969) has described how children construct knowledge about the world in their own personal way. They gather up all the experiences that happen to them and try to fit them into some sort of framework for understanding them. This period of development is often referred to as the period of creativity and ideas. Toddlers are dedicated to finding out, first through a rather intense trial and error approach, and at the end of this period through a more systematic mental form of trial and error. For example, the little scientist becomes increasingly able, because of those infuriating preliminary experiments performed for months, to think about which method would be most successful for getting the cat to jump and screech and run away. This ability to hold ideas in mind and sort through them, combine them in new ways, is a major cognitive breakthrough. No longer does the toddler have to do something in order to think about it.

This intense need to know is what is commonly known as curiosity. Jewel & Zintz (1986) have identified curiosity as "the major characteristic initiating all learning for the young child, both cognitive and affective" (p. 72). Toddlers' thinking can be seen in their behavior as they ask questions like these:
"What happens when I do this?"
"Why does this go like that?"
"How could I get it to do this?"
"What is another way to do this?"
Allowing toddlers to ask those kinds of questions and discover the answers themselves encourages the development of creativity. Caregivers are in a unique position to influence this process in a fundamental way. They can in fact sup-

port curiosity and the creative process, or they can nip it in the bud.

Some adults appear to think that curiosity is the last characteristic which needs encouragement in a toddler. It is tempting to take this attitude. After all, a caregiver working with toddlers generally aims to civilize these little humans, to minimize their often dangerous and destructive impact on the ordered, sensible world. A caregiver working with toddlers may view as a major goal helping the small, entirely individual, somewhat obsessive, often demanding and inescapably egocentric toddler to conform a little more each day to the unavoidable realities of the world, such as gravity or night time.

Is there room for such subtleties as creativity? How can anyone support a curiosity which manifests itself in such acts as eating soap or flushing toys down the toilet? Cataldo (1983) urges caregivers to remember that character and attitudes are being formed very early. She says, "... the behavior that is respected, the qualities that are valued—these grow into positive self concepts and feelings of worth that help the baby grow up confident and capable" (p. 50).

Adults can recognize and nourish the qualities, if not the acts, of curiosity and creativity, and conversely, they can inadvertently discourage these qualities by simply overlooking them or by frequent negative reaction to them. A look at what happens in a program that regards creativity as a low priority may highlight this point. What are some well known methods of nipping the creative bud? Caregivers would have to watch their role with children very carefully. Encouraging conformity of behavior is one of the most obvious ways of discouraging creativity. For instance, they would make loud comments about how much better Sally is threading her beads than those slow pokes over there. Lots of comparison of children really helps them to conform. They would want to have a lot of group activity where the expectation is that everybody participates and does the same thing at the same time. When toddlers wriggle and squirm, disrupting these activities, caregivers would be sure to point out how badly they are behaving, make a bit of an example of one child, ban that child from the group, or cause embarrassment in some way. This seems to impress the point with other children. When a toddler insists on listening to the story standing up the adult would make sure the child is not allowed to get away with it. She would ensure that children do not waste a lot of paper by allowing them to experiment with only one piece occasionally, she would hang up one of the better scribbles, the kind that resembles something recognizable, so that children will know what she considers to be the "right" kind of drawing. This illustration is not so terribly far-fetched, unfortunately, as the author has seen many programs that seem to follow these principles.

It is what adults say, do, and provide that gives a child the foundation needed to become a creative person. These examples are so small and perhaps seem so insignificant when slotted into the maze of experiences a young child has in a week that it may seem silly to give them much importance. The job of caring for children and supporting their social, physical and cognitive development is such a complex and overwhelming task at times. Creativity and its development seems a frill. Adults try to remember this aspect of development, but there is so much else to do! Is creativity so important after all? What is it anyway? Piaget (in Duckworth, 1969) states:

> The principal goal of education is to create men [and I am sure he meant women too] who are capable of doing new things, not simply of repeating what other generations have done—men who are creative, inventive, discoverers. (p. 5)

Creative thinking on a personal level is required now much more than ever before. This is because the world is changing so fast; it is no longer the secure, predictable place that it has been. Many of the old rules have changed. People move around more, they change their jobs, perhaps their careers, many times in their lives. Traditional sources of guidance such as schools, church, state and family no longer speak in harmony. There is no longer a clear consensus on what is ethically and legally "right". Individuals must make decisions that previously the system made for them. It is the early years that determine to a great extent the kind of adult that will emerge to face this challenge!

A creative person has a much better chance of coping and living a happy and productive life. What kind of person would this be? Many of the characteristics listed by authors on the subject of the creative personality (Torrance, 1965; Austin, 1977) sound very much like many two year olds. These are some of the characteristics they highlight:

- an awareness of and interest in unsolved problems;
- an ability to generate a large number of ideas;
- a willingness to become engrossed, to concentrate;
- the ability to connect things in unexpected ways;
- courageous perseverance, individuality in the face of conformity;
- curiosity, the decisive trait that stands out above the others.

This list gives an idea of what a creative person might look like. The next question is, how do caregivers go about supporting the little person who exhibits these characteristics in order to keep alive that sense of wonder and curiosity? Rachel Carson (1956) gives a good starting point. She states:

If a child is to keep his inborn sense of wonder without any such gift from the fairies, he needs the companionship of at least one adult who can share it, rediscovering with him the joy, excitement and mystery of the world we live in. (p. 45)

Adults do this by who they are, which is reflected in what they do, say, and provide. Adults who value curiosity have an extremely powerful tool to use in teaching, by simply being curious themselves, by using everyday opportunities to demonstrate how a curious and creative person acts.

It is possible to adopt methods and techniques that can support spontaneity and creativity in children. For instance, adults can show approval of children's original thoughts and actions by their verbal and non-verbal responses. They can demonstrate that they not only accept different ideas but expect them, by recognizing and applauding differences. They can enjoy a joke, for instance, when a child uses a piece of equipment in a silly way. It is not going to upset life too drastically, for example, if a child decides to have morning tea while sitting backwards on the chair. When a child insists on wearing his new robot-emblazoned underpants outside his shorts, the adult can try to see this as a unique, yet urgent personal statement, rather than a power struggle, a deliberate effort to be defiant. There will be time enough to adhere to adult dress conventions later.

Cleaning up with toddlers can be a challenge, especially when one child insists on nudging a block in the general direction of the shelf, pretending to be a bulldozer. There is not much point in engendering the panic of clock watching ("Oh! No!" the caregiver says with mock horror, "It's nearly lunch time. Hurry and pack up!") This causes the panic without the constructive hustle that she hoped would accompany it. There are many legitimate ways to get blocks on to a shelf. At snack time caregivers can restrain themselves from chastising the child who bites two holes in a sandwich, sticks two fingers through the jammy cavities, and spends the next five minutes marching this "thing" around the table greeting the other sandwiches. These examples show how adults can respect children's ideas and protect their confidence in their own ideas.

Another way to stimulate creativity is to ask questions that have no predetermined "right" answer. Most adults have been educated by schools and by society to value highly the possession of facts. Witness the immense popularity of the game "Trivial Pursuit", which asks for rapid recall of facts. Often the curriculum in early childhood seems to focus on this recall capacity. Caregivers ask such questions as "How old are you?", "What color is your shirt?" "What does the cow say?", "Where's your nose?" These are all closed questions that demand closed answers. Closed questions ask for:

Facts: How many cups are there?
Labels: What kind of animal is this?
Recall: What did we have for lunch?

There is obviously a fundamental place for these questions in any program for young children, so these are not totally inappropriate questions. The problem is that adults may tend to overuse this teaching device at the expense of more open questions which demand an entirely different kind of thinking. Open questions have no "right" answers. Even very young children can

58

benefit from questions of this sort. Ask observation questions such as "What can you see?" This encourages the child to really look. It is a very simple game that toddlers love. It gives them a chance to use their limited vocabulary and practice their labels and of course, there are many different "right" answers. Allowing all answers, including "elephants" and "monsters" encourages imagination.

Ask analyzing questions such as "I wonder why Jamie is crying?" Answers may include "Wants his Mum" or "Bottle". When adults accept and consider all answers, including those that go beyond the obvious ones, they are developing creative thinking. Ask problem solving questions: "Oh, oh, there's milk on the floor. What can we do to fix that?" Toddlers love to do real work. Give them a chance to think a real problem through and come up with their own solutions. Obviously, toddlers vary considerably in their ability to express themselves verbally. These games can be played by pointing too. Be prepared for lots of repetition. Children are less in need of facts than they are in need of the ability to think. Children are fluid, original, creative thinkers until they learn that questions have "right" answers. They are quite prepared to consider the irrelevant or what adults might consider illogical data.

Open questions have an emphasis on the *process* of thinking, rather than the *product* of answers. Process and product are issues in another creative pursuit, expressive art. Very young children are relatively unskilled users of materials.

They dabble, experiment, and generally muck around with art materials just to gain experience. They rarely start out with a clear plan of what they will create, and even when they do, the process will often suggest something that alters the plan. The scribbles of toddlers appear to be totally random and meaningless. Yet they are a necessary prerequisite to

more advanced drawing and creative art work, in much the same way as crawling leads to walking. Through scribbling

a child discovers how lines link up to form shapes. These shapes, drawn inadvertently and then purposefully, begin to be named by the child, who sees a resemblance to something recognizable from real life. There is some evidence that even very young children of two years are trying to represent real things in their scribbles (Winner, 1986). Their attempt at representation seems to be gestural rather than pictorial. An example of this would be a child zooming the crayon all over the page as a way to represent a car, or in the case cited by Winner, a child who "hopped it around on the page, leaving a mark with each imprint and explaining as she drew, 'Rabbit goes hop-hop'" (p. 28). At this age, eighteen months in this example, the child is not concerned with making the drawing look like the thing. Young children draw what they know rather than all the details of what they see, probably because "... drawing is difficult for them, but also because they have not been fired up by the peculiarly Western pictorial ideal of realism." (Winner, p. 32)

An emphasis on realism in a child's drawing can be a real impediment to creativity. When adults emphasize process, it frees them from the temptation to provide models for children to copy. Copies, in any arena, are usually poor substitutes for the original. Anyway, when the expert is on hand, why bother with laborious copying? It is all too easy to be involved in children's art as the originator rather than the helpful assistant. In pursuit of "What will I do with them tomorrow?" adults often present cute ideas found in one of those "make-and-do" books which masquerade under a title such as "Creativity for Busy Hands". Caregivers sometimes give children an activity in kit form. It is a marvellous exercise for the adult's creativity, because they are doing all the creative thinking. They spend hours preparing masses of cut-outs of pre-drawn component parts, and the next day they instruct children on the method of assembly. The ubiquitous egg carton caterpillar is an example:

"Now children, we're going to make caterpillars today. First put the feelers on his head like this. These spots are for his eyes. No silly, his eyes don't go on his feelers, do they?"

The next day, the resulting products are laboriously patched up by the adult because the feelers keep falling off. Then they dangle off an attractive tree, drawn by the adult at 10:30 the previous night. Eventually the adult has produced a delightful wall display. Parents arrive in the morning, immediately recognize the product as a caterpillar, and are thrilled at their child's skill, and at the caregiver's ability to channel their rampant energies to such constructive ends. The name tags help immensely to remind everyone which caterpillar belongs to which child. There is an immediate talking point

between caregiver and parent, and a concrete answer to the inevitable question, "What did you do today?"

The product seems to represent learning. The child who has produced a caterpillar has learned something. When asked, the adult can point to color recognition, facts, ability to follow directions, and the exercise of small motor skills. These are, in fact, learning goals, very worthwhile, that adults may have in mind, and there is no harm in the very occasional "kit" type activity. But the danger is that when these become a daily diet, children will learn a whole set of attitudes that may not be particularly desirable. Attitudes, as well as skills, are taught through activities. In the future these children may become dependent on adults for ideas. They may begin to ask or wait for ideas to come from the adult, who may be put into the role of a magician delving into a bottomless bag of tricks. Eventually, the children learn to distrust their own capabilities. The "I can't" syndrome seen in school children sets in.

Perhaps most importantly, these kinds of activities clutter up their minds with symbols that do not belong there. Piaget (in Duckworth, 1969) describes the process of forming schema or mental representations of the world. A young child may be working at developing a mental model of what a dog or caterpillar is like, by drawing it over and over. Experience with the object gives the child more to work with in terms of details. It is a personal process, based on personal experience and learning. Each child does this in a unique way until someone interferes with the process and gives a formula or their own personal schema for the object. To give an example of this, if adults are asked to draw a tree, chances are good that many of those trees are the lollipop variety. Yet a glance out the window is unlikely to reveal many trees of the lollipop sort. Lollipop trees can be blamed on coloring in books, or teachers, but most adults stopped bothering to try to represent trees in a personal way a long time ago. This does not imply that children should never be interrupted, or that adults have nothing to teach. Caregivers are not expected to simply stand by and watch the "process" take place. In the same way that caregivers help children to learn how to eat, how to get dressed, how to hammer a nail, they can help them with creative materials. Firstly, they give technical help when necessary. They show children how to hold scissors the right way up and how to wipe a brush when painting. They demonstrate various ways to use a crayon to get different effects. They take the time to discuss a problem a child might be having instead of taking over and doing it for the child. They provide plenty of time, space and suitable materials.

Perhaps the most difficult aspect of working with toddler art is trying to think of something reasonable to say about their efforts. It is important to avoid those natural yet closed questions. "What is it?" or "Is it a duck?" can cause embarrassment, discomfort, or even rejection when "it" is not anything at all, or "it" is a picture of mummy, not a duck!

This line of questioning also implies that every effort must be *something* and, once labeled, it will continue to be referred to as such. The safer and more beneficial approach is to comment on what can be seen, such as lines, dots, colors or shapes, and to comment on what the child is doing, such as swirling, zig-zagging, filling up the corners: "You certainly have made a lot of long, red lines haven't you?" Adults who can deliver these slightly strange comments with a note of admiration and approval in the voice are often rewarded with an explanation by the artist of the thinking process behind the work. Of course, some pictures should be allowed to speak for themselves.

Adult-conceived, adult-directed, and in too many cases adult-executed, activities are a whole lot more attractive to the untrained eye than are the messy little nondescript lumps of creativity that children produce. It is difficult to know how to display them because they are usually fragile. But there are ways to do it. Special display areas can be designated and made attractive with backdrops of fabric. Aspects of the creative process of the activity can be highlighted by putting up a notice that describes

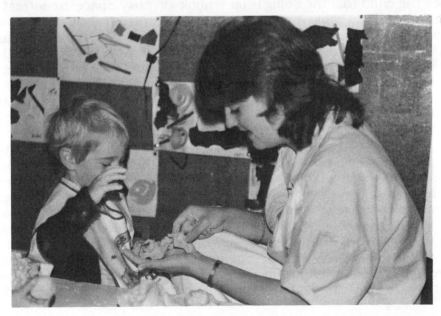

what was done and the way materials were used. It is unlikely to become too time consuming, because not everyone will produce something every day. Every drawing or object will be recognizable to its owner because it is an expression of its owner, and of no one else. If a child does not recognize a personal creation then it may not be important, in which case it is not worth keeping. After all, in most cases young children focus primarily on the doing, and much less on the product. Adults complicate this by raving excessively about the product, instead of commenting on the skills and ideas the child used in order to make the product.

The very real problems of producing attractive wall displays and parent expectations cannot be ignored. Staff in child care centers operate much more in the public view than do schools. Parents are invited to participate freely in programs. They are likely to be more involved on a day-to-day basis than they will be again as their child grows older. Consequently it may require a fair amount of courage to offer creative art experiences.

Parents may expect a product every day. When they ask for it, they further convince the child that the doing is far less important than what there is to show for it. Staff should talk to parents about this, informally at the end of the day, or even better, at a meeting where examples can be shown and answers to their questions provided. The use of small information posters attached to a wall in the creative arts area of the room may help. Such a poster describes what the child care worker considers to be the value of that particular experience, and sometimes it gives suggestions to parents or other visitors about how they can help children without taking over.

Creativity is the "sinking down of taps into our past experiences and putting these selected experiences together with new patterns, new ideas and new products" (Smith, 1966, p. 43). Children under three do not have a lot of past experience to draw on because they have not been around for very long. However the experiences they have with their parents and in child care are in many cases the primary materials they have to work with, so it is very important that they are provided with new as well as familiar experiences.

Human beings need and prefer novelty—not surprisingly! Research with small babies confirms that when shown two objects, one familiar, the other new, the baby usually reaches for the new object. Almost anyone experienced with babies will have noted this. What do adults do with a distressed baby? They try to comfort and distract the baby with a view of something new. But awareness of children's appreciation of novelty is not always reflected in environments planned for children. The place in which children are cared for can become static and boring, not only for children, but for staff too. A rich and varied environment must be provided such as that experienced by children in a home environment of high quality. A child at home does not spend all day in one room and one yard. There is probably a favorite nook or cosy space to retreat to for private contemplation. There would not be 16 siblings of a similar age clustered about all day. There would be daily excursions out to the supermarket or to a friend's house. There would be lots of different textures to investigate and relish—the shag-pile in the lounge room, the cool linoleum in the kitchen, the cold tiles in the bathroom, the scratchy cement on the verandah. There would be lots of drawers and cupboards set aside and available for investigations, a special place for toys or crayons and paper.

In a study done of three year olds, White (1978) tried to discover why some of these children had already acquired an "edge", were already more competent than their peers. He concluded that it

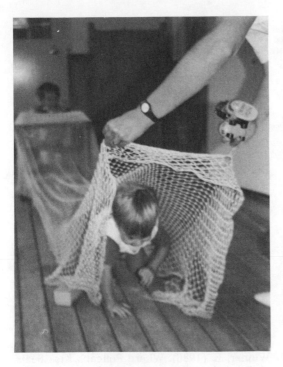

*Total Learning for the Whole Child.* She suggests that adults should provide plenty of unstructured materials that children of various ages can use in various ways. By this she means boxes, planks, sheets, bits of hose, containers of all sorts, junk materials. When children are confronted with open, unstructured materials they make them into whatever they need and explore freely. This process is easier when the object is not defined too closely. When a plastic train comes complete with cars, wheels and driver pre-moulded into place, there is not a lot of room for variation. This object will always be a plastic train. A cardboard box, given the suggestion of a wheeled vehicle by sticking on or drawing on circles, can become any form of transport. It can be changed and adapted to the whim of the driver.

Old familiar objects can be combined in new ways. Putting small plastic animals on a table with a set of stacking cups may change the way both items are used. Suspend a collection of materials, such as a steel pipe, a metal tray, a cheese grater, a block of wood from the climbing frame. The noise will be less annoying outside, and the child can experiment with different sounds while an adult points out what sounds are being made: "That sounds so soft. Can you make a really loud sound?"

Toddlers can have a wonderful time with a tape recorder. They love to hear their own voices, just as most other people do. It is a good opportunity for children to hear themselves as others do and encourages much use of language. When a large number of empty cartons of various sizes are provided, toddlers can spend hours determining how they fit or not into them. There are endless possibilities to stimulate thinking and encourage exploration by imaginative choices of play materials.

The area of dramatic play offers many chances to enhance and extend the ba-

was the designer of the child's environment, human and physical, that made the difference. He states that:

> The most competent parents provided ready access to living areas. The child could roam and explore to her heart's content. In doing so, her curiosity was broadened and deepened, new interests developed and sensory data for building new meanings and generating new language were greatly expanded. (p. 137)

Another effective way to express this same idea is provided by Jewel and Zintz (1986), who say, "The raw material that builds meanings before she has words is 'vacuumed' from the environment in her endless quest to satisfy her curiosity about the environment" (p. 22). Child care centers and other spaces specifically designed for children have to have this variety of qualities, and allow freedom to explore them; centers for toddlers must be "sensory rich".

Joanne Hendrick (1981) gives some excellent guidelines for encouraging imaginative, creative play in her book sic and rapidly emerging ability to play roles. This process of pretending exercises the intellect, and allows the child to pretend to be other people. It gives opportunities to experiment with emotions, to solve problems. It is serious work. Caregivers can show respect for children's work by giving them the props they ask for, by keeping interlopers from interfering, and by allowing plenty of time for this type of play.

In summary, young children can express their creativity in three ways. They put together ideas based on past experience when they:

- Think creatively
- Use self-expressive materials creatively
- Pretend to be or do something they have seen others being or doing.

Caregivers can help them by being curious, spontaneous people themselves, by asking open questions as well as closed, by respecting differences, and by providing enough time, interesting spaces, and open materials. Children who have the good fortune to spend their early years in this kind of supportive and stimulating environment will be in a much better position to contribute creatively to the world of the future.

## REFERENCES

Austin, J.H. (1977). *Choice, Chance & Creativity*. New York: Columbia University Press.

Bradford, M. and Endsley, R. (1980). *Developing Young Children's Curiosity: a Review of Research with Implications for Teachers*. Athens, Georgia: National Institute for Education.

Carson, R. (1956). *The Sense of Wonder*. New York: Harper & Row.

Cataldo, C.Z. (1983). *Infant and Toddler Programs*. Reading. Mass.: Addison-Wesley.

Duckworth, E. (1969). Piaget Rediscovered. In R.E. Ripple and V.N. Rockcastle (Eds.), *Piaget Rediscovered*. Ithaca, N.Y.: Cornell University Press.

Hendrick, J. (1980). *Total Learning for the Whole Child*. London: C.V. Mosby Company.

Jewel, M. and Zintz, M. (1976). *Learning to Read Naturally*. Dubuque: Kendall/Hunt.

Torrance, E.P. (1976). Education and Creativity. In A. Rothenburg and C.R. Hansman (Eds.). *The Creativity Question*. Durham, N.C.: Duke University Press.

White, B.L. (1978). *The First Three Years of Life*. New York: Avon Books.

Winner, E. (1986). Where Pelicans Kiss Seals. *Psychology Today*, August, 25-35.

*Photographs:* Lady Gowrie Child Centre, Brisbane; Bev Olsson; Lady Gowrie Child Centre, Perth.

# Chapter 7

# Discipline

## Faye McKay

*The most important component of effective discipline is what Mary Elizabeth Keister (1972) calls "a spirit of alliance" with the child, an attitude communicated in the adult's behavior and words that says to the child, "There are some rules that you have to follow. I know it will be hard for you to follow them, and I will do everything I can to help you follow them. You will not appreciate my firmness sometimes, but I am on your side". This approach comes from an understanding and acceptance of the developmental characteristics of toddlers as they are in the present, and a belief that they are treated with care and sensitivity, they will learn from that treatment, and eventually will develop the capacity and the desire to treat others that way. (Keister, M.E. (1972) Discipline: The Secret Heart of Child Care. Greensboro, N.C.: The University of North Carolina at Greensboro.)*

*Discipline is undoubtedly the most frequently requested topic for in-service discussions for caregivers of toddlers. This suggests that it is an aspect of care that caregivers never feel "on top of," or totally confident about. It also means, as McKay states, that there are no easy answers or foolproof procedures.*

*The following chapter contains a very practical, down to earth approach to discipline, one that shows great sensitivity to the reality of toddlers. The implicit assumption behind it, and behind any sensitive treatment of the topic, is that discipline is not something negative or punitive, but rather that it represents a very large and important part of the teaching that adults do with the children they care for. Examination of the strategies and guidelines suggested in the chapter reveals that teaching children how to get along, how to respect themselves, other people and the physical world around them, which is what discipline is all about, is really not drastically different from the other kinds of teaching that are undertaken in a caring adult-child relationship.*

"Don't climb on that, it's dangerous."

"Come here at once when I call you

"Stop splashing water or you'll have to find something else to do."

"I thought I told you not to do that."

"I'm not warning you again."

"Didn't you hear me tell you not to do that?"

"Take that out of your mouth at once."

"Go and sit on that chair until you've learned not to throw sand."

"There! I told you that would happen."

Comments like these are often the product of a tired caregiver, who for the tenth time in one morning has tried to stop a toddler from climbing onto the table, grabbing another child's toy or throwing sand up in the air because it is windy.

Children need discipline, but it should be appropriate discipline, applied in an appropriate way, for appropriate reasons. Discipline should help children learn what is acceptable behavior and what is not. Discipline is a necessary part of caring for children and it is probably one of the most difficult and confusing issues of early childhood, for adults as well as children.

Adults tend to be influenced by discipline experiences from their own childhood, and many attitudes are difficult to discard or re-arrange. Children may find adult behavior strange at times and their expectations unreasonable. Sometimes adults say one thing and mean another, or respond in a certain way to an incident one day and treat it differently the next.

Because of their immaturity, children may find it difficult to learn and understand the rules of behavior, especially when the rules seem to change or are applied differently to individual children. A three year old is expected to exercise some restraint and not continually interrupt a conversation, for example, while a baby who crawls through a toddler's Duplo™ construction gets protection from the caregiver with comments like "Don't get angry, he's only little, he doesn't understand". Adults accept babies making slushy messes of themselves and everything within a three meter radius as they attempt to feed themselves, while toddlers who up-end their glass of milk on the table are in trouble and are expected to clean it up.

Amazingly, most children do eventually learn what is expected of them and how to behave in different situations, and they come out of their early years behaving more or less in socially acceptable ways. Whether or not the process of learning was supportive and positive, with the children retaining good feelings about themselves and basic trust in adults, is largely dependent on how the rules were taught during the learning process.

## AIM OF DISCIPLINE

As children grow in understanding, they can gradually learn to take responsibility for their own actions and make

their own decisions, but to be able to do this they need to have confidence in themselves and confidence in their caregivers. They need to be sure their efforts will not be laughed at and that their decisions will be accepted when they have been given a choice. With help, children can gradually develop a respect for the rights of others and learn socially acceptable ways of expressing their needs and feelings.

## WHAT SORT OF DISCIPLINE AND WHY?

The type of discipline that is used and how it is applied makes a big difference to the ways children respond.

First of all, discipline does not necessarily mean punishment for wrong-doings, although that is how it is often seen. In its most positive sense, it means helping children take responsibility for their own actions, control some impulses and learn to respect the rights of others. This requires learning rules and being able to apply them appropriately. The easiest way for this to happen is by having realistic rules based on reasonable limits, and ensuring that they make sense not only from the adults' perspective but also ultimately the children's. Caregivers' decisions about what to allow children to do depend very much on what they see as important, or in other words, what their priorities are. Basically, it makes sense to set limits for all of the following reasons:

**1. Safety:** If children are to be safe from harm, they must learn many things.

a) *Selves and other*—Children must learn, for example, that some things may not be touched, that roads can be dangerous, and that some animals bite or scratch. Children must also learn not to hurt others, so certain rules need to be imposed for the protection of other children in the group and the adults who work with them.

b) *Surroundings*—Children need to learn to care for the physical environment, including play materials, furniture and equipment, their own and other people's work, as well as the natural world.

**2. Security:** Children need limits to develop a sense of security. They need to know how much freedom is allowed them and to be sure of getting help when they try to go beyond those limits. The limits need to be reasonable and consistent, and should allow for a fair amount of freedom and flexibility.

Children who have no clear guidelines to follow tend to feel insecure and unloved. It is as if they perceive that the adults responsible for them do not care enough to keep them safe. Children know when an adult is "on their side" and prepared to help them if their behavior gets out of control. Often children will test the limits, watching for adults' reactions, to see how far they can go, almost asking to be stopped and to be assured that they will receive help when they need it.

**3. Society:** Because most children thrive on acceptance, they need to be taught acceptable behavior. It is good to be an individual with an interesting personality, but society usually frowns on certain behavior. Most people find it distasteful to sit next to someone who does not use a handkerchief when necessary. Children who are constantly demanding, rude or showing off, tend to be avoided. Many people get upset by children's natural frank comments. So gently and gradually adults help them adapt their behavior to the expectations of society.

**4. Sanity** (the caregiver's!): Retaining caregiver's sanity may involve protection from a splitting headache or hearing loss! Teaching children that other people have feelings and rights is a gradual process which stems from letting children know what upsets them. They can learn to respond positively to being told, "That noise is too loud" or "That hurt", provided it does not become a constant nag.

Once caregivers sort out what the appropriate limits are and feel confident that they are reasonable and fair, they should relax and allow as much freedom as possible within the confines set.

## TESTING THE LIMITS

Helping children to behave in a responsible way is not easy and becomes more difficult when they try out the limits that have been imposed. For example, a toddler might disappear down the passage when a door has been left open inadvertently, watching out of the corner of the eye to assess the caregiver's reaction. This may be a way of exercising growing autonomy by finding out what the reaction will be. This can be frustrating and even infuriating for a busy caregiver who knows that the child knows it is out of bounds. To make matters worse, it always seems to happen when the caregiver is feeding the baby or holding a dish of water, which, if put down, will be quickly investigated by several crawling babies.

67

Sometimes this type of behavior can be treated as a joke, with a gentle reminder such as "you *know* you can't go off down there by yourself. Come and help me empty this dish and we'll find something for you to do."

If this does not work and there is no one else about, there is only one course to take—the caregiver must go after the toddler (taking the baby or putting the dish down), resisting the temptation to shake the toddler soundly, and remembering that this is normal behavior for a curious toddler whose confidence in the caregivers allows investigation in this way.

## ADAPTING EXPECTATIONS

Some adults expect far too much, far too early. They expect children to behave in a grown-up way, before they have the understanding, experience or control of an adult. Too often little children are expected to wait for things—wait for food, wait for turns, wait to be picked up, long before they have the social and emotional skills necessary for waiting, or before they have formed a basic trust in their caregivers that their needs will be met. The necessity to wait should be minimized in a program for toddlers, and when waiting periods cannot be avoided, toddlers should be given something interesting to do—singing simple rhymes or finger plays, for example—to help the waiting time go more quickly.

Sensitive caregivers will adapt their expectations to match the particular stage of development the children have reached, gradually helping them to learn control of some behavior and expression of feelings in socially acceptable ways.

*Expecting too much too soon can lead to aggressive, defiant behavior which caregivers find difficult to manage. These habits, once established, can be very hard to discourage.*

## SHARING AND TAKING TURNS

One of the outstanding characteristics of toddlers is their egocentric nature. To them the world seems to (or should!) revolve around their needs. Because of this, they are possessive and find it difficult to share people as well as play ma-

terials. They do not yet appreciate that others have rights and feelings. This point must be kept in mind when planning for this age group.

In day care, a toddler can become attached to a particular toy belonging to the center and, in a matter of seconds, consider it personal property. Woebetide another child who tries to take it. Telling the child, "This doll belongs to the center; we must all share the center toys", will not help change this attitude. In fact it may encourage the toddler to hold on to this precious object even harder. The toddler's difficulty with sharing poses problems for a caregiver who regards it as a mean streak and one which has to be dealt with. However, if this caregiver were asked to list the main characteristics of the age group, reluctance to share may be at the top of the list! It requires great skill to successfully blend theoretical knowledge with its practical application in work with young children. *Expecting a group of toddlers to cope in an environment that does not allow for their egocentricity creates discipline problems.*

## Some Points to Remember

1. When multiples of favorite toys are provided, the number of situations requiring sharing is reduced, and two toddlers fighting over one toy can quickly be offered one each. (There are some wonderful ways of adapting junk materials to make interesting and worthwhile toys for toddlers, at little or no cost. Providing duplicates of these will not strain the center's budget.)

2. When a toy or piece of equipment which cannot be duplicated creates problems, it is probably best to distract the toddlers and remove it altogether, making sure the distraction is worthwhile and interesting. Removing the equipment should not be carried out as a punishment, but as a help.

3. The process of learning to take turns and to share is a gradual one, so adult expectations should change gradually too. Short periods of waiting, rewarded with "Now it's your turn", can be tolerated more easily by the older toddler, providing the reward comes when promised. A busy caregiver can tell an impatient toddler, "I'll be there as soon as I've changed the baby", thus acknowledging the toddler's need for attention, but letting him know also that there are other demands on staff time. In many situations that are not potentially dangerous, caregivers can help children recognize that others have needs and rights in this way. Of course, it is important to follow through with what has been promised and not get side-tracked. Toddlers should have the opportunity to learn to trust that the wait usually brings the desired result.

4. Waiting periods, whether it be waiting for attention from a caregiver or a turn at the water table, should be made as interesting as possible. Waiting which cannot be avoided can be made more interesting if the toddler is encouraged to come and watch or help, or to find a book which can be read when the caregiver has finished. In other words, the adult can *help* the toddler learn to wait.

## BITING

Biting can be a very emotional issue, more so probably than other types of children's undesirable behavior. Somehow it seems a more personal and venomous act than punching, pinching, hitting or scratching. It can certainly inflict a great deal of pain and often brings a quick, dramatic response.

A toddler whose language is not well developed may resort to biting as a quick means of expression, often without malice. It may be a direct reaction to frustration, a method of forcing another child to relinquish a toy, or a reliable way of gaining attention.

Sometimes biting can be a "once-off" attack, the biter getting as much of a shock as the victim if the reaction is explosive. If the response is gratifying—that is, if the biter gets the toy from the other child or finds biting to be the best or only way to get the caregiver's attention, it can become a successful way to communicate needs. Unfortunately, biting in a group of toddlers can reach almost epidemic proportions, as children can learn quickly from modelling behaviors that are rewarded (Craig, 1979).

Biting at times can be simply an experimental act—a nice, pink, juicy, bare thigh belonging to the baby nearby may seem very enticing to the toddler who pats, prods and sucks almost everything within reach. As the toddler's teeth sink into that inviting pink thigh, what a reaction! The baby screams, caregivers come running from every direction demanding to know what happened, while the toddler stands back, probably amazed at the reaction.

So, there is a biter in the group! What can be done to help that child and also discourage others from doing likewise?

Unfortunately, there are no magic or infallible management methods, but the following guidelines may help. *Remember there is no quick cure, and a calm approach and patience are probably the caregiver's most valuable assets.*

1. Because biting *is* nasty, show the biter than this is definitely "out-of-bounds" behavior. At the same time, the biter may be distressed and confused by the reaction the biting has caused, and may need comforting too.

2. Save big reactions for big offences such as biting. A child who is constantly being told "No", being yelled at, or removed for minor offences will not appreciate the difference.

3. Use facial expression, tone of voice and touch to communicate with a toddler who needs guidance. A stern facial expression and tone of voice can convey a clear message of disapproval. Removal of the biter, along with firm words such as "Biting hurts!", are often sufficient.

4. Give attention quickly to the victim (two caregivers are useful here.)

5. Give the biter something to do that is satisfying and reduces the need to bite.

6. Try to work out the reason behind the biting—experimentation, frustration, difficulty in verbalizing needs, fatigue, or need for attention, and try to change the situation accordingly.

7. Remember, prevention is better than cure. Try to assess what triggers the biting and endeavor to get there before it happens.

In some cases of persistent biting, ignoring behavior has been used successfully. A caregiver who makes a great fuss of the victim, totally ignoring the biter, may modify the behavior of a child who is seeking attention and/or sensation. This is suggested only in extreme cases when biting persists. *It would need to be sensitively balanced with praise, encouragement and attention at times when the child's behavior is acceptable.* Caregivers should make every effort to understand why the toddler is demonstrating very real needs in this way.

## A Word of Warning!

Caregivers should never be tempted to retaliate either by biting biters, encouraging victims to bite back, or trying to make aggressors bite themselves! Toddlers are not mature enough to understand the pain they have inflicted and biting back in fact teaches the behavior that is being discouraged. Apart from that, there would be no surer way of destroying a toddler's trust in the caregiver.

## Should the Parents Be Told?

Caregivers often feel ambivalent about how much parents need to be told. A decision should be based on knowledge of the parents and how they are likely to react. If their help is required to try and reduce the need for biting, then they should be told about the incident. They can be reassured that, although unfortunate, it is perfectly normal for some toddlers to bite. If it is a "first offence" it may never happen again, and telling the parents may only make them anxious unnecessarily. It is important, though, that the parents of the bitten child know, particularly if the skin is broken or teeth marks are obvious. Parents would naturally get upset when they find bite marks while undressing their toddler for the evening bath! They also should be told that biting is fairly common at this age and that while they cannot promise, staff will try to prevent it happening again.

## Older Biters

Experimental, non-malicious biting from toddlers is different from the deliberate, aggressive biting of an older child who has not learned to direct anger into acceptable channels or communicate needs and feelings verbally. Sometimes it can be predictable behavior from a child who has lived with too much aggression and/or frustration for too long. Some management procedures in this case, would, of course, be different from those suggested above, with more emphasis on discussion of feelings and reasons behind the aggression.

## TEMPER TANTRUMS

There are two main types of temper tantrums. The majority are the result of frustration common to toddlers. Others may be an attention seeking device, often used by older children.

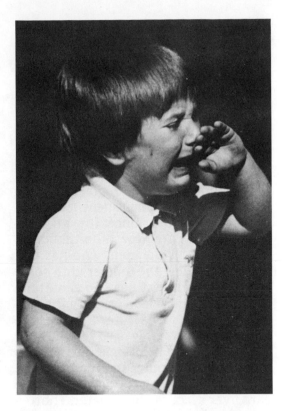

## Toddlers' Frustration Tantrums

Tantrums born of frustration can be likened to a bottle of champagne which has been shaken and pushed about and warmed up over a period of time. A final tiny nudge can then produce an explosive reaction—the cork flies off and the fluid spills over to allow the expanding gas to escape. Eventually, it settles down, leaving the remaining champagne still and flat. Picture a toddler who throughout the day may have been continually told to do this, to stop that, to put that down and to eat that up; may have been hit by another child and had a favorite toy taken; tried to put shoes on only to be told "they're on the wrong feet"; and may have spent a long time pasting only to have the finished work fall to pieces. The 'final straw' comes when the caregiver removes the toddler from the bathroom because she/he was getting

71

wet...the toddler explodes: goes red in the face, becomes rigid and throws herself/himself on the bathroom floor screaming and kicking, unaware of the wet mess. The caregiver watches in amazement having merely suggested that the tap be turned off and tried to lead the toddler out of the bathroom!

## Management Suggestions

This type of tantrum requires sympathetic, sensitive management. It can be a frightening experience for all concerned—the caregiver, other children, but most of all the child who has lost control. Holding the toddler until some control returns may help. To allow time to regain dignity, lead or carry the toddler to a quiet area. After a tantrum, a toddler will probably need reassurance that everything is all right and that no one is angry. A quiet soothing activity, like water play or a story on the caregiver's lap, can follow later. The toddler may be quiet and seem exhausted for some time, so if agreeable, a sleep may be in order.

Although temper tantrums are fairly common between one and a half and three years, when they happen constantly, caregivers should look closely at their programs and their attitudes to routines. *Rushing children too much or having unrealistic expectations of their developing abilities causes frustration, which contributes to tantrums.*

## The Attention-Seeking Tantrum

The second type of tantrum is usually a more conscious act than the first. A child who seeks attention or has been denied a particular pleasure may whip up a dramatic temper tantrum in a matter of seconds. If successful, that is, if the attention or the biscuit or the toy is forthcoming, the toddler will probably use this method to gain gratification again and again.

## What to Do

Ignoring unacceptable behavior at times can be used as an appropriate form of discipline, and attention-seeking tantrums can usually be treated in this way. The caregiver should find something to do close by, ignoring the child as far as possible. The caregiver should not be tempted to give in to the demands that precede tantrums, as this only reinforces the behavior. After the child has calmed down, the caregiver can offer something interesting to do, remembering to *always praise and encourage the child's acceptable behavior.*

It requires great skill and sensitivity on the caregiver's part to decide correctly when a temper tantrum is a legitimate expression of inability to cope, and when it is a more calculated bid for attention. It must be said that caregivers tend to overuse the excuse that a tantrum is a bid for attention. Ignoring the child should be used sparingly at this age. Most young children are frightened when their emotions get out of hand and usually need comfort and reassurance.

With encouragement, children can gradually learn to express their feelings verbally and it is important that caregivers accept and acknowledge those feelings. It is also important that caregivers let children know very definitely that some behavior is unacceptable.

## "SAY YOU'RE SORRY AND GIVE A KISS"

Children can often resolve their own fights and, within reason, should be encouraged to do so. A caregiver close by can step in quickly if the fight gets nasty and either child is in danger of being hurt, or when one child is being forced into submission by another stronger, more assertive child. Stepping in quickly and saying, "That's Sam's. I'll get one for you. Come and help me find it", can often divert a threatening situation.

A toddler who has either willfully or accidentally hurt someone else will not readily appreciate the pain caused. Insisting on an apology, a hug and a kiss, is asking for empty words and actions—an expression of feelings which may not be there. These social courtesies should be learned by modelling and should be based on sincere feelings. Adults should apologize to children when they have upset them or have made a mistake, the same as they would to another adult. Acts of hugging and kissing should stem from feelings of warmth and a desire to be close to someone, whether it be to greet them, as an apology for hurting them, or simply as an expression of feelings.

A child who has learned to say "Sorry" without feeling, can use it to a great advantage. A loud "Sorry" and a noisy kiss (making sure a caregiver is watching) can absolve a child from feelings of responsibility for what has been done. In fact, it can be viewed by the child as the go-ahead to keep doing it, as long as an apology follows the thump!

In situations where children need to learn some restraint and to be taught not to hurt others, removal in a firm manner, with words like "That hurt and I can't let you hurt Kim"can be used. Watching the caregiver comfort the victim can also help the toddler's understanding. Some appropriate alternative should then be offered and efforts made to try and prevent it happening again. If it does happen again, firmer action may be required, such as removal to another room or outside for a while with something active to do.

*Remember, toddlers hurting each other is fairly normal behavior. It is a way they have of expressing themselves quickly, at a time when language is limited and self-control difficult. Often there is no malice behind the act and it is a way of finding out how things work.*

## REASONING AS A TOOL FOR DISCIPLINE

Young toddlers' language comprehension may not be well enough established for them to engage in much verbal reasoning, and anyway they have little patience to be still and listen to lengthy explanations at this stage. Often a caregiver's firm tone and stern facial expression is enough deterrent. With potentially dangerous situations, quick removal, accompanied by "I can't let you do that", is probably most appropriate. Words like "gently", "slowly" and "careful" can be used from a very early age, and caregivers can reinforce these words with appropriate gestures. In this way a toddler can learn to play with a baby without being rough or to handle a fragile shell without it breaking.

Explanations should be given, but kept brief for younger toddlers. Most children, by the time they are three, can begin to appreciate reasoning, and if they have a basic trust in their caregivers and discipline is appropriate and consistent, they should be able to accept most of the limits that are set.

## SOME GUIDELINES FOR EFFECTIVE DISCIPLINE, OR APPLIED COMMON SENSE

- *Only expect the expectable.*
  This is the golden rule for discipline. This means that expectations must match the children's stage of development and particular abilities. Because toddlers are egocentric, they should not be expected to share things and wait for turns too readily. Programs should have multiples of favorite toys available, and waiting should be cut to a minimum.

- *Use a positive approach.*
  Practice discipline in a positive way, rather than a negative way. That is, tell children what they *can* do, rather

than what they *cannot* do. Tell a toddler "The towel hangs on the hook over there", rather than "Don't drop the towel on the floor", or "You can bang the drum outside" instead of "Don't bang the drum inside".

- *Always be honest.*
  Avoid ever lying to or deceiving chil-

- *Offer appropriate alternatives.*
  When there is a need to discourage certain behavior, do offer something else that is similar, but acceptable. Suggesting to the child who is racing around kicking other children's block constructions to sit down quietly and look at a book is offering a poor substitute and probably will not work. A

dren, as this destroys their trust. Telling a toddler "Mummy will be right back", when in fact she has gone for the day, is not only dishonest but damaging to the caregiver/child relationship. It can also create unnecessary anxiety for the toddler, who keeps expecting the absent mother to appear any moment. Allowing a parent to sneak off without the child's knowledge is equally destructive. Even when it is certain the child will be upset when the parent leaves, it is important that the child knows and is able to see the parent go.

moist ball of clay to pound and punch or a turn on the trampoline may be much more satisfying. A toddler who is keen on throwing toys about can be given a soft woolly ball or some bean bags to throw.

- *Encourage decision making.*
  Offer children choices when appropriate, *but only when you are prepared to accept their decisions.* For example, offering a choice between cleaning up and wiping tables may bring a positive response. Most children will choose one or the other, whereas a straight request to clean up may be disregarded.

Offering choices like "Would you like a banana or orange?" demonstrates a regard for the child's opinion. "Will we put your socks on next or your sweater?" helps children take some responsibility for themselves. But do not overdo it! It can be too confusing for young children to be constantly having to make decisions.

- *Be consistent.*
It is not good practice to stop a child from doing something one day and allow it the next. It may be difficult for toddlers to understand rules that change—for example, shoes and socks off in hot weather is allowed, but not when it is cold. Throwing balls is all right, but not blocks. These rules will eventually make sense to the children, and in the meantime cannot be avoided. But being angry when a toddler uses a colorful swear word on one occasion and smiling behind your hand and winking at another caregiver when it is repeated is unacceptable. Reprimanding a child who slops food all over the table, giving a warning to stop it, and then ignoring the behavior when it continues, is not good follow through. Much "try-out" behavior is best ignored anyway from the onset, and often does not go any further, for who wants to continue "showing off" when no one will watch? Inconsistencies can also arise between staff members who have different expectations and attitudes. Discussion and agreement on management procedures is important, so that inconsistencies are kept to a minimum. Difficulties may arise for children who experience one set of rules at home, with a particular type of discipline, and a completely different set of conditions in day care. Many of these children may even experience different standards within the home, for example, an authoritarian father, a timid mother and doting permissive grandparents, so try at least to give the child some degree of consistency within the center.

- *Do not shame or embarrass.*
Shaming or embarrassing children or comparing them with others in a bid to get co-operation is mean, destroys their self-esteem and often results in resentment. Do not say to a slow-eating child, "Look how Lucy's eating up and she's only two!" Never call a grubby toddler "little pig", even if it is said fondly, and do not send a toddler into the babies' room to shame her into behaving "properly". This kind of discipline decreases confidence and self-esteem and often increases disruptive behavior.

- *Avoid painting yourself in to a corner.*
Try to word requests in a way that allows both adult and child a graceful way out of a sticky situation. No matter how reasonable requests seem to the adult, at times they will be met with a negative response. Often toddlers will respond negatively to test their growing independence or to find out what will happen. If an adult says to a two year old "Are you going to bed now?" and the toddler says "No", what happens next, if in fact it is bedtime? Will the adult pick the child up and pretend that a choice has not been given? Will the situation be ignored in the hope that no one else heard the toddler's refusal? Will the caregiver plead with the toddler? Whichever method is chosen, it turns into an "I win, you lose" situation and one that should be avoided. Simply stating the facts, "It's sleep time. I'll help you get ready", is a more positive approach and more likely to be met with acceptance.

- *Give explanations.*
  Tell children simply the reason for a rule. Even very young children can appreciate simple explanations. A toddler, block in hand, approaching a baby in a threatening manner, can be quickly gathered up and told "Blocks are for building; come and we'll build a tower together", thus diverting the child's attention in a positive way. An older toddler throwing sand about can be told "Sand hurts when it gets in your eyes; let's dig a tunnel". The older the child, the more complex the explanation can be, with the child being encouraged to work through the reasons behind the rules.

- *Acknowledge children's angry feelings.*
  Children often appreciate someone understanding their angry feelings. When aggressive feelings have been provoked, a sensitive caregiver can say, "I know you are angry, but I can't let you hurt another person." As children grow in understanding and gain skill with language, they should be encouraged to talk about their feelings.

- *Do not play on children's emotions.*
  Adults caring for children must be careful not to use emotional blackmail. If the children are to grow up expressing genuine feelings, adults must be genuine in expressing their feelings to children. When a child refuses a request such as "Give me a cuddle" or "Come and help me", caregivers sometimes fake tears, saying "Look, you've made me cry!" or "You make me unhappy when you won't give me a cuddle". It is usually said in fun, but is really loading the child with responsibility for the caregiver's emotions! Coercing children into co-operation by threatening to cry is also unacceptable.

*Emotional blackmail is upsetting and confusing for small children and can form the basis on which they measure feelings and model their own behavior.*

- *Acknowledge adults' rights*
  Letting children know adults have rights and feelings too encourages the development of empathy. A caregiver should not pretend that a deliberate pinch did not hurt. It is okay to say firmly, "That hurt and I don't like being hurt!" Of course, another pinch may be administered, possibly a little softer, as a "try-out". If this happens, the adult can hold the child's hand firmly, without hurting, and repeat, "That hurt and I don't like being hurt. *Please don't pinch!*" in an emphatic tone, looking the child in the eye.
  Caring for toddlers can be exhausting, and a caregiver may need to say to an energetic toddler who wants to use the caregiver as a jumping board, "I'm tired. Let's sit here quietly and look at a book".

- *Be confident.*
  Try to be confident and reasonably assertive when necessary, as if the toddlers are expected to listen and cooperate! Saying firmly and confidently, "It's time to clean up for lunch" is more likely to be met with acceptance and co-operation than a timid, "I think perhaps we should clean up now". A toddler is more likely to ask for and accept help from a confident caregiver whose manner is reassuring. One of the skills inexperienced caregivers must develop is the ability to appear confident when they are not!

- *Don't overdo the warnings.*
  "Didn't I tell you...?"
  "I thought I told you..."
  "If you do that again..."
  "Did you hear me...?"

Try not to fall into the trap of warning children over and over and over again. Of course they hear, but they choose not to heed! This continual warning practice almost dares a child to keep doing what is forbidden. When children are old enough to understand, two reminders should be enough. For example, the adult says, "Sand is for digging, not throwing", followed by "If you keep throwing sand, you will have to find something else to do". If it happens again (and it probably will) remove the child, physically if necessary, and offer something else to do. Very young toddlers who continually misuse materials are probably too young for them anyway and should be diverted immediately and given something more appropriate. Eating large quantities of dough or sucking on felt tipped pens or wandering away from the easel with a dripping paint brush are good indications that the children are not developmentally ready for these materials.

- *Ignore some behavior.*
Taking no notice of some attention-seeking behavior can be an effective form of discipline. Adults do not have to respond to everything children do. When unacceptable behavior is not damaging or dangerous, ignoring it can influence the child to behave in a way that is acceptable and that can subsequently be acknowledged and encouraged.

- *NEVER hit, bite or otherwise physically punish a child.*
Physically hurting a child can no doubt stop undesirable behavior, but only because the child is frightened of being hurt. That is certainly a destructive way to try to teach acceptable behavior, and does not help the child understand why the behavior was unacceptable. Physical punishment can have two far-reaching effects, both of them negative. It can reinforce aggressive behavior (often the very behavior the caregiver is trying to stop) and destroy feelings of trust the child may have for the caregiver.

## AND FINALLY

Most of the contents of this chapter have been written to minimize the need for discipline, for that should be the aim. But caregivers can follow all the rules and still be faced with a two year old who runs away when told apples are for biting but not babies' legs, a three year old who keeps the whole group awake by continually calling out at nap time, and a toddler who insists on climbing the only unsafe piece of furniture in a room full of safe climbing equipment.

Unfortunately, there are no magic or foolproof answers. Every situation has to be handled individually and immediately. Children cannot be expected to wait for discipline to happen, while a caregiver considers the options.

Limits should be set to provide a safe and happy environment for the toddler, but to be effective, limits must be realistic and allow for exploration and learning, in relation to people and the physical world. Caregivers, when planning for toddlers, should make allowance for conflicts and try to minimize them, keeping in mind that conflicts, when they arise, help children learn about others and grow in understanding themselves.

**REFERENCES**

Australian Early Childhood Association Inc. (1985) *Handbook For Day Care*. Canherra: Australian Early childhood Association Inc.

Craig, G.J. (1979). *Child Development*. Englewood Cliffs, New Jersey: Prentice Hall, Inc.

Hurlock, E.S. (1978). *Child Development*. Tokyo: McGraw-Hill, Kogakusha Ltd.

Leach. P. (1977). *Baby & Child—A Modern Parents Guide*. London: Dorling Kindersley, Ltd.

*People Growing: Issues in Day Care*. (n.d.) North Carlton, Vic: The Lady Gowrie Child Centre.

Stone, L.J. and Church. J. (1975). *Childhood and Adolescence—A Psychology of The Growing Person*. New York: Random House.

*Photographs:* Educational Media Unit, Prahran College of TAFE, Victoria

# Chapter 8

# Toddler-Centered Routines

## Marcelle Psaltis
## Anne Stonehouse

*It is often said that a good experience for young children is one that proves a healthy mix of the novel and new and the comfortable and familiar. The younger the child, the more benefit there is to be gained from the familiar. Toddlers are notorious for making the most of any situation, or at least making something different from what the adult had in mind. They can transform even the most mundane activity or situation into something interesting and engrossing. Because they are keen to make sense of their world and their existence in it, if adults will allow it, toddlers will relish the opportunity to wring out of daily routine activities a number of enjoyable and worthwhile play and learning experiences.*

*Routines are the times when programs can become "unstuck" because of lack of teamwork, organization, inconsistencies between staff members, lack of communication and coordination, or lack of appreciation by staff of their potential value to the children. As was stated in Chapter 2, programming, however it is undertaken in the center, must provide opportunities for staff to focus on the routine activities and times, with the aim of maximizing their use on behalf of the developmental needs of the children.*

There are many days when child care workers with under three year olds feel that they have done nothing but assist the children with routine activities. These include eating, toileting, changing diapers, dressing and undressing, washing, sleeping, and resting. At best, these routine activities take up a large amount of time in care programs and therefore deserve attention and careful consideration. More importantly, they are part of the toddlers' experience, an excellent arena for learning self-help skills, experimenting with and exploring the world around them, and increasing general understanding of the way things work.

In the past, child care programs for babies and toddlers were criticized because they often did not extend beyond a concern for the physical care of children. There was sometimes undue and inappropriate emphasis on hygiene and efficiency at the expense of making available developmentally appropriate play and learning experiences. While current thinking about quality care stresses the need for children's experiences to extend far beyond routines, it is essential that caregivers develop ways to make routine times safe and hygienic but also to incorporate them into the range of play and learning experiences offered. In other words, in a program of high quality for toddlers, routines are viewed not as time away from the program, but as an important part of the program, full of rich, colorful opportunities for learning and growth by toddlers. In as much as toddlers are especially interested in taking part in the meaningful everyday activities going on around them, routines play a particularly important role. Using routines to their fullest advantage requires slowing down, taking more time, adjusting to "toddler time".

Routines have been described as the necessary parts of the day, the experiences that are always there. In planning the overall timetable or daily program, child care workers need to take into account the value to children of establishing a predictable daily routine. Knowing what to expect gives children a sense of security and a much needed feeling of having some control over their experiences. Giving toddlers' days a framework, the opportunity to predict successfully what come next, will develop self-confidence, independence, and trust, and enable better understanding of the world around them. At the same time, it is important that the timing of routines and the ways they are carried out should be based as much as possible on individual needs rather than "group norms" or, what sometimes seems to be the case, what fits conveniently into the adults' concept of a timetable. In other words, staff should have as an aim in their programs to *individualize routines as much as possible*. Ideally, in a program for toddlers, children could eat, sleep, and toilet when they need to. This is hardly ever possible for a variety of reasons, but it is something to be aimed for.

Children in care should not feel a sense of urgency in routine activities, feel themselves being rushed through them, or be passive participants as routines are done *to them rather than with them*. Similarly, children should not waste their time in routine activities and this means that waiting and being bored should be eliminated. It is not appropriate to build into routines any lining up and waiting, for the toilet for example, or sitting and doing nothing for example, while waiting for the food to arrive at the table at lunch time. Staff should examine their overall program with the aim of eliminating all of these wasted times.

## Arrivals and Departures

The beginning and end of the day in care are critically important times for children, staff, and parents, and careful thought needs to be put into ensuring that they go smoothly. Obviously, staffing must be adequate to allow setting up and cleaning up to happen along with greeting parents and children, aiding separations, and assisting children to make the transition from home to care in the morning and care to home at departure time. Unfortunately, because funding arrangements and therefore staffing patterns do not often take into account the critical importance of the "edges" of the care day, arrival time is in many centers a chaotic, stressful time, with too few staff racing around trying to do necessary chores, children distressed because they have not been helped to separate and there is nothing very interesting to engage their interest (unless they are fans of "Sesame Street" or "Playschool"), and parents feeling unsure and not welcomed because the staff hardly have time to acknowledge their brief presence, much less engage in a friendly, meaningful conversation with them. The end of the day may have a similar feeling. Everyone is tired, staff are still racing around doing their end-of-the-day chores, children have little to do because the play materials have been packed away, and parents are feeling rushed and weary.

It is essential if care is to be of high quality that programming takes into account the importance of the "edges" of the day. This implies the following:

1. Staff require some setting up and cleaning up time before children arrive and after children leave. Involving one or a few children in preparation and cleaning up is a good idea, but staff cannot be expected to open up a center, set up activities, talk to parents, and care for several children at the same time. It is essential that a welcoming environment with attractive experiences for children to go to be available as soon as children start arriving. Separating from parents and making the transition into care is so much easier when there is something interesting to focus interest and attention on.

Setting up and clearing away equipment as well as doing laundry, washing dishes and bottles will require a caregiver's attention at these times. It is therefore desirable that staff rosters allow at least fifteen minutes for these tasks before and after the children's day. Again, it should be kept in mind that where possible caregivers should involve toddlers in these tasks, as would happen with a toddler at home. The tasks will not be completed as quickly or efficiently if toddlers "help", but the ben-

efits to the children of being involved in the meaningful work of the center outweigh by far the disadvantages. Counting the clothes pins as a caregiver hangs up the laundry, helping to take the dishes out of the dishwasher, folding diapers and countless other routine tasks would be very enjoyable to toddlers.

2. Priority should be given to welcoming parents and children, to staff being available and *appearing to have the time* to talk to parents. Parent-staff relationships are discussed elsewhere in this book, but the importance of daily informal contacts between staff and parents cannot be stressed too much. These interchanges between staff and parents should be aimed at making parents feel welcomed, a part of the center, nourishing and sustaining feelings of belonging to and pleasure in their child. In addition, an exchange of daily information relevant to the care of the child is essential for both staff and parents to care well for the child. The mutuality is important, with parents being encouraged to impart information to the staff as well as receiving it from them.

As most child care workers work shifts, so that the person who talks to the parent at the beginning of the day is usually not the one who is there at the day's end, a system for recording information is essential for both parents and staff. Parents will not feel very secure about their child's care if, in response to a question about whether or not the child ate lunch, the caregiver says, "I really don't know; I only came on at one o'clock." A daily information sheet is outlined in Chapter 13: Parent-Staff Relationships. As suggested in that chapter, staff and parents in a center can design their own form to meet their own particular needs. It must be stressed, however that the use of a form for the exchange of written information should supplement *but in no way replace* conversation between staff and parents.

3. Separating may be stressful for both parents and children, and both may need sensitive and sympathetic help from staff. Staffing must allow for this help to be given. There could be no worse start to the day for both parent and child than for the parent to have to pry the crying child's arms away, put the child on the floor, and race out quickly while being pursued. A caregiver's greeting and assistance in engaging the child in an activity often prevents distress at separation, but help is even more essential for the child who is tentative or overtly distressed about coming to care The child's distress will be minimized by the assurance that someone is doing all that is possible to help, and the parent's stress will be lessened.

4. The end of the day has its own peculiar character and challenges. A quiet, relaxed environment will be appreciated by everyone. Some special activities and materials should perhaps be reserved for this time of day, when children are tired, have "done everything there is to do", and are waiting for parents to arrive. The last children at the center will need special attention.

For a variety of reasons, children may "play up" when parents arrive, with some actively protesting going home with their parents. Staff need to be available to "smooth over" this awkward time, and to reassure parents that this annoying behavior is unfortunately perfectly normal and does not mean that the child prefers the center and the caregivers to home and parents.

## Toileting

Learning to use the toilet independently and consistently is usually highlighted as one of the major developmental milestones of toddlerhood. Parents and caregivers may feel a great deal of pressure to teach toddlers to use the toilet, or to "train" them as early as possible. Therefore it is particularly important that center staff have a relaxed, individually oriented attitude toward this area of routine care. As with the learning of any new skill, adults should wait for signs of interest and readiness from the toddler before attempting to teach the use of the toilet. Obviously, as is true of the emergence of any new skill, the age at which toddlers are ready and interested to start using the toilet will vary tremendously. Therefore, a policy of embarking on a program of toilet training as children turn eighteen months, for example, is totally inappropriate, as it ignores individual differences. It is widely known but sometimes ignored that children must be physiologically ready before control of elimination is possible. Other signs of readiness include being able to indicate in some way the need to eliminate, and being able to remove necessary clothes to use the toilet (Leach, 1979).

One of the great advantages of having toddlers in a group is that, because of their fondness for imitating each other, they are likely to take a natural interest in using the toilet as they see other children doing so. Encouraging this natural interest in a relaxed way, without applying pressure, is the most desirable approach. If using the toilet becomes unpleasant, involving the use of threats, it is certain to become full of power struggles between adults and willful toddlers, and this in the long run interferes with the successful completion of the task, namely, getting the toddler to use the toilet. (Imagine how it would feel to be told at a particular time to go to the toilet, and that you couldn't get up until you had produced something.)

Reminders and encouragement are different from pressure, and often the presence of an adult, the company of another child, or a book to look at will make the time on the toilet or potty more pleasant. Successes can be noted, but accidents or other signs of lack of success should be treated in a matter of fact way. As in other areas of care, *there is no place in learning self toileting for shaming, embarrassing, or making a toddler feel guilty.*

The importance of the bathroom and toileting areas being appropriately designed and set up for toddlers' size and skill level is stressed elsewhere. Both toddler-sized toilets and potty chairs should be accessible to toddlers at all times, encouraging independence and routines based on individual needs. Of course, adult help should be easily accessible to the toddler, to encourage as well as to ensure that considerations related to hygiene are acted on.

There are numerous treatments of "toilet training", a term that Penelope Leach says is inappropriate if adults wait until the child is ready. These treatments vary tremendously in quality. Two that are recommended highly by the authors of this chapter are those by Leach (1979) and Weinstein and Flynn (1982), cited in the references for this chapter.

## Diaper Changing

It is important for staff to remember that changing a toddler's diaper or assisting with toileting usually provides a rare opportunity in the day for one-to-one attention, for conversation and affection. If this is to happen, the changing area must be organized, and a carefully thought out routine that all staff are familiar with in place, so that the adult's energies can go toward making it a pleasant time for the toddler. There should be a low changing table to allow eye contact between adult and child, a mobile or picture of interest to the child (this should be changed regularly), and something interesting for the child to hold.

In addition, all supplies needed to carry out the diaper change in a hygienic manner must be nearby. This includes a sink with running water, spray disinfectant, easily accessible buckets or other containers for soiled diapers, and a stock of clean diapers and wash cloths.

Detailed consideration of health and safety related issues, while of paramount importance in child care centers, is beyond the scope of this book. However, an example of a detailed diaper change procedure, as used at the Lady Gowrie Child Centre in Perth, is outlined below. Other centers may want to make alterations to fit their individual situation, but this may serve as a guide to ensure that there is a routine that is followed that minimizes the risk of spreading infection.

1. Wash hands under running water and dry.

2. Run a small amount of water into sink.

3. Place clean folded diaper and drying cloth onto change table. Be sure wash cloths and container for soiled diaper are correctly placed.

4. Gather child to be changed, remove diaper, place closed pins on shelf and diaper into container.

5. Wash child's bottom with wash cloths, using water from sink, and wiping from front to back. Place cloth into container with diaper. Dry child with a drying cloth.

KEEP ONE HAND ON THE CHILD AT ALL TIMES.

6. If appropriate, have the child use the toilet or potty.

7. Stay with the child. Note whether or not the child passed urine or faeces.

8. Encourage the child to flush the toilet and wash hands. Explain why.

9. Place a clean diaper on the child, with the open end of the pins facing away from the umbilicus.

10. If possible, pass the child on to another caregiver, or place the child in a safe place with something interesting to do.

11. Rinse diaper under sluice, and place in bucket to be laundered. Empty/rinse potty under sluice also.

12. Wash hands in water in sink. Discard water.

13. Clean used area thoroughly with spray disinfectant. Include potty chair if used, nozzle and button on sluice, and container soiled diaper was placed in.

14. Wash hands under running water.

Another practical point, which will also help to ensure that a high standard of hygiene is maintained, is that centers must ensure that various cleaning cloths, mops, and sponges are always kept separate and labeled clearly so that caregivers will know which ones to use in the toilet area, the diaper change table, work tables in the play room, and kitchen benches. A system of color coding will indicate which equipment is to be used in each area, as follows:

yellow sponges—sink in kitchen area
blue sponges—floor only
green sponges—activity tables
orange sponges—eating tables

blue disposable cloth—toilet/potty cleaning
yellow disposable cloth—disinfect change table
white wash cloths—washing bottoms
yellow wash cloths—washing faces, hands

Once these systems and routines are in place, they become second nature to staff, who carry them out automatically, thereby freeing them to concentrate on the children.

## Transition Times

Movement from one part of the day or one area of the environment to another should happen naturally and in a relaxed manner. Staff should aim to eliminate abrupt dramatic changes, hurrying children, interrupting their play unnecessarily, lining them up, and wasting their time by making them wait. All of these situations, if they occur on a regular basis, add significantly to children's frustration, and increase the likelihood of undesirable behavior such as lack of cooperation, interfering with other children's play, or generally being disruptive.

Lining up to wash hands or go to the toilet, sitting at the table with nothing to do until the food appears, and sitting at the table after finishing eating are all an unnecessary waste of children's valuable time.

Toddlers should be warned about cleaning up time in sufficient time for them to bring their activity to a close. They are much more likely to cooperate when they know what is about to happen. While helping to clean up or pack away is a valuable experience for toddlers, in that it gives them a feeling of responsibility for caring for their environment, it does not help if caregivers badger and threaten and try to force toddlers to help. Besides, it just does not work, and there is no way to force toddlers to pack away, even if that were desirable. Inviting and encouraging help from toddlers, acknowledging it gratefully, and making it into a pleasant fun part of the day is the best way to enlist the assistance of toddlers. Caregivers of toddlers should do some cleaning up and tidying up continuously without interfering with toddlers play, thereby maintaining an attractive environment and decreasing the job at the end of the activity. Attempting to enforce a policy that each child packs away what he or she gets out is impossible, and even if it could be enforced, it is a deterrent to constructive, creative play, as it is an overt disincentive to use lots of materials.

The overall plan of the day with toddlers should have a kind of integrity, and should flow naturally for the individual child. In other words, in keeping with the premise that programs of high quality for toddlers are planned for individuals and not for groups, transition times should be for individuals rather than for groups. Unobtrusively taking two or three toddlers who have finished playing in the sand pit to wash their hands while another staff member stays outside with the rest of the children, is far preferable to marching the entire group to the bathroom and making them wait for a turn at the sink. As Davidson (1983) says:

> Adults who often make children wait for them or the group, or who otherwise waste children's time, convey a basic lack of respect for children, which may well have a detrimental effect on the way children view themselves. (p. 196)

## Meal Times

The way that meal and snack times are handled in a center is a good indication of the overall quality of the program, as these are perhaps the best examples of the rich variety of opportunities available in routine activities.

As with all activities, the smaller the group at meal time, the more pleasant

the occasion for toddlers. The noise level and other distractions of a large group may interfere with toddlers eating sufficiently and pleasantly. Attention must be paid to the physical environment. Seating should be comfortable, allowing feet to touch the floor and providing support at the sides for young toddlers. Tables should be large enough to prevent crowding and reduce the temptation to eat from the next dish rather than ones own! Several small tables establish a more pleasant and manageable atmosphere than one large one. The table setting should be attractive, and place mats may be more sensible than a cloth, as they help to delineate individual space. Bowls with straight sides are better than plates for children who are trying to use a spoon. Cups should have wide bottoms.

Assisting in setting the table affords toddlers a valuable opportunity to do some "real work". Similarly, priority should be placed on letting toddlers serve themselves and clear their own cutlery and dishes, scraping leftovers into a bowl. Sensitive caregivers with this age group accept a fair degree of mess as toddlers struggle to feed themselves. As with other routines, being organized with buckets, sponges, and some wet wash cloths nearby makes meal time go more smoothly. While it

may be appropriate to discourage toddlers from playing with food, there should not be undue emphasis on table manners and the usual conventions associated with eating. Spills and other mess should be treated in a matter of fact way, and toddlers can be involved in cleaning up the mess. Children can be encouraged to try new foods without being pressured or coerced. If the menu is a healthy, well-balanced one, there is no need for some foods to be used as rewards for eating others. If this is happening in a center, the menu may need to be re-examined.

While some toddlers may need assistance with eating, adults should avoid hovering over toddlers at meal time, constantly giving orders or telling them to hurry or to stop being messy. Sitting with a small group of children enables the caregiver to provide help at the same time while interacting with the toddlers.

"Individualization" and "flexibility" are key concepts to apply with all routines, and they apply to eating as well. As some children are speedy, no-nonsense eaters and others are slower, it makes sense to allow toddlers to leave the table as they are finished. Staff need to be organized for this, and to have something for the children to go to after morning and afternoon tea. Similarly, the child who is exhausted before lunch should have a sleep and have lunch upon waking, and the child or children who are very involved in an activity should be able to finish it and have their morning or afternoon tea after.

After lunch, children need help to wash their hands, brush their teeth, and prepare for a rest after lunch. The transition from lunch to rest and sleep time needs to be gentle and relaxed, to help the toddlers unwind from the excitement of the morning in order to relax enough to go to sleep.

## Sleep and Rest Time

Atmosphere and room arrangement must be considered for sleep. The area should not be too busy, and the light, temperature, and ventilation must be adjusted to assist children to sleep or rest. Noise must be kept to a minimum, and some quiet gentle music may help children to relax. As mentioned previously, some children may need sleeps at times other than when the majority of children do, and this should be accommodated.

What can caregivers do to assist toddlers at sleep time? Firstly, they can encourage the toddlers to help with the preparation of beds. Each child should have a bed, so that linens are not shared. For health and safety reasons as well as to assist toddlers to settle, beds or mats should be spaced apart from each other. Toddlers' individual preferences and the sleeping arrangements at home must be taken into account. For example, some children are moved from a crib to a bed at a much earlier age than others. Some restless toddlers who have difficulty settling will cope better in a crib or on a cot than on a mat on the floor, where it is very easy to just get up and walk off. A favorite soft toy, a pacifier or blanket may help the child go off to sleep. Caregivers should find out from parents what the bedtime routine is at home and duplicate it as closely as possible at the center. Some children may want clothes removed, while others will object. Most children will enjoy having their back patted or rubbed, and will appreciate the closeness of a special caregiver to help them to sleep.

Some children wake up distressed, so a caregiver should be there to comfort them immediately. It is important that staff pay attention to the atmosphere as children wake up. Some children wake up slowly, and nothing could be worse than being half awake and being thrust

suddenly into the busy, noisy atmosphere of the child care center. Staff should allow children time to wake up at their own pace, and try to arrange a peaceful atmosphere with quiet activities for them to come into as they are ready. Adults should be available to give comfort and affection to children who need it. Going off to sleep and walking up are times when young children are especially vulnerable and in need of security and comfort.

## Other Routines

This chapter does not include detailed discussion of other important routines that are part of the toddler's day in care, including dressing and undressing, brushing teeth, brushing and combing hair, hand washing, and bathing or showering. As with the routines discussed more extensively in this chapter, the concerns for health and hygiene and the use of routines as times for learning and the development of self-help skills must be kept in mind. Developing workable systems that ensure that wash cloths are not used for more than one child, that tooth brushes are kept separate and are not shared, that a healthy balance is struck between allowing children to become messy and dirty and an appropriate emphasis on cleanliness, all are major challenges in a child care center. Meeting those challenges successfully requires dedicated teamwork, a commitment to communicate with each other, and a willingness to compromise on the part of staff who work together.

## Conclusion

Carrying out routines in a toddler centered way requires a great deal of flexibility and will create many challenges for caregivers. However, with careful thought and planning, staff can plan routines which take into account the abilities and needs of the children, and provide an environment where the child's feelings of self worth are enhanced. Rational principles, practical planning, and being on the side of the toddler will enable routines to be part of the total developmental program.

**REFERENCES**

Davidson, J. (1983). Wasted Time—the Ignored Dilemma. In J. Brown (Ed.). *Curriculum Planning for Young Children*. Washington, D.C.: National Association for the Education of Young Children, 196-204.

Leach, P. (1979). *Baby and Child*. Ringwood, Vic.: Penguin Books Australia Ltd.

Stonehouse, A.W. (n.d.) *People Growing: Issues in Day Care*. Melbourne: Lady Gowrie Child Centre.

Weinstein, M. and Flynn, M.S. (1982). Developmental Issues Important for Group Infant/Toddler Care. In R. Lurie, and R. Neugebauer (Eds.). *Caring for Infants and Toddlers: What Works, What Doesn't*, Vol. Two. Redmond, Washington: Child Care Information Exchange.

**ADDITIONAL REFERENCES**

The Creche and Kindergarten Association of Queensland (1984). *Routine Survival*. Brisbane: The Creche and Kindergarten Association of Queensland.

The Lady Gowrie Child Centre Melbourne (n.d.). Routines—Discussion Guide Sheets. Carlton: Lady Gowrie Child Centre.

Sebastian, P. (1986). *Handle with Care*. Blackburn: AE Press.

(Note: Some of this material has been borrowed from "People Growing: Issues in Day Care", Melbourne Lady Gowrie Child Centre, n.d., Sheet Numbers 8, 9, 11-13).

*Photographs:* Lady Gowrie Child Centres, Perth and Brisbane

# Chapter 9

# The Play of One to Two Year Olds

## Pat Patterson

*It has been said that one to two year olds are "in-betweeners". While most of them are toddlers in the literal sense, in that somewhere between twelve and twenty four months they become very mobile, in other arenas of development there are also major changes that signal the end of babyhood and therefore the need for a new set of requirements for quality care for the age group. Patterson spells out sensitively the nature of play in this age group. This is the background against which an appropriate program must be planned.*

Play certainly has many facets, and it is possible to relate toddlers' play to a number of them. It can be described very well as spontaneous and voluntary (Garvey, 1977), for young toddlers may not imitate the actions of adults who try to explain play materials or dictate their use to toddlers. For example, the adult takes pieces from a puzzle and tries to replace them. The young toddler picks up a piece, puts it in the mouth, carries it round or drops it on the floor. Toddlers experiment with equipment in their own way. Later in their development they are influenced more by imitation and by verbal directions.

Toddlers are for the most part "actively engaged" (Garvey, 1977) in their play with equipment—they push, pull, squeeze, hug, throw and hammer. While it is obvious that the adult has an "extrinsic goal" in the building of a tower, or the completion of a puzzle, toddlers' play with the same equipment may show no such desire. Their responses appear to be very "non-serious" and "joyful" (Dearden, 1967). When left to occupy themselves without interference, toddlers play with whatever happens to be in the immediate vicinity. Their innate curiosity determines what it will be.

With under three year old children, particularly the young toddlers and the early two year olds, the definition of play could be taken from Garvey (1977). It will be active, should in most instances be joyful, spontaneous and self-initiated and lead to real involvement through personal interest and natural curiosity. Toddlers are fascinated by their environment. To them all is new and interesting. It is the task of the adult to ensure that the environment is a safe one, and that it remains challenging and sustains interest.

## How Level of Development Affects Play

Toddlers are at the stage of achieving autonomy (Erikson, 1950). As babies become toddlers who can walk, run, climb and jump, they develop socially and emotionally into less dependent individuals. Their physical abilities enable them to move independently, and with this new capability comes an overwhelming desire to do things for themselves to take charge of their own lives, including their play. They want to explore the world, to touch, taste, feel and see everything around them, and as they learn what effect the environment has upon them, they also learn that they have power within themselves to influence the people and the objects around them.

Within the toddler there is developing a strong feeling of personal importance as the child seeks to establish identity, and to find a place both within the family group and probably within a larger group of peers. The toddler in this stage of autonomy is beginning to know the pleasure of ownership, and the word "mine" often becomes one of the most used words in the growing vocabulary.

The toddler stage of autonomy and of developing pride in personal ownership means that they should not be required to share equipment with others. Actually, at this stage the child is often intent on gathering as many articles as possible for personal use. Though this desire may have to be curbed at times, a play situation for toddlers needs to provide several articles of the same kind, so that pressure to share can be avoided. The child who seizes a truck from another child should not of course be allowed to keep it, but should be provided with another similar one. Toddlers are too young to understand sharing.

"No" expresses the toddler's ever increasing knowledge of personal impact upon the people and the objects in the environment. It also expresses the desire for personal independence and acceptance as an individual with particular ideas, thoughts and feelings. This stage of autonomy is a very important one, and its characteristics are often misinterpreted by adults.

The "no" that so clearly expresses a toddler's desire for independence also affects the play and the play equipment. The equipment must be such that it can be used effectively by one person. A toddler wants to climb alone—the adult can stand near and be available if needed, but the child needs the opportunity to try alone. All too often adults lift children of this age over obstacles and off equipment that they were anxious to negotiate on their own. Adults are in-

clined to provide toys and demonstrate their use. Toddlers want to explore for themselves.

## Physical Development

The toddler's level of physical development influences play. Skill and coordination in the use of large muscles is growing, so the play environment should be uncluttered. Co-ordination is still imperfect but toddlers are highly motivated to practice their skills. Some falls and bumps are unavoidable at this stage and toddlers are very resilient, but they can also become frustrated when mishaps are frequent, and angry upset feelings can be the result. Some sensible organization of available space will ensure that the toddler meets the minimum amount of frustration. Toddlers need to succeed, so the area in which they play should encourage them to use new-found physical skills and also to avoid the frustrations that arise from physical hurt and failure to achieve goals.

Toddlers like to run freely, to ascend and descend stairs, to climb over obstacles and to crawl through them, to jump on soft gym mats, and from low boards and trestles. The height of the board means little to the toddler, and of course safety must be considered. It is the feeling of balance and the sense of rhythm and personal freedom that accompanies the jump that is of importance, and this can be achieved with a board that is only centimeters above a soft gym mat.

Because young toddlers are enjoying the new-found freedom of walking and running, "push and pull" equipment is appropriate for this age group. Baby buggys, carts, and large push-along toys with strong axles and wheels are ideal, and the children need equipment that is strong and durable. Toddlers meet frustration through their own lack of skill. They should not have more of it thrust upon them by toys that do not

work properly, or wheels that break. Their developing self confidence is too important to be at risk over such incidents—nor should it be threatened by scoldings or accusations over broken toys that were not strong enough in the first place.

While large muscles are becoming strong, skill with small muscles will take much more time and practice. Equipment designed to produce skill in coordinating small muscles lacks the appeal of the large push and pull wheel toys to children in this age group. When playdough is provided, one to two year olds enjoy pounding it with hands or fists, squeezing, squashing and poking it. Mallets for pounding and flattening may be more suitable than the rolling pins and cutting utensils that are provided for older children.

When toddlers paint they need thick-ened paint that will not run. Large paint brushes that achieve a result rapidly, and rollers used in house painting can be used by toddlers to paint large card-board cartons. At this stage it is the "doing" that is important, and a large utensil assists small hands that lack some fine motor skills.

Equipment such as baskets and bags of varying sizes are valuable for toddlers who go walking and gain confidence by carrying articles similar to those that adults use. As this stage is also one of picking up, carrying and throwing out, the value of baskets and bags is obvious.

Building blocks appeal to all ages, and assist in developing physical skills. Toddlers make good use of large foam blocks than can be built up, knocked over, sat upon, jumped on, and enjoyed in other ways. The foam can be covered with brightly coloured cotton material so that it looks attractive and can be washed easily. Toddler play includes much knocking down.

Because of their particular stage of physical development, play with balls at this age generally amounts to running chasing, kicking and rolling. The balls, like the blocks, need to be large and colorful. Catching and bouncing skills come later.

## Cognitive Development

In their mental development young toddlers are, according to Piaget (1951), in a sensorimotor stage. Their own ac-tions in the most literal and physical sense of the word are the beginnings of their intellectual growth. They actually take control of organizing their experi-ences themselves. At this level of de-velopment there is some early co-ordi-nation of sensation and movement. Those two words "sensation" and "movement" are the foundation for the structure of their play. Babies and young toddlers develop thinking skills through

their actions, just as older children use language. Toddlers look, feel, touch, taste, listen to, push, poke, drop and, in various ways, manipulate objects. This is their way of playing—it is the type of play that is natural and right for this level of development.

Objects with which the toddler plays should provide different sensations, and the young toddler may use both mouth and hands to explore. Natural objects that are part of the outdoors, such as sand and water, leaves, twigs, flowers, seed pods and stones are all playthings that offer great interest, challenge and joy. Birds, insects and small wild or do-mestic animals are part of the scene—objects to look at and examine within the boundaries of safety. Young children have a high level of both visual and auditory acuity. The smallest seed will attract their attention, and they respond joyfully to sounds within their environ-ment. Objects that provide sound when moved are interesting play things, and encourage the toddler to develop skills. Percussion instruments—drums, bells, tapping sticks, tambourines and shak-ers—have a universal appeal in the playroom. Bags of small objects that look and feel different provide the tod-dler with different sensory experiences, and satisfy the natural desire to pick up, carry round and tip out. Bags of waste material collected as collage for older children can be a source of wonder to the toddler, who is able to tip out and examine the different objects at will. All parents know the joy that the toddler finds amid the utensils in the kitchen cupboards. Such a cupboard could be deliberately assigned to the toddler at home, or equipped with appropriate utensils for toddlers' use in the group care situation.

## Autonomy

Essential to this stage of their devel-opment both mentally and emotionally

is their growing desire to take control of their own experiences. Those who observe, supervise and provide for toddlers at play need to remember that the toddler is not ready for adult-organized situations. They need to wander freely, to pick up, experiment, put down and to handle an object in their own way. They are not yet ready to copy the adult method of using equipment. The adult will sit, take out, and replace pieces of a puzzle in an attempt to show the child its purpose. The young toddler will pick up the pieces, put them in the mouth, carry them round, and drop them on the floor. The adult will draw with crayons on paper—the child puts the crayons in the mouth, hits them on the table, rolls and rattles and in other ways enjoys their sound. The adult rolls and cuts out shapes in dough. The toddler squeezes, hammers and manipulates it. Much free experimental use of the equipment must precede its final use in the accepted form. Pressure on toddlers to accept the adult method of play usually produces complete indifference in their response, or anger, frustration, and emotional upset. Knowledge of the stage of development enables adults to accept the toddler's natural play, and to provide better for it.

## Social Skills with Peers

Socially the toddler shows interest in other children and there may be contact, but the contact is usually brief and can not typically be described as truly social play, especially when compared with that of older children. A study of the pro-social behavior of two year olds in the context of play situations (Patterson, 1980) found that all children spent the highest percentage of their play time in non-social play, and the lowest in social play. Only eight per cent of this time was devoted to social play. One might expect that a study of the play behavior of under twos would find a still smaller percentage of time spent in actual social play. Because of the drive for autonomy the play is highly individual and egocentric. Indeed the task of the supervising adult involves the arrangement of space so that toddlers are not pressured into constant close contact, and the provision of many similar pieces of equipment, so that each toddler has the use of one. The toddler is busy establishing personal identity. Social play will develop once this initial task has been achieved.

## Language and Communication

Though young toddlers and twos are developing speech, their communication is mainly non-verbal. This, too, has an effect on their play situation. If they are to avoid the frustrations that arise from unfulfilled needs and desires, their caregivers must be constantly aware of their non-verbal communications, and be able to respond appropriately.

## Effect of the Adult

In toddlers' play the adult provides:
- a security base
- an encouraging, approving presence
- a companion for play.

The adult plays an all-important role in providing for the toddler, and from this security springs feelings of well-being and self-confidence, and the desire to take the initiative, to experiment and explore. The familiar, trusted adult is the central point of the circle from which the toddler moves out to explore.

Toddlers' play then is often somewhat dependent upon the presence of the adult. Equipment carefully selected to meet all the toddler's needs may be ignored completely if the child feels unsure. A toy may distract attention briefly, but no piece of equipment can provide a substitute that will completely satisfy this most essential need for security. Soft furry toys, bunny rugs blankets and sometimes pieces of material can provide comfort and an association with the caring adult, but there will be no real play until the child is comforted and confident.

A young toddler generally spends a limited time with any one piece of equipment, as there are too many interesting things to see and do, but the presence of the adult encourages them sometimes to sustain interest, or to return to the point of interest.

The toddler who has learned to trust an adult enjoys sharing what may be described as physical play—the friendly tickling, touching, stroking and jouncing that extends the affectionate bond between them. It is a sharing of contact and enjoyment, a very different concept from the sharing of equipment that should not be required of the toddler. Games such as "I See" with the adult hiding and quickly returning; "Ride a Cock Horse" with the child sitting on an adult foot, or being jounced gently on a board, or a trampoline; "Round and Round the Garden" with the appropriate movement of fingers and tickles; and play with a mirror with child and adult close together, all have a place in play between a toddler and an adult.

The adult role in toddler play also includes a friendly voice that encourages, reassures, and approves, and a physical presence that can be relied upon to be aware of safety and the toddler's undeveloped sense of caution, and lack of physical coordination. The adult needs to be available—aware of, but in no way intrusive upon the child's play. It is often difficult for an adult to watch a young child climb, jump, ascend and descend steps and climbing equipment. The temptation to interfere is strong. A child, though, can be easily inhibited by the presence of concern in the adult's voice or body posture. The result could be a timid child who develops a lack of confidence in personal ability; or a battle of

wills between adult and child that leads to a constant struggle, with the child insisting on autonomy and returning again and again to the object of concern. The adult needs to remain confident and to project this feeling to the child. The toddler may accept a hand extended casually as an extra piece of equipment, but will fight against interference with that all important independence during the play.

## Effects of Peers on Toddler Play

Though some research indicates that toddlers and twos spend only a relatively small percentage of their contact time in social play with their peers, the presence of peers does have both negative and positive effects on the play. One toddler in a group who becomes overstimulated or frustrated, and touches, hugs or bites, certainly affects the other children's play. The behavior could frighten the recipient to such an extent that the whole group play situation is frightening to and therefore avoided by that particular child.

However, Patterson's (1980) study of two year olds indicates that some positive social responses are also apparent in the behavior of toddlers during their play, although the frequency may be low. Considering the definition of pro-social as "involving sharing, helping, defending, sympathizing, rescuing and cooperating", one would not have been surprised to find that there were few of these responses. This pro-social behavior during the play must be considered to be a very positive effect of the presence of peers—one that should balance any negative effects.

Obviously, some social play with peers exists in groups. In the research cited previously (Patterson, 1980), the children spent eight per cent of their play time in social play. Although not conclusive, the results of the study suggest that the nature of the group in which a child spends time could be an influence on the play as well as on the amount of pro-social behavior that occurs. Two groups, one a vertical age, and one a peer group, were studied, and the results indicate that the frequency of pro-social responses was higher among children in the vertical age than in the peer group. It is certain that the group affects toddlers' play, even though the toddler may spend only a brief time in play that could be described as truly social.

## Play Things

Toddlers' play involves much gross physical activity in the form of walking, running, climbing, jumping and crawling. Large boxes of timber, strong cardboard or plastic provide safe, stimulating play equipment, and ladders and slides can easily be adjusted to safe heights. Where children climb and jump, gym mats can provide for safety, and they can also be used for rolling, tumbling and playing with the adult. Trampolines can be used effectively if they are equipped with padding over the springs and their use supervised carefully. A seated child can enjoy a gentle rocking or bouncing movement provided by adult pressure, and thus gain confidence to stand and jump alone. The trampoline provides for active play, and leads to muscle and total body co-ordination. Openings, like windows, made in the large cartons, or cut into the wooden boxes, suggest climbing in and out and crawling through. Toddlers generally make good use of them.

Steps and ladders can be safely used by most young toddlers, but slides present some difficulty. Here, for some time, there needs to be adult assistance, for even a short slide made deliberately for their use immediately throws them off balance, and they are not sufficiently coordinated to control their own movement. A safe pit of sand at the base of the slide, or a gym mat, is needed while the children practice.

Earth, sand and water are all play things that offer wonderful touching experiences and joyful messy play. Toddlers enjoy the different sensations offered by grass, sand, soil, fallen leaves, bark, stones and gravel. The natural world is a child's birthright. It offers fascinating experiences to the toddler.

Wheeled toys such as wheelbarrows, baby buggys, bicycles and wagons meet the young child's needs for individual, self-initiated play, and rockers that can be climbed on and self-propelled are popular, for children enjoy the climbing on and off and the rocking sensation.

Young children also enjoy the sensation provided by a swing, but have to be helped by an adult. The young child is passive in this situation. By age three further development enables some self-propulsion, but until then the swing provides only a safe place with a pleasurable feeling of movement. It does not really fit into the concept of play for active toddlers.

Balls and bean bags encourage activity, and toddlers enjoy using large brushes to paint with water on walls or fences, and with paint on cartons and large boxes that can be easily disposed of.

## Water Play

Water to young toddlers means immersing the whole body—it is literally playing in water, so the most likely place for it is the bath. Here they can enjoy dumping out, filling up and squeezing, and the play with soap and bubbles that water offers. Another place is a small pool where two or three young children can get into the water and be fully involved in play with safe plastic containers and floating toys. The conventional water table where children stand up and play with water equipment is better suited to the next age group. Such play, of course, requires careful adult supervision. When toddlers play in water the adult must be very aware and totally immersed in the task of supervision. All children under three enjoy the routine of hand washing, and this too can be regarded as part of their play, as well as the practice of a physical routine. Caregivers are often hurried and anxious to complete the routine. Children love the experimental play with the water, the soap, and the taps.

## Books

Books are part of the play environment even before the child begins to walk, and toddlers base their use of them on their own previous experience. The books themselves need to be "untearable" for very young children, with a gradual introduction of other types as the child develops. Many one or two year olds use books as they do other play equipment—they pick them up and carry them around. Those who have experienced the closeness of an adult lap combined with bright, interesting pictures and a warm adult voice enjoy selecting a book and carrying it to the adult, with perhaps a non-verbal, but unmistakable, invita-

gestion of pretending play as the toddler picks up the cup and lifts it as though expecting the liquid inside. Where there are beds provided for dolls they need to be large enough and strong enough for children. Toddlers will get into and out of the beds themselves. Equipment that will fold up, such as ironing boards and some chairs and bassinets, need to be stabilized for use by toddlers. Cupboard doors should open and close easily, for this is how toddlers will use them. They also need to be firmly based so that they will not fall when the toddler pulls at doors and drawers. Toddlers enjoy play in the home corner, for it provides familiar articles often inaccessible in the real home environment, at the child's own level and adapted to the child's size.

tion. From this closeness arises the interest, and the toddler handles the book, turns the pages and becomes increasingly aware of content.

## Home Corner

The equipment in the traditionally organized home corner is of interest to the toddler, but it will be used by children in their second year of life and often into the third primarily as a collection of articles to be examined and manipulated rather than for imaginary or pretending play. Telephones fascinate, but observation shows many toddlers pulling around the dial and holding and dropping the receiver rather than talking into it. Dolls are usually placed by adults into baby buggys or beds. Toddlers push the baby buggys and on occasions take the dolls out. Just as books are carried from the library shelves to a trusted adult, so the dolls are sometimes lifted out and carried and presented to the adult.

Cups with which the home corner is often equipped are treated by toddlers as the genuine article. There is no sug-

## Crayons and Paper

Art materials such as large lumbar crayons can be provided for toddlers and the children left to experiment. There will be a variety in their own play with the crayons. They pick up and drop, feel, taste, carry around and sometimes use on the paper. A low table, fully covered with paper, limits the area to be used for drawing.

## Manipulative Equipment

Play material can also include manipulative equipment such as bead frames, puzzles, small blocks and pieces designed to be fitted together. Large puzzle pieces are required, and many are now being made with a knob for small hands to hold. Toddlers delight in pulling apart, but as their own co-ordination develops they begin to use the equipment for more constructive purposes.

Toddlers experiment, enjoy and play with everything with which they have contact. Equipment need not be expensive. Lids that clip or screw on to safe containers, and other articles from the average kitchen cupboard provide satisfying play experiences indoors. In their play toddlers show preferences that arise from individual differences in personality and ability. Some are more active and agile than others. They climb on everything that presents a hand or foot hold. Others are less adventurous by nature and content to keep both feet well grounded. All are influenced by their environment, in that they are curious about the new and strange. They are also drawn to the familiar, and observation in toddler groups invariably shows many of them picking up and patting dolls and immediately pushing baby buggys—articles with which most are familiar from an early age. They are also drawn to familiar household articles such as telephones, frying pans, irons, rakes and mowers.

For the toddler there is no dividing line between play and work. Almost everything they do is fascinating and enjoyable. Their days, unlike those of older human beings, cannot be divided into play times and other times, for toddlers play even during routines. They play in the bath; they often play with food; they play when dressing and undressing. In fact, some of their happiest play times with adults are during these routines. Play is an essential part of their whole existence. Toddlers' play is living, being and doing.

## REFERENCES

Dearden, R.F. (1967). The Concept of Play. in R.S. Peters (Ed.). *The Concept of Education.* London: Routledge and Kegan.

Erikson, E. (1950). *Childhood and Society.* New York: W.W. Norton & Co, Inc.

Garvey, C. (1977). *Play.* New York: Fontana/Open Books and Open Books Publishing Ltd.

Patterson, P. (1980). *Pro-Social Behaviour of Two Year Old Children in Mixed and Same Age Groupings.* Brisbane: Lady Gowrie Child Centre.

Piaget, J. (1951). *Play, Dreams and Imagination in Childhood.* New York: Norton.

Watts, B.H. and Patterson, P. (1984). *In Search of Quality: Home and Day Care Centre Complimentary Environments for the Growing Child.* Brisbane: Lady Gowrie Child Centre.

*Photographs:* Lady Gowrie Child Centres, Brisbane and Hobart; Michael Taylor

# Chapter 10

# Programming for Two to Three Year Olds

## Barbara Nielsen
and the C Nursery Staff Team
Lady Gowrie Child Centre,
Adelaide

*Enormous developmental changes occur in the second and third years of life. Consequently, a group of "almost threes" will be very different and will require a different program from a group of predominantly young toddlers, slightly over a year old. In the following chapter, Nielsen and the Adelaide Lady Gowrie Centre staff look at programming for two to three year olds in a broad context. While they include attention to the principles and underlying philosophy that sound programming must be based on, they also provide specific suggestions for activities, experiences, and materials. Older toddlers require a program that allows them to explore, experiment, and discover, one that acknowledges the particular developmental needs of the age group, and that gives priority to the importance of play.*

## Preface

The ideas that follow are the product of the 1985 staff team's work with children two to three years of age in full day and regular part-time care at the Lady Gowrie Child Centre in Adelaide.

This practical guide, based on a common philosophy of caregivers and teachers, indicates how beliefs can be put into practice in a daily program for young children.

The process of preparing such a document is probably as important as the product. However, time often does not allow each caregiver to have this opportunity. Through recording and showing the work of one staff team it is hoped that others may benefit and find this material a useful resource for their own staff discussions when planning some aspects of the program.

*E.T. Mellor*
*Director*
*Lady Gowrie Child Centre, Adelaide*

## ABOUT CHILDREN

(Adapted from Weeks, B. et al., 1983).

### We believe:
- Children are unique, curious, knowledgeable, feeling, thinking people.
- It is important that children feel good about themselves.
- Learning begins at birth and continues throughout life.
- Language is central to children's learning.
- The attitudes formed in the early years are crucial for living and schooling.
- Children are naturally curious and want to learn.
- Children learn through play and through active involvement with others.
- Children should be encouraged through specific positive feedback as success brings further success and motivation.

- Children between two and three years old are at a stage when development is particularly rapid.

have had stories read to them from 10 months of age whilst others may have had no book or story experiences.

## CHARACTERISTICS OF CHILDREN 2 TO 3 YEARS OF AGE

It becomes obvious when working with a group of children between the ages of two and three plus years in care that there is a broad range of developmental levels within the age group. Because of the cultural background, the physical environment in the home, and adult expectations, each child will experience the center environment uniquely, and may find it to be very different from that provided at home. Some children may be ready to climb over anything and everything, others may not want to venture beyond the parent or caregiver. Some will want to go to bed straight after lunch, while others will not have had a daytime sleep for some months. Some will go to sleep in a bed, while others may not have ever gone to sleep except in their mother's arms. Some will still be reliant on a bottle or pacifier; some will have given them up long ago. Some may

This diversity is normal, and it serves as a reminder to child care workers that each child is an individual. The center program, whilst taking account of the home situation and the child's experience, cannot replicate the home environment for each child—but it can supplement it to the child's advantage. Child care can help to facilitate a child's development.

## INDIVIDUAL DIFFERENCES IN DEVELOPMENT

Each child develops at an individual pace. It is not possible to predict that a child will be at a certain stage of development at two years of age. Not only are there differences between individual children of the same age, but each child may be at different stages of development in specific areas. For example a two year old child may have the gross motor development of a 1-1/2 year old,

100

the fine motor development of a one year old, the language development of a three year old, the self-help skills of a two year old and the social-emotional development of a two year old. Development in different areas proceeds in spurts and stops. This is often clearly visible when a child who may have been saying a few single words starts to walk. The talking may not advance for a time while the child practises the new physical skill and goes off exploring the wider world.

To provide appropriate learning experiences and activities for the stage rather than simply the age of the child, caregivers need to make some assessment of the child's developmental level in specific areas. To do this caregivers should be sensitive and interested observers, always evaluating as an ongoing process so that children can be given the opportunities to succeed at their own level of development. For example, if some children are using scissors and one child cannot make the hand movements, then the caregiver can encourage the child to gain satisfaction from tearing paper for glueing. Conversely, if several children are tearing paper and a child is showing the need to be more precise, then scissors can be introduced for that child.

## ON PLAY

(Adapted from Weeks, B. et al., 1983).

### We believe:
- Play is the way children make sense of their world, and is the natural way they learn.
- Play is a child's work.
- Play is:
  - self-initiated
  - spontaneous
  - a way of finding out about people
  - a way of learning to live with people

- a means of thinking
- a means of developing and practicing skills
- an opportunity for children to use their curiosity to explore, experiment and test ideas
- an aid to developing concentration
- a way of nurturing creativity
- a means of self-expression.

### This means that:
- We provide an environment conducive to play, an environment which contains materials which are stimulating, challenging, changing, varied, familiar and loved.
- We provide an environment which encourages different kinds of play, such as construction, role playing, gross motor movement, fine motor movement, problem solving, discovering, communicating, creating, imagining, and activities involving reading, writing and number, space and measurement.
- During play, caregivers:
  - allow uninterrupted concentration
  - intervene when appropriate
  - extend learning
  - stimulate the child and arouse curiosity
  - support the child, sometimes by becoming involved
  - observe the child
  - encourage involvement in a variety of activities
  - promote children's self-esteem by valuing their efforts
  - encourage children to value their own efforts and the efforts of others.

### THE IMPORTANCE OF ROUTINES
Much of the child care day is occupied with routine activities, such as eating, cleaning, toileting, sleeping and resting, dressing and undressing. These are important for a number of reasons.

101

## We believe:

- Eating habits established in the first years of life lay the foundation for future health.
- Children know when they have had enough to eat.
- At this stage children are developing independence and want to be able to feed themselves.
- A good diet is the best way to care for teeth.
- Children should have a dental examination for the first time at two years of age.
- Children's teeth should be cleaned properly once a day by an adult.
- Most children will usually require a sleep during the day, commonly after lunch.
- During this stage children develop control of bodily functions and learn to use the toilet.
- During this stage children develop an awareness of their own sexuality.
- At this stage children are unaware of many potential dangers in the environment.
- Home routines and cultural background must be taken into account when helping young children adapt to new routines and expectations in child care centers.

## This means that:

- Children need a balanced, dentally sound diet, without unnecessary salt or sugar.
- Children who do not feel hungry should not be forced to eat and may need extra food before the next meal time.
- Most foods should be finger foods or easily managed by the child with a spoon.
- Caregivers should promote good health with the parents.
- The program and physical set-up of the care environment must allow for the differing sleep needs of the children to be met; both the differing needs of different children, and the differing daily needs of each child.
- The physical set-up of the care environment must incorporate:
  - diaper changing facilities
  - potties and/or training chairs
  - low toilet(s)
  - low hand basin(s)
  - paper towels or named hand-towels for each child.

- Caregivers should have a relaxed approach to helping toddlers learn to use the toilet, with gentle encouragement of regular toileting as a part of the daily routine.
- Children's interest in their own sexuality, and the sexuality of others, is accepted by the caregiver as the natural growth of body awareness.
- The environment must be monitored so that situations which might be dangerous to the children's health can be avoided.
- In encouraging children to explore the environment, the caregiver needs to maintain a middle road between overprotection which produces fearful, timid children, and allowing children to take foolish risks.

## THE CARE ENVIRONMENT

In providing a care environment for children under three years of age we aim to create a nurturing environment which

102

complements a loving and stimulating home environment.

This implies an environment in which:

- each child is treated as an individual.
- each child is treated as a growing, thinking, feeling person.
- each child feels unconditional acceptance and warmth.
- there is a balance between loved and familiar toys and new or changing toys and activities.
- each child is challenged to think and to try.
- each child is able to develop the skills and attitudes for accepting, understanding, interacting with, and working effectively with others.
- each child develops competence in motor skills.
- each child is encouraged to use language for communication.
- each child has the opportunity for experimentation with and self-expression through language, drama, music, dance, movement and art.
- children are involved in the world outside through frequent, short excursions and visits.
- there is close liaison between parents and caregivers.
- the caregivers recognize the developmental stage of each child and develop a program which reflects the developmental stages of each of the children in their care.

## CREATING THE INDOOR ENVIRONMENT

The indoor environment can be a never-ending source of interest to the young child. It is contained by fixtures such as walls, but can be filled with things just waiting for sensory exploration and discovery by a young child.

The *boundaries* are walls, ceiling, doors, windows and floors.

The *contents* include:

| | |
|---|---|
| space | pictures |
| furniture | decorations |
| lights | heating |
| storage places | animals |
| water | toys |
| toilets | food |
| people | smells |
| a cooking place | music |
| tools (e.g. brooms, hammers, wooden spoons) | sounds/noise |
| | books |
| special places | color |
| notice boards | textures |
| shapes | art materials |
| junk | |

ALL OF THESE CONTRIBUTE TO AN ATMOSPHERE.

## Organization of the Contents

In the home environment all of the fascinating contents of the indoors are naturally arranged in special places because houses are made up of rooms. In the care environment it is necessary to create special places, or centers of interest, and it is also usually necessary to use areas for a variety of activities during each day. Some centers of interest, or special places, include cosy places, quiet places, book corner, kitchen, dress-up corner, art area, wet area, place for each child's possessions science and nature corner, woodwork bench, sand, block and construction area, music center, space for movement, puzzles and manipulative materials area, adult places (especially chairs) and a sleeping place.

## Defining Areas or Centers of Interest

These may be quite large and complex, such as a home corner, or may be quite small and simple, such as a special shelf for puzzles. Some areas may maintain their identity throughout the day. For example, a quiet corner may be developed with cushions and books into a book corner, and although the books are changed each week, the corner retains its atmosphere and identity from week to week. Other areas, such as a table top, may change their identity several times during a day, and may even be shifted to different places in the room. The children need a balance between the security of familiar things and the novelty of changing things or areas.

Some ways and places to make centers of interest are:
- on a mat (small) or a carpet area
- use of furniture to divide or partition an area
- on a table top
- under a table
- in a box
- on a cart
- on a sheet of plastic
- on a lino area
- by hanging streamers from the ceiling (to just above adult head level)
- on a shelf
- in a cupboard (open the doors to open the center)
- in a water table or sink
- in a corner
- on a window ledge
- on the wall
- with a pile of cushions
- by draping a sheet over a table or chairs
- on a mattress

- on a sheet
- with a story cushion (e.g. a long snake).

## The Role of the Caregiver

The caregiver plays a most important role, both in developing the indoor environment, and as the focus of child-adult interactions. Listed below are some of the ways in which the caregiver can develop children's play and facilitate their learning, while always observing each child's play and identifying the level of each child's development physically, emotionally, socially and intellectually.

*In all areas:*
Rotate materials
Participate in conversation
Ask questions to stimulate play
Assist with cleanup
Use positive reinforcement.

*In the home corner:*
Assist with clothes
Model behavior of the parent
Participate in the play.

*In the block area:*
Assist the child in playing safely.

*In the book corner:*
Select books to suit the child
Sit close to the child
Involve the child with the story.

*In the music center:*
Sing songs
Dance to the music
Assist with instruments or music making
Assist with cassette or record player.

*In puzzles and manipulative materials center:*
Complete puzzles
Provide a variety of manipulative materials
Assist with opening and closing containers.

## Questions that may be used in evaluating indoor play activities:

(Adapted from Leeper, et al., 1974.)
- Are several groups or centers of interest active at the same time?
- Is there time for individual and small group play at a leisurely pace, or is the time too tightly scheduled?
- Do the materials and equipment stimulate dramatic play?
- Are the materials arranged so that they are accessible to the children?
- Is there a variety of play equipment available (for example, wheeled toys, blocks, dolls, soft toys, house-keeping equipment, puzzles, books, and dress-up material)?
- Does the play equipment vary in level of difficulty so that it challenges children and leads to the development of new skills?

## THE OUTDOOR ENVIRONMENT

The outdoor environment offers the young child many opportunities for physical activity, exploring, discovering and learning. The play area needs to be interesting and safe.

*An ideal play area would include:*
- space in the sun and space in the shade
- a hard surface area for wheeled toys, balls, and blocks
- both open and secluded areas which can be easily supervised
- grass for playing, running, rolling and crawling
- plants—trees (fruit, deciduous, evergreen), shrubs and flowers
- areas of sand play, water play and mud play
- a digging patch
- a gardening patch
- pets
- special features such as slopes, mounds, undulating paths
- 'real' cars, tractors, trains, boats, etc.

- tunnels, climbing equipment, cubby house, swings
- movable equipment such as tires, drums, climbing equipment, blocks.

## Outdoor Activities

### 1. Sensory Play

The outdoors holds a multitude of sensory experiences for the small child. These include:
- the feel of the wind
- the sound of leaves
- birds singing
- the smell of flowers
- the feel of mud
- dappled light through the leaves
- the heat of the sun
- the textures and tastes of leaves.

As well as all of these incidental sensory experiences, the children enjoy sensory play which is planned.

*Water Play*

Children love playing with water. The water trough, bucket, baby's bath or bowl can be an ever-changing source of sensory experience. Interesting additions include:
- color
- soap flakes for bubbles
- hose pipe (with funnel and spray)
- pieces of wood or "sardine" tins for boats
- a "floating and sinking " kit
- sponges
- squeeze bottles
- pipes
- sieves
- rubber gloves with holes in the fingers
- ladles and spoons
- jugs, kettles, saucepans.

Other experiences include a sheet of wet plastic for sliding, an aqua-lab (a canal system for boats), and small individual tins or buckets of water with a brush for "painting".

*Sand Play*

Sand play in a sand pit tends to be different from sand play in a sand tray.

All sand play can be an enriching experience for the child.

Toys and items useful for sand play include:
- spades, long and short handled
- spoons, scoops
- sieves
- buckets, saucepans, plates and cups
- flour sifter
- small garden forks and trowels
- tires and reels
- pipes
- scales
- sand wheel
- dump trucks, graders, trucks and cars
- shells and stones (make a beach in the sand pit).

Other experiences include treasure hunts, drawing with sand, and water in the sand pit.

*Mud Play*

Mud can be fascinating for the young child as it has quite a different texture from wet sand. Mud may be in the digging patch, in an old wading pool, baby bath, sand tray or bowl.

Interesting experiences with mud include:
- body painting (followed by a hose down. Choose a hot day!)
- using cake decorating tools to squeeze mud out
- covering a table with plastic and doing mud finger painting.

## 2. Play for Developing Large Motor Skills

Most outdoor play helps the child to develop balance, physical strength and coordination.

*Climbing Equipment*

Some climbing equipment may be fixed, and some moveable. It all needs to be firmly secured, with no rough parts or protruding screws or nails. The ground below needs to be soft enough to cushion any falls.

Some useful climbing equipment:

| | |
|---|---|
| A-frames | ladders |
| blocks | trees |
| reels | ropes |
| planks | scramble nets |
| monkey bars | knotted ropes |
| ladder-ropes | |

*Gymnastics*

For gymnastics use an old mattress or gym mat, a small trampoline, and rocker boards.

*Balls*

Have a variety of balls, including different size beach balls, soccer balls, tennis balls, and bean bags. Use these to throw and catch, bounce, throw at or through targets. Some additional suggestions include hanging a ball in a stocking for hitting, trying a bat and ball, playing croquet or cricket, and playing skittles or bowls.

### 3. Manipulative Play (Fine Motor Skills)

Woodwork is a great outdoors activity. The children can make a lot of satisfying noise, as well as develop fine motor skills. The children can hammer with or without nails. Tacks or screws make an interesting change. The children can hammer corrugated cardboard, foam rubber, cardboard cylinders and wood scraps.

### 4. Science or "Real Life" Activities

Children can be involved in setting up and maintaining their outdoor environment.

For example, they can:

- clear the sand back into a pit
- water the plants
- prepare and use a digging patch
- hang out washing
- paint equipment (shelves, tires, sleds)
- plant trees (fruit trees and deciduous trees are especially good)
- sweep paths and rake up leaves
- cart rubbish away.

- dig for earthworms
- set up a wormery
- enjoy a visit from a mother animal and her babies
- find that bird singing
- chase butterflies
- find interesting insects.

### 5. Cubbies and Quiet Places

These can exist in parts of the garden, or may be created for short periods of time. A changed position creates fresh interest.

Some ideas for cubbies and quiet places are:

- under low-hanging trees and shrubs (always prune from a child's point of view)
- in an old boat
- under a beach umbrella with vision curtaining pegged around it
- built from small cardboard cartons
- in a large cardboard carton
- curtains (shower curtains and vision netting as well as opaque curtains) pegged from tree branches, a trellis, clothes line or draped over tables or climbing equipment.
- a tarpaulin or camping mat attached

*Gardening*

As well as helping with weeding, watering and planting, children love to have their own gardens. Children can have a garden in a tractor tire (cut in half), trays, jars, margarine or cream containers, or a small identified garden plot. Some plants which grow quickly are watercress, alfalfa, bean sprouts, sunflowers, daffodils, and ranunculi.

*Animal life*

Children enjoy keeping pets, and they love investigating all the insects and bugs which can be found in any garden area.

They can:

- keep guinea pigs, rabbits or lizards in a hutch
- have an aviary
- keep turtles, frogs, snails or fish in an aquarium
- 'hire" a pet from a resource center
- go on caterpillar or snail hunts

to a fence, and then pegged to the ground using tent pegs, about one to one-and-a-half meters out from the fence.

Caregivers can be flexible and creative about where they offer activities.

## TAKING THE INDOORS OUTDOORS

- Let the children sleep outdoors, under a tree, in a cubby area.
- Make an enclosed area for books. Use tables and chairs, or a rug with cushions.
- Eat outdoors on chairs and tables or on rugs.
- Take puzzles onto the lawn.
- Set out a rug with cushions and soft toys, especially late in the afternoon.
- Tell stories on the lawn or under a tree.
- Have felt board stories.
- Set up a home corner under a tree or in a corner in the yard.
- Have some small blocks on a rug.
- Paint — with feet
    — on paper around a tree or on a fence or wall.
- Do crayon drawing on paper on the ground, against a tree trunk, wall or fence.
- Provide chalk drawing on blackboards or on the footpath.
- Have an outside nature table.
- Drape old curtains for a puppet stage.
- Include dress-up clothes in a "cubby house".

## TAKING THE OUTDOORS INDOORS

- Have an inside sand tray.
- Have a water table, sink or baby's bath for water play.
- Use a large container of sawdust or wheat as well as, or instead of, sand.
- Use a balance beam, mini-trampoline or rocker board.

- Bring in large wooden and plastic blocks.
- Set up an obstacle course indoors.
- Bring in push-along toys.
- Have woodwork indoors.
- Set up an inside nature table.
- Grow plants and vegetables on cotton.
- Have inside animals—birds, fish, mice.
- Use leaves, twigs, etc. for collage, printing and pasting.
- Use seed pods for "food" in the home corner—supply some tongs.
- Build cubbies inside using tables, chairs, rugs, blocks, boxes, etc.

## EVALUATION OF OUTDOOR ACTIVITIES

Some questions (adapted from Leeper, et al., 1974) to use to help evaluate outdoor activities are:

1. Are the equipment and space adequate for the development of motor skills and muscular coordination?

2. Is the equipment placed for easy supervision and to minimize the possibility of accidents?

3. Is there a variety of activities for the children?

4. Are all of the children challenged by their environment to develop new skills?

5. Can children choose from among a variety of activities?

6. Is concentration encouraged or do children have to change
    activities because another child wants to use materials or equipment?

7. Is there sufficient space for the particular activity?

## SENSORY AND MANIPULATIVE EXPERIENCES FOR TODDLERS

Children need a wealth of sensory and manipulative experiences if their sensory motor development is to be facilitated. As these experiences continue they lead naturally into self-expressive skills.

Materials which promote this sensory-motor development are:

| | |
|---|---|
| play dough | soap suds |
| clay | finger paint |
| sand | glue |
| water | paper (different |
| mud | colors and textures) |
| blocks | crayons |
| mosaics | paint and brushes |
| materials for | pencils |
| threading | solid point felt pens |
| woodwork | chalk |
| hole-punches | charcoal chunks |
| scissors | |

Enjoyment and success in tearing and pasting using fingers and hands should precede the use of scissors and brushes, which require greater precision. There are stages, too, in pasting. The younger child or a child inexperienced in the activity will pile one piece of torn paper or pre-cut colored paper on the other using much paste. Provide scraps of cardboard or the base paper will disintegrate. After lots of experience the child will scatter the pasted items over the paper, and later will use these to form a picture or ordered theme. Instructions should not be given.

The following lists are examples of inexpensive, often discarded items from homes, factories, offices and workshops, or they are found in the natural environment. They can be used effectively for toddlers' sensory exploration, experimentation, and construction experiences. The collection of materials takes some ingenuity and sense of imagination on the part of the adults. The materials for children's investigation, manipulation and construction should be examined carefully for sharp edges and other dangers. Some smaller items will need to be closely supervised, particularly if children in the group are still at the stage of putting things in the mouth.

## Large Construction and Play

Boxes of all shapes and sizes;

Wood scraps—smooth edged;

Carpet pieces and lino scraps;

Burlap, old blankets, curtains;

Second hand dress-up clothes, belts, handbags, school bags, brief cases, hats, hard hats, ties, tool carriers, baskets;

Cardboard cylinders from paper, material, mailing tubes;

Hose pieces, funnels cut from juice containers.

## Small Construction and Decoration

*Natural materials*—apple, orange and pumpkin seeds, acorn caps, pine cones, pine needles, feathers, flowers, petals, egg shells, pebbles, seed pods, rocks, gum nuts, bamboo, leaves, bark, sea shells.

*Material scraps of various textures*—burlap, velvet, nylon, silk, cotton, wool, gauze, cotton balls, fur samples, flock, laces, braids, bias binding, rick rack, felt scraps, cotton balls.

*Wood and paper products*—computer paper, streamers, colored papers, magazine pages, cellophane scraps, blotting paper, shiny cardboard scraps, gummed labels, gift wrapping, crepe paper, small boxes, packets, egg cartons, sawdust, small wood pieces, sandpaper, newspaper, wood shavings, brown paper, milk cartons, cans, confetti, flint paper, ice cream sticks.

*Sewing and craft aids*—raffia, yarn, sequins, pipe cleaners, ribbons, artificial flowers, elastic, beads.

*Home type items and disposables*—
sponges, plastic bottles, steel wool,
plastic spoons, forks, knives, lids, food
trays, clothes pins, stockings, cupcake
papers, saucepans, chopsticks, parts of
broken toys (e.g. wheels), wooden
spoons, bottle tops, nails, spices, inner
tube scraps, keys.

*Office*—staplers, punches, sticky tape,
franked stamps, envelopes, paper clips,
paper dots, strips computer paper, rubber bands, typewriter spools.

*Factory*— Investigate local industry
waste materials.

## Evaluation of Sensory and Manipulative Experiences

(Adapted from Leeper, et al., 1974)

1. Observe children to see who does
and does not enjoy getting messy.

2. Observe the child's movements—
free or restricted, experimental or dependent on encouragement.

3. Observe each child to establish
which type of activity the child prefers
and/or if the child is avoiding any activities.

4. Reflect on the variety of experiences offered at the center over a period
of two weeks.

5. Keep anecdotal records on individual children.

# ART ACTIVITIES

## We believe:

- Art activities provide opportunities for sensory exploration and experimentation.
- Art activities strengthen the child's ability to observe and to imagine. They increase the child's sensitivity to self and to others.
- Through working with art materials, the child assumes responsibility for choosing and shaping them, and learns judgement and control.
- Successful experiences with art materials help develop the child's self-esteem.
- The child can express feelings through use of art materials.
- Children grow socially through using art materials.
- Intellectual growth takes place through art experiences.
- Exercise, the development of motor coordination, visual discrimination and hand/eye coordination take place through art experiences.
- Art for the young child develops into a means of self-expression.

## This means that we:

- Offer experiences every day which encourage sensory and manipulative investigation and practice.
- Offer a choice of several activities at a time.
- Recognize staff limitations by offering only one "messy" or new medium requiring close supervision with several familiar activities which the children can handle more independently.
- Allow time for unhurried, satisfying exploration and practice.
- Provide a variety of activities which allow the child to make tactile explorations, using hands as tools.
- Plan an environment to stimulate creative activity, an environment which is challenging, stimulating, and gives

opportunities for the beginnings of aesthetic appreciation and sensitivity.
- Understand the child's developmental level and respect it.
- Recognize that it is the process, not the product, which is important to the young child.
- Allow children time to watch an activity before trying it, if that is what they need.
- Understand how to stand back...and do stand back and observe.
- Provide enriching experiences— books, pictures, excursions, nature walks, etc.
- Help each child to experience success each day, give approval of the child's sensory/manipulative experimentations and gently encourage, support and offer technical help when needed.
- Raise questions to stimulate thinking.
- Help the child to assume an increasing responsibility towards maintaining the orderliness and attractiveness of the room, and for clearing up after activities.
- Create a feeling of security that leaves the child free to think, select, make decisions and imagine.

- Realize that children need many experiences in similar activities to develop beyond the experimental stage in that activity.

- Do not show the child how to paint, where to place pasted items on the base board or paper, or suggest that the child does more on the page.
- Do not use adult patterns for coloring in or models to copy.
- Help parents to understand that children's experience in sensory manipulative activities, not the end result, is important at this stage.

## Developmental Stages of Drawing

| | |
|---|---|
| Up to 1 year | Accidental and imitative scribbling |
| 1 1/2 years | Refines scribbles, vertical or horizontal lines appear. Produces multiple line drawings and likes to scribble over visual stimuli. |
| 2 years | Produces multiple loop drawings with spirals and crude circles. Begins to name scribbles. |
| 3 years | Figure reproduction appears, especially circles and crosses, and combines these. |
| 4 years | Can make simple pictures with combinations of symbols, recognizable to adults. |
| 7 years | Drawings become gradually more intricate as knowledge increases. |

The child's developmental stage depends not only on the age of the child, but also on the previous experiences of the child. For example, a three year old child who has not had any opportunities to paint or draw, will have to go through the exploratory/manipulative phases before naming scribbles and then beginning figure reproduction.

## BOOKS, THE BOOK CORNER AND STORYTELLING

Through books, the book corner and storytelling, we aim to:

- Introduce each child to the concept of books, that is that books are stories written down.
- Help each child develop a love of books.
- Teach each child how to handle books.
- Help develop each child's listening skills.
- Introduce the child to the rhythms of language.
- Help develop each child's visual discrimination skills.
- Help develop in each child a sense of anticipation and the skill of prediction.
- Help each child identify with stories.
- Teach concepts such as sharing, belonging, matching and one-to-one correspondence.
- Help each child develop consideration for others through group story times.
- Help the child begin to understand the book-making process.

### This means that:

Each child needs to have a wide variety of experiences with books. Some of those experiences are:

- Looking at books with an adult and learning by modelling how to handle a book, turning the pages, looking at pictures, identifying and naming pictures.
- Looking at books alone.
- Listening to a story being read in a small group.
- Having a story told instead of read.
- Sharing a book with another child.
- Helping the child make a book either with blank paper or with drawings or other art work.
- Making group books about shared experiences, for example, excursions, lunch time, sequence of the day, pets who visit. Real photographs are useful.

- Felt board stories.
- Dramatic play to retell stories.
- Storytelling with puppets.
- Story tapes.
- Seeing adults enjoy books.
- Having their spoken words written down, for example, about a painting.

### Selection of Books

For very young children books can be divided into two broad categories:
- those books which are strong and durable enough to sustain handling by fingers which are often not only poorly coordinated, but also grubby;
- and those books which need to be kept aside for use with adult supervision.

### Other points to consider:

1. Story length (children of this age usually need short stories).
2. Simplicity of language.
3. Clarity of illustrations (photos are excellent for very young children).
4. Strong, durable books, readily accessible to the children.
5. Special books available for use with adults.
6. Other toys, such as soft toys and puppets available in the area.
7. Sometimes quiet activities such as threading or lacing available there.

### Handy Hints for Storytellers

- Use voice with expression.
- Use facial expression and body language.
- Keep the language simple, and the story simple.
- Try using props, for example, a puppet, dress-up, a musical instrument or other object.
- Mime actions.
- Keep the story moving.
- Use rhyme and rhythm.
- Tell the story to a small, compact group of children.
- Give eye contact to all of the children.
- Be prepared
  —know the outline of the story
  —have a good line to begin
  —have a good line to finish.
- Personalize the story sometimes, for example, by using the children's names, or telling a story about one of the children.
- Pick up on children's cues, be spontaneous and flexible.
- Prepare stories for outings.
- Tell stories anywhere and everywhere.
- Talk about things you feel comfortable with.
- Enjoy yourself!
- Use repetition.
- Encourage involvement through the repetition of a phrase or a song.
- Encourage prediction... "and then

what do you think happened?"

Remember there is a big difference in the interests and concentration abilities of children two and three years of age.

There may be an even wider difference if children are developing two languages.

## Themes for Stories

- The child's own world and experiences in the past, present and future
- A family's experiences
- Holidays
- Group outings
- An animal
- An animal that only talks to children
- A toy
- A tree or flower
- A puppet tells of its adventures
- A piece of furniture, e.g. a chair
- People and occupations
- A child who is always getting into trouble
- Expansion of ordinary, everyday activities

## MUSIC AND MOVEMENT

## We believe:

- Musical experiences are enjoyable.
- Music contributes to the development of each child.
- Music offers the child opportunities for listening, rhythmic responses, singing, creating and playing instruments.
- Listening to music helps the child to develop an awareness of and sensitivity to sounds.
- Through singing, the child increases the range and flexibility of the voice.
- Movement to music helps the physical development of the child.
- Movement to music helps the child learn about space in relation to self.
- Through music the child can express feelings.
- Experiences with music can promote musical appreciation.

- Music can help the social growth of the young child.
- Music is a medium for creative expression.
- All young children have musical capacities and should have the opportunity to develop this potential.

## This means that we:

- Use music during play and routine activities.
- Have special music activities every day.
- Ensure that each child has opportunities for a wide range of musical experiences: listening, moving to music, singing, making and playing instruments.
- Recognize and respect the child's developmental level.
- Sing as we work and play with the children, encouraging them to sing along.
- Allow the children to watch and listen before joining in.
- Base the early musical experiences on beat, rhythm, and pitch.
- Use language and dramatic play to encourage movement responses.
- Ensure that children have opportunities for listening, performing (singing, playing, moving), and creating.
- Plan a program which allows the child to experience music of varying types, and begin to develop musical appreciation.

## Developmental Sequences

(Leeper, et al., 1974)

### A. Singing

1. Enjoys listening to someone singing, may sing spontaneously while playing.

2. Responds with actions to song sung by another.

3. Joins in with an occasional word or phrase as someone sings.

4. Sings with an adult or group, but not necessarily in time with them.

114

5. Sings along with an adult or group. Is able to match pitch, but with a limited range.

6. Sings alone.

7. Selects and requests favorite songs.

8. Recognizes songs sung or played by others.

9. Develops a repertoire of songs.

10. Sings accurately with an expanded range.

## B. Listening

1. Engrossed in own activity, but listens just enough to be aware of what is being sung or played.

2. Enjoys a short song, recording, or an instrument, either alone or with an adult.

3. Enjoys a short song, recording or an instrument along with a small group of other children.

4. Listens and analyses what is heard.

5. Can distinguish between loud and soft or happy and sad music. Can listen for details and answer questions.

6. Can listen to own singing or playing and match pitch.

## C. Movement (to rhythms or music)

1. Makes random movements, using large muscles.

2. Moves rhythmically in own way for short periods of time.

3. Responds when an accompaniment emphasizes movement.

4. Moves at fast tempo, but finds slower tempos more difficult.

5. Listens before participating.

6. Adjusts body movements to keep the beat.

7. Adjusts body movements to an accompaniment which involves contrasts.

8. Acquires musical concepts of high-low, fast-slow, short-long and is able to express them through movement.

## D. Playing instruments

1. Manipulates and experiments with instruments.

2. Recognizes the sounds of various instruments.

3. Uses an instrument as an accompaniment to movements, but not necessarily in time with own steps.

4. Can play an instrument and keep

the beat with another instrument or recording.

5. Is interested in and curious about instruments that adults play.

6. Plays instruments along with a small group of other children.

7. Learns the names of some of the better known instruments.

## E. Creating

1. Chants to accompany an activity. This may be a play on words, or experimenting with sounds.

2. Experiments with instruments and sounds.

3. Will suggest new words for a song.

4. Makes up extra verses for a song.

5. Dramatizes a song.

6. Interprets the mood of music through movement.

7. Creates own melody or tune.

## Some Ideas for Music and Movement

### 1. Music in Play and Routine Activities

- Sing while children walk, march, skip from place to place.
- Use songs and chants during daily activities, for example, "This is the way we...
  ...wash the dishes"
  ...pick up the blocks"
  ...go to sleep".
- Sing songs while travelling.
- Sing to distract and soothe an upset child.
- Encourage children to listen to sounds and music in the environment.
- Bring songs into storytelling.
- Use rhythmic chants during routine activities. For example: And now it's time to pick up the puzzles, pick up the puzzles, pick up the puzzles, And now it's time to pick up the puzzles, Come and help us too.
- Sing to the beat of a bouncing ball, skipping rope, the movement of the swing.

- Play musical statues.
- Encourage the children to sing to each other.
- Sing "Happy Birthday" when they make cakes in the sand pit or from play dough.
- Tape children as they sing, do everyday activities, play instruments...and then play it back to them.
- Make musical instruments with the children.
- Play musical games with the children, for example "Ring around a rosey", "Row your boat" (with children facing each other).

### 2. Sound in the Environment

Encourage the children to listen to:
- doors closing
- water running, dripping (fast and slow), splashing
- hand washing
- teeth cleaning
- a toilet flushing
- body noises
- footsteps
- a refrigerator
- kitchen utensils in use
- frying
- boiling
- a telephone
- a radio, stereo, or television
- a washing machine
- people eating, crunching, mushing, slurping, etc
- sounds in the street—trucks, cars, buses, motorbikes
- sounds when crossing the road
- animal sounds
- thunder and rain
- wind in the trees
- leaves falling
- seaside noises
- a train station
- rivers
- planes
- birds
- sirens of fire engine, etc
- sounds in the park.

### 3. Experiments in Sound-Making

*Mouth sounds:*
- tongue clicks
- fish 'pops'
- changing the shape of the mouth to make different sounds
- pitching the voice at different levels.

*Body sounds:*
- clapping
- stamping
- flapping arms
- slapping legs
- tapping head.

*Using objects:*
- chairs moving on carpet, lino, concrete
- chant rhyming words
- balls hitting the ground
- kitchen implements, such as eggbeaters, tongs, bowls and spoons, saucepans and lids
- sand paper
- tapping on tables, concrete, wood, tin, cushions, with hands or spoons
- water play, pouring, shaking using different sized containers
- running or walking on different surfaces
- the sound of seeds or grain in tins and plastic bottles.

### 4. Using Rhythm

*Voice:*
- finger plays
- poetry
- action rhymes
- chant to accompany daily routines

*Body:*
- play the beat or rhythm using hands while singing or listening to music.

*Tambour/Tambourine:*
- keep time with the child
- play a beat for the child to move to
- vary the beat for the child to vary the movement
- accompany rhymes and stories.

### 5. Singing
- Sing as the children play, move around, clean up.
- Use finger puppets with nursery rhymes and songs.
- Use finger plays, clapping and body movements to accompany singing.
- Remember the young child's limited voice range when choosing songs (middle C—A, 6 notes).
- Use repeated choruses in storytelling.
- Accompany singing with musical instruments.
- Allow individual children who wish to sing to the group.
- Tape record singing and play it back.
- Incorporate children's language into the singing.
- Initiate singing and dancing games.
- Keep a list of songs the children know.

### 6. Movement
- Use language and drama to stimulate movement to music—for example, "Clap Handies", "I'm a great big tiger".
- Use body parts to keep the beat.
- Use songs to stimulate gross motor movements.
  Examples: "I am walking, walking, walking..."
  "Clap, clap, clap your hands..."
  "This is the way..."
- Dress up, or use accessories to stimulate role-play.
- Develop space awareness through group activities.
- Listen to the music or beat, then move to it.
- Encourage the development of balance through movement activities such as standing or walking on tiptoes, standing on one foot.
- Help children develop body awareness through movement to singing games.
  Example: "Heads, shoulders, knees and toes."

## 7. Creativity

- Teach songs where children can partake in a real-life situation.
- Encourage them to become animals when singing animal songs.
- Use language experiences and encourage each child to develop a unique interpretation of action rhymes.
- Help children to act out stories with repeated choruses; create musical sounds to represent the characters.
- Create new words to well-known tunes.
- Provide taped music of different types, instruments, and props such as scarves and hats, and allow the children to express themselves.

## PROGRAM PLANNING

By now readers may be thinking "Where to go from here?" Young children are usually curious and active participants in an environment especially planned for them. Every experience the young child has is part of the program and every adult working with children plans in some form. Any decision about what experience and/or activity to provide for children or a child is "planning".

When children are in group care and there is a staff team responsible for the majority of the child's day, communication and planning become even more important. Experiences in group care should complement the young child's home experiences. There should be a balance to the day; times when the child has access to familiar experiences and times when new experiences can be introduced. Not too many new experiences should be offered at once.

Staff team planning in child care is essential to the provision of quality care programs so that each child has developmentally appropriate and meaningful experiences which lead to success.

## We believe:

- Planning and observation are basic to an effective program.
- Planning is the active development of the program.
- We should plan activities which are appropriate to the developmental stages of the children in our care.
- People working with the same group of children need time together for planning.
- Shared responsibility leads to the best possible program for the children.
- The most effective way to share responsibility is for child care workers to each have areas of responsibility.
- A written program is both a way of planning for the future and a record of past ideas.
- The written program should be easy to use, useful and not time-consuming to write up.

## This means that:

- We aim to plan every week for the coming week, and to develop plans for excursions, themes, big events (for example the Christmas festivities) several weeks ahead.
- We plan together where possible and share ideas on individual children and their needs. Sometimes plans must be done by individuals, as time when all staff can be together may be limited.
- We have divided our program into the following areas of responsibility:
  - Outdoors
  - Home corner/quiet activities
  - Art activities
  - Books, stories, finger-plays.
- Each child care worker has an area of responsibility for the week. The area of responsibility changes each week. Each child care worker has a small group of children as a primary care group to ensure that special relationships are developed between each child and a caring adult.

118

- We keep a written plan of each week's program.
- We have developed a way of writing our program which is useful, easy to use, and takes very little time to write up.
- We plan to allow each child care worker time for child observation.
- Ongoing communication between child care workers, and between care staff and parents, which relates to individual children's needs and progress is essential.
- Some planning will take place daily or even during the day; hence some plans may be recorded after the event.
- Basic activities may not be recorded unless there is to be a special emphasis, change of venue or particular stimulation.

## REFERENCES

Cherry, C. (1972). *Creative Art for the Developing Child*. Belmont, California: Pitman Learning Inc.

Derham, F. (1961). *Art for the Child Under Seven*. Canberra: The Australian Preschool Association Inc.

Leeper, S.H., bales, R.J., Skipper, P.S. and Witherspoon, R.L. (1974). *Good Schools for Young Children*. New York: Macmillan Publishing Co. Inc.

Lindberg, L. and Swedlow, R. (1985). *Young Children—Exploring and Learning*. Boston: Allyn and Bacon Inc.

Pile, N. (1973). *Art Experiences for Young Children*. New York: Macmillan Publishing Co. Inc.

Playgroup Association of SA Inc. (1979). *Sand and Water Play*. North Adelaide: The Playgroup Association of SA.

Roberts, P. (1980). The Playground—an Outdoor Environment. *Australian Early Childhood Resource Booklet* No. 1. Canberra: Australian Early Childhood Association Inc.

Seefeldt, C. (1976). *Curriculum for the Preschool Primary Child*. Columbus, Ohio: Charles E. Merrill Publishing Co.

Sheridan, M.D. (1975). *From Birth to Five Years—Children's Developmental Progress*. Windsor: Nfer-Nelson.

Stonehouse, A.W. (1979). Toddler's Play. *Australian Early Childhood Resource Booklet* No. 5. Canberra: Australian Early Childhood Association Inc.

Turner, J. (1973). *Creative Play*. Sydney: Belair Publications.

Weeks, B., Nielsen, B., Nankervis, C., *et al.* (1983). *Focus on the Early Years of Schooling*. Adelaide: Central Southern Region Education Office.

# Chapter 11

# Experiences for Toddlers— Some Practical Suggestions

## Bev Olsson

*"More ideas of things to do with them" is a familiar request of caregivers of toddlers. Although caregivers sometimes project their own boredom with familiar, tried-and-true activities to the toddlers the care for, it is of interest and benefit to both children and adults to have new and different experiences, and variations on the familiar. It is important in searching for "something new and different", however, to maintain the link between characteristics of the age group and the materials and activities being offered to them. It is equally important to think of offering experiences that are meaningful, that make sense to toddlers, and to avoid gimmicks that appeal only to adults because they are novel. In the following chapter, Olsson suggests some appealing variations and innovations, but bases them solidly on the needs, characteristics, and interests of the age group.*

Toddlerhood is a period of rapid change. Children pass from one developmental stage to another very quickly; consequently, interests change frequently.

It is time for pre-occupation with motor learning, a time for intense curiosity, a time of striving for autonomy, and a time when language development, although still very limited, takes great leaps forward.

The toddler is a physically active learner. Increased mobility, together with an insatiable curiosity, bring the toddler into close contact with a wide range of materials to explore, touch, look at, taste, climb on and through, sit in, push, pull, carry, bang together and take apart.

Toddler are imitators, wanting to do everything adults do, such as sweeping, pouring, washing up and cooking.

Toddlers strive for independence, needing to do things for themselves attempting to take control of their bodies.

Although the following practical suggestions for program planning for toddlers have been presented under different areas such as motor, sensory and language ideas, all areas are inter-related and no area develops in isolation.

In the preparation of this material it has been assumed that toddler programs have access to such equipment as sand pits, swings, climbing equipment, home corner furniture, comfortable adult-sized tables and chairs, and to materials such as paint, dough, crayons and paper.

## Practical Ideas for the Development of Motor Skills

As the toddler learns each skill, it will be repeated frequently until mastered, so particular pieces of equipment and activities may need to remain in place for some time to allow for practice and repetition.
- Set up an obstacle course, selecting from some of the following items: large

outdoor blocks, tyres, wide planks, tables, chairs, large cardboard boxes, sheets, hoops. The course should involve such activities as crawling, walking, climbing, sliding, jumping. Plan it so that the youngest as well as the oldest can take part successfully. Obstacle courses can be planned as both indoor and outdoor activities.

- Make a stepping stone trail. Materials could include carpet squares, paper, foam plastic sheets, cardboard, vinyl and tiles. Use a variety of textures.

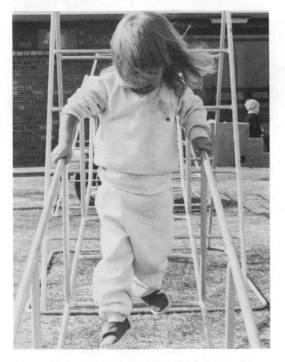

- Stand a ladder sideways by tying it between the swing frame or wedging it between tyres, boxes or blocks. Hang strips of material, plastic, paper (crepe, cellophane, newsprint), vinyl, or rope mesh. Children will experience a variety of textures as they crawl between the rungs.
- Use boxes of all sizes, including boxes large enough to stand or sit in, to crawl through or push around. Attach a rope and it can be used to create a pull-along toy. Provide boxes that are small enough to carry around. Boxes are favorite playthings, and any household kitchen can provide a wide assortment.
- Make an activity board. Attach to a board a selection of the following objects—door knobs, push bike bells, a variety of light switches, door knockers, telephone dials, clock faces, hooked door catches, small hinged doors.
- Provide large materials for construction, for example large cardboard boxes, sheets of cardboard, sheets and hoses.
- Take a small bag, or make one from brightly colored material, and stuff it with paper. Hang it inside or from a tree branch. It can be used for batting or kicking.
- Provide a thick foam mat or mattress for rolling and tumbling.
- Cover various sized pieces of foam plastic with strong material. These make excellent soft building blocks, and no matter how large are safe for toddlers to use.
- Make a collection of screw-top plastic jars. The toddlers will enjoy screwing and unscrewing lids. Put a treasure, for example, dried fruit, inside to encourage this activity. Ensure success. (If provided with two or three jars and lids, the older children might try to fit the correct lid to the jar.)
- Use paint rollers or brushes and water to "paint" outdoor equipment.
- Movement skills are increasing constantly. Make moving fun. Attach crepe paper tails to children's clothing or to their ride-along toys. They fly as the children run or ride.
- Provide wheeled toys to push, pull, ride on, ride in or carry favorite things in.
- Blow bubbles, and encourage children to run and catch them. Always ensure the smaller children can catch some too. Be aware of the safety issues involved in the use of soap and deter-

gents.

- As children develop the skill of jumping, use tires as jumping circles.
- Make bean bags of various sizes for throwing, tossing, or just carrying around.
- Balls of various shapes and sizes should always be available—tennis balls, plastic balls, footballs, ping pong balls. Push a large colored ball as far as possible into a stocking. Suspend it from the ceiling or tree branch so that it is within easy reach. Watch how the children use it.

through.

- Save clear plastic two-liter juice containers. They can be filled with colored, noise-making objects. Attach string to the handle and this makes a pull-along toy for the younger toddler.
- Tins (with sharp edges removed) from the kitchen can be painted to make simple nesting tins. The younger toddler may use only two, and more could be added for use by the older children. Some of the tins could have handles attached for carrying things.
- Hang a hoop horizontally. Give the

- Make balls from scrunched up news-aper or onion bags stuffed with cellophane paper (this makes an interesting sound), or small lengths of stocking stuffed with paper and secured at either end with rubber bands. Provide cardboard tubing (for example, aluminium foil rolls) for hitting.
- Sew bells onto elastic bands that fit the child's wrist. The children are aware of the sound as they move.
- Play chasing and hiding games.
- Partly bury tyres in an upright position so that they stand firmly. This provides an archway for crawling

children balls, balloons and bean bags to drop through. If the hoop is hung vertically children can crawl or walk through it.

- When using crayons with toddlers tape the paper to the table. It can be difficult for the toddler to hold the paper as well as draw on it.
- Provide the toddler with things that can be manipulated, such as telephones, clocks, keys and purses.

Toddlers learn by "doing". They gain information by watching, touching, tasting, smelling and listening. Development of sensory skills enables a child to discover more about objects through exploration—how things fit together, how objects can be classified, how they are alike and different, cause and effect, and constancy and change. There are many everyday articles that can be recycled to become toddler toys. It is not necessary to rely on expensive commercially produced equipment.

An understanding caregiver lends support and encourages toddlers in their need to find out as much as they can about their environment. The arrangement of the playroom and outdoors should allow for freedom of movement and freedom to interact with objects and people. Placing too many restrictions on a toddler's explorations will cause conflict, anger and tantrums.

## Practical Ideas for Sensory Experiences Within the Programs

*Water*
- All programs need water. It can be provided in a variety of ways—for example, in a large trough or in smaller dishes for individual play. Add an assortment of plastic bottles, cups funnels, jugs. The list is endless.
  - Add color.
  - Add soap to make the water bubbly.
  - Punch holes in various patterns in tins. The flow of water provides an interesting effect.
  - Add sponges to water activities.
  - Use sponges of various thicknesses and density. Colored water adds to the interest.
- Use watering cans to water the garden.
- Turn the hose on and let it trickle.
- Play in the puddles after rain, or play under the sprinkler.
- Fill or partly fill small balloons with water. Children can experiment with throwing, dropping, rolling, pushing and kicking.

- Make wet footprints. Soak a large sheet of foam. Children can make discoveries about hand- and footprints on concrete, wood, a table top or other appropriate surfaces.
- Give individual dishes with flour or similar material together with water and spoons. Allow children to use in ways of their choice. Children may choose to mix it together, dump it out, explore it with fingers, taste it. There is no "correct" way to use materials such as these. Adults should allow free experimentation and give approval to whatever method children choose.
- Provide a dish of warm water and a dish of cold water side by side.
- Wash dolls' clothes and bath the dolls. Notice the difference between the warm soapy water and the cool rinsing water.
- Make large ice blocks in an ice cream can. Turn them out for the children to feel, observe, bang, slide.
- Put several items in large clear containers of water. Sometimes things look different under water. Occasionally the water can be colored.
- What happens when various papers such as newsprint, cellophane or

crepe paper are put in water?

- Make a collection of various squeeze bottles. Allow experiments with these. Squeeze bottles can be plastic salt and pepper shakers, sauce bottles, trigger action spray bottles, or old shampoo bottles.
- Fill a clear plastic bottle with some colored water and place it on a window sill where the sun can shine through it. Also experiment with cellophane paper on windows. Take cellophane paper outdoors and look through it.

*Sounds*

- With the children's help rake together a pile of autumn leaves at the base of the slippery slide. This makes an interesting landing surface.
- Make a collection of seed pods from trees such as the poinciana and jacaranda. Listen to the sounds they make when shaken.

  Different shakers can be made:

  (a) Pour rice or sand inside two large coffee bottle lids and join them together with insulation tape. Stickers can be added to make it look attractive.

  (b) Plastic sauce or similar bottles can be filled with stones, dried peas, rice or sand. A piece of dowel securely fitted into the neck of the bottle makes for easy handling. The lids should be fastened securely for safety reasons.

  (c) Put noise makers into small fruit juice plastic bottles. Secure lid firmly.
- Give a child a stick or a piece of dowel to walk along a fence or verandah rail for a noisy activity.
- Collect items that make noise. Listen to watches, clocks, an alarm clock, a radio, bells, a typewriter, a music box, or a telephone.
- Hang a musical triangle in the room. Give the child a striker and listen to the sound.
- Other items such as horse shoes, wooden blocks, plastic bottles, cardboard rolls, saucepans, and lids can

be hung on a rope and stretched across a verandah or along a fence. Make various striking objects, such as wooden and metal spoons, available to produce different sound effects.

- Experiment with how the children's voices sound through a cardboard tube, plastic tubing, rolled up paper, or when shouting or whispering.
- Make "drums" from large boxes or tins.
- Hang wind chimes from a tree branch in the playground.
- Draw attention to all environmental sounds and display pictures of things that make sound.
- Listen to the sounds as children eat 'crunchy" foods—for example carrots, celery and apple.

*Tastes*

- Squeeze oranges and make orange juice.
- Use the blender and make banana smoothies and other milk drinks.
- Make a collection of "no-bake" recipes suitable for use with toddlers.
- Put pineapple pieces, strawberries, grapes or other fruits in ice-cube trays and cover with fruit juice.
- Cut small pieces of celery and spread cream cheese or peanut butter in the hollow section. Add some raisins. Spread cream cheese on whole meal biscuits and decorate with raisins.
- Enjoy a picnic lunch occasionally.
- Change the way apples and oranges are served occasionally. Remove the core from the apples and slice thinly. Oranges can be peeled and cut thinly in slices.

### Discovery Through the Senses

- Use discovery bags. Place all kinds of interesting items into large paper shopping bags. Leave them in the room for children to discover and delve into. The same can be done using a "feely box".

- Sew buttons of various colors, sizes, shapes and textures onto a strip of ribbon or material. Make it into a wall hanging. Make sure the buttons are stitched securely so they will not come off with constant handling. Buttons can also be stitched into a cloth book.
- Put some sand in a large dish or tray. Special things can be hidden for children to find, such as shells, stones, leaves, straws, popsicle sticks, small cars.
- Explore around the playground:
  - Lift up a log or stone to see what is underneath.
  - Look at leaves on the trees and smaller plants.
  - Feel the bark on the trees.
  - Search for bugs.
  - Collect colored stones.
- Encourage birds to come to the playground by making bird feeders. A simple way to make a feeder is to mix bird seed with peanut butter, stuff the mixture into a pine cone, and hang it outdoors.
- Have an assortment of containers that can be carted around, such as ice cream containers, cans, small baskets, all kinds of household items with handles added, and small buckets. Collecting things and carting them around is a favorite toddler activity.

*Language* permeates all early childhood programs and can be encouraged by adults who surround children with meaningful language experiences. Time needs to be spent with individual children, labeling actions and objects, giving descriptions, and having detailed discussions. Adults who respond readily to children in their attempts to use language and who listen attentively encourage language development. Toddlers are eager to share their discoveries with their caregivers.

## Experiences That Will Assist Language Development:

- Looking at books and reading simple stories.
- Making picture books of familiar objects and activities. Actual photographs can be used.
- Giving children the words to communicate with when they do not have them. This does not imply interrupting them, finishing their sentences for them, or pressuring them to speak quickly or "properly".
- Playing simple games—for example, naming body parts.
- Singing songs and finger plays.
- Talking to a child about what you are doing—encouraging the child to be a participant, not only an observer.
- Corresponding words with actions—for example, "We are washing the table".
- Giving older toddlers some simple choices which encourage a verbal response.
- Assisting the child to be a good listener. Listening is part of communication and helps the child become sensitive to language. Create an awareness of sounds in the environment.
- Using finger and hand puppets.
- Being available to listen, to talk, to play, to respond, to share in excitement.

*Imitation* is a way in which toddlers learn. They observe parents, caregivers and other children and often imitate these actions. Ensure there are enough props available to encourage this. These could include:

- Mirrors.
- Dress-up clothes for both boys and girls, including handbags, hats shoes. Toddlers enjoy chomping around in a pair of cast off shoes.
- Jugs, saucepans, spoons, cups, plates.
- Brooms, mops, buckets, sponges.
- Telephones.
- Brushes.
- Washers, towels, soap, water.
- Dolls, prams, strollers.
- Food packets.
- Magazines, books.

Throughout toddlerhood children are becoming increasingly independent. They are learning to master their own bodies, practising and improving and becoming increasingly competent in motor development. They are becoming more aware that they are people in their own right. They are individuals. They are learning what they can do and what they can make happen.

- Provide finger foods which allow the children to feed themselves, and allow plenty of time for eating, making it a non-hurried occasion. Some favorite finger foods include carrot and celery straws, cheese cubes, raisins, small sandwiches, chicken drumsticks, meat cut into small cubes, and apple slices.
- Be tolerant of the inevitable messiness that comes when toddlers are learning to feed themselves. Give younger toddlers help when they want it, and avoid pressuring them to feed themselves.
- Ensure there are mirrors in the playroom placed at child level. Toddlers are learning to recognize their own image.

- Provide opportunities for the toddler to master objects, such as flicking the switch to make the lights come on, or walking down the steps instead of being carried.
- Lend encouragement and support to a child's striving to master self-help routines. Allow time for taking off shoes and socks, washing hands and face, including turning taps on and off, opening the door, and note all accomplishments.
- Be responsive when a child seeks help, as the toddler is learning to use adults as a resource.
- Make sure the playroom is adequately equipped, as toddlers cannot be expected to share, and they tend to be possessive about their own belongings.
- Toddlers can help with the playroom chores. It may take longer but will give satisfaction and a sense of achievement. They can:
  - Use a sponge and help wipe the tables.
  - Help pick up the toys from the sand pit and water play table and put them in appropriate containers (also a useful tool for developing classification skills).
  - Rake up leaves.
  - Water the garden.
  - Sweep the floor.
  - Wash the dishes.
  - Set the table.
  - Carry things for staff.
  - Relay simple messages.
  - Put rubbish in the rubbish bin.

The caregiver has the responsibility for setting the scene, for organizing the environment that provides the stimulation, materials, and experiences that will ensure positive growth and development. The caregiver provides the emotional climate which has a direct influence on each child's development. The children need an adult who is sensitive to their needs and responds appropriately, with warmth and consistency.

In order to provide a developmentally appropriate program the caregiver must first:

(a) know how toddlers grow and develop

(b) recognize what they need to do

(c) give consideration to the purpose of the program, together with its goals and objectives.

It is helpful if regular time can be set aside to observe children closely, to watch for skills that have already been mastered and those that are being attempted, to listen to language, to observe how materials are being used, to watch for the responses to the program as presented, and to recognize individual differences.

It is through observation, together with a knowledge of development, that caregivers come to know and understand children. Understanding ensures that activities and learning experiences can be introduced at a time when they can be handled competently. In any group it can be expected that not all children will have reached the same developmental level, so it is necessary to bear this in mind in the preparation of the program.

The most important contribution caregivers make to the program is themselves—their warmth, sensitivity, enthusiasm, knowledge, understanding patience, support, and most of all, their TIME!

*Photographs:* Lady Gowrie Child Centre, Perth; Bev Olsson

127

# Chapter 12

# Parent/Staff Relationships

## Cynthia a'Beckett

*Some child care center staff, when asked about parent involvement or parent/staff relationships in their center, reply with statistics about attendance at parent meetings, participation on the management committee, and help provided with fund raising and at working bees. While these are meaningful activities for some parents and should be available, they circumvent the most essential and meaningful parent involvement that must exist if a center is of high quality. The day-to-day relationships and interactions that exist between parents and staff must be based on mutual respect and regard, willingness to compromise, and the child's best interests as the uppermost concern. What happens at arrival and departure times, the quality of the talk that goes on between parents and staff, the extent to which parents spend time in the room with their child, the degree of shared decision mak-*

*ing that goes on, the compassionate help that children and parents who are having trouble separating receive, and other daily considerations matter so much more than formal participation in the work of the center.*

*There is among a number of professionals in the field of child care a strong feeling that the quality and quantity of involvement experienced by a parent on an ongoing basis over a period of time may have lasting effects on the parents feelings of investment in and attachment to their child.*

*The following chapter sets out clearly a model of parent/staff relationships that begins with the strong assumption that close, warm relationships between parents and staff are vital to the provision of quality care.*

Providing quality day care for toddlers involves far more than planning appropriate experiences for the child. It includes consideration of the child, the parents, siblings, extended family members and close family friends. These people make up the toddler's world, and staff have a special role in taking the initiative and establishing a warm supportive relationship between the whole family and center staff.

Yes, the task of working with the whole family can be demanding and a real challenge, but it can also be the most rewarding, exciting and meaningful aspect of work in child care. If there is a concern for quality, no options exist about whether to work exclusively with the children, with the immediate family, or with the whole family. It is important to unlock the closed door notion which some people, both staff and parents, have towards the child care center. Staff must create an open door policy, not just as an empty line in an information handbook, but as a reality in the center.

Implementation of a center's open door policy provides an important starting point for strengthening parent-staff links. Placing a young child in full time care can be very stressful for a parent. While parents may outwardly appear capable, many families today are isolated and anxious about their parenting roles. When families know that they are welcome at any time to be part of their toddler's day in the child care setting, they will view parent-staff relationships in a positive way. They will start to see that they can work with staff as part of a mutually supportive team. Stonehouse (n.d, No. 5) describes this as "working with parents and sharing the care of the child rather than substituting for parents".

Unlocking the doors, bringing the whole family into the center and working together as a team, rests on some important understandings on the part of staff. The first one involves recognition of the parent-child relationship as the basic unit, the vital starting point for the toddler. The second understanding relates to respect for and acceptance of all families, reflecting an appreciation of the individual differences between families. This second understanding enables staff to provide a program which welcomes contributions from the entire range of families attending the center. Australian society consists of diverse socio-cultural and ethnic groups, which is often reflected in child care settings. All families have a special, unique contribution to make to the program, and respect and acceptance will enable all parents to contribute in their own way.

An open center where people reach out to new families in this accepting,

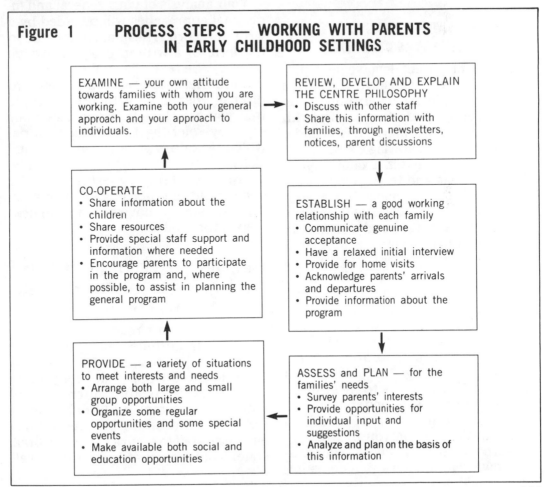

**Figure 1**   **PROCESS STEPS — WORKING WITH PARENTS IN EARLY CHILDHOOD SETTINGS**

EXAMINE — your own attitude towards families with whom you are working. Examine both your general approach and your approach to individuals.

REVIEW, DEVELOP AND EXPLAIN THE CENTRE PHILOSOPHY
• Discuss with other staff
• Share this information with families, through newsletters, notices, parent discussions

CO-OPERATE
• Share information about the children
• Share resources
• Provide special staff support and information where needed
• Encourage parents to participate in the program and, where possible, to assist in planning the general program

ESTABLISH — a good working relationship with each family
• Communicate genuine acceptance
• Have a relaxed initial interview
• Provide for home visits
• Acknowledge parents' arrivals and departures
• Provide information about the program

PROVIDE — a variety of situations to meet interests and needs
• Arrange both large and small group opportunities
• Organize some regular opportunities and some special events
• Make available both social and education opportunities

ASSESS and PLAN — for the families' needs
• Survey parents' interests
• Provide opportunities for individual input and suggestions
• Analyze and plan on the basis of this information

receptive and appreciative manner lays the foundations for effective parent-staff relationships. The construction and maintenance of these effective relationships have been the focus for many writers and practitioners connected with early childhood settings. These concerns have prompted the following model, which is the culmination of various theoretical perspectives and the years the author spent working directly with families and staff in various early childhood settings. The model is designed to separate certain steps which are experienced as a number of interwoven complex processes. It is dangerous to simplify this process. However it may enable child care workers to focus on their own situation and develop an individual model based on this one.

## EXAMINATION OF PERSONAL ATTITUDES

Successful parent involvement programs start with sensitive staff. This sensitivity requires careful examination of attitudes towards the families with whom you are working. These can be examined in the following ways:

**General Approach.** Examine your thoughts, ideas and feelings in relation to the general family population at your center. You will find yourself taking into account the location and community personality of your center. Is the center situated in a busy inner suburban area of a capital city or in a small country town? Have you worked in this location or in a similar location before, or is it a new situation for you? What are your overall feelings about the families? Do you need to find out more about groups whose ethnic background differs from your own? The answers to these questions will help you to understand and clarify your own general approach to the families with whom you are working.

**Approach to Individuals.** Your attitude towards individual parents is important, and it will vary a great deal. It is not possible or desirable to relate to every parent in the same way, and some parents may relate better to another staff member. It is useful to analyze firstly how you are relating to individual parents and then to clarify why you might be interacting in that particular way. This examination will help you to build up a general picture of the way you interact, thereby extending your self awareness. Reviewing both your verbal and non-verbal communication with others can be enhanced through the use of a video camera. Many groups and individuals now own or have access to camera equipment, and taping your interactions either within the center or with friends outside the center can be most informative.

Your analysis of your general and individual approaches will be aided by a written record. These notes may be in the form of a written diary of events, they may be reflective and involved, or in quite brief note form. You may want to discuss your style with other people that you are close to, or analyze your style by referring to written material which describes general interpersonal skills. When you feel confident and ready, share some of the key features of your style with the other members of staff. This will signify movement to the next step in the model.

## REVIEW, DEVELOPMENT AND EXPLANATION OF THE CENTER PHILOSOPHY

When staff are ready, they should share their attitudes and ideas with others in a positive, constructive way. Reference to existing philosophy statements provided by the center will provide an important additional focus. Written records of the discussions will enable all staff to contribute to the draft statement for a revised policy. When all

130

staff feel that the statement reflects a reasonable consensus, it can be finalized. The director's role in this process will be crucial as it will be important to ensure that all staff views are considered. This may prove to be extremely complex in a situation where staff views are diverse. It may be necessary to bring in an outside facilitator. This may be an advisor attached to the center or a professional, skilled in the area of human relations, who has links with the center.

This process should be undertaken regularly, to ensure that practices reflect policies and philosophy, that new staff are familiar with the philosophy, and that old staff are reminded.

**Handbook:** The center's handbook is an important source of introductory information for families, as it contains the center philosophy, general information about its operation, policies and staff. Sebastian (1986, p. 82) provides useful information about this document. Watts & Patterson (1984), in the review section of their research report on quality care, emphasize the importance of "a written description of philosophy and practices... and orientation procedures" (p. 173).

**Newsletters:** A short statement which reiterates the center's general philosophy can be included in the newsletter. Any changes to the previous statements can also be shared through an effective newsletter.

**Notice Boards:** A short notice reflecting a section of the philosophy can be displayed on the notice board and perhaps changed from time to time. If the statement is short, some simple graphic support can extend the message.

**Parent Discussion and Communication:** Small group discussions about the center philosophy as well as daily individual communications are effective ways of familiarizing parents with the staff approach at the center. Brief daily exchanges are important in assisting this step in the model and later steps.

## ESTABLISHING A GOOD WORKING RELATIONSHIP

Parents will now have some guidelines about the center's general approach, and staff and parents will then be able to move to the next step whereby an effective working relationship is established. You will need to take the initiative, to welcome parents in an open accepting manner. Practices which encourage parents to view staff as experts should be avoided. The removal of the "expert" barrier will enable the parents to relate to you on a more equal basis. Since they know their own child best, they will be less daunted and more willing to offer information about their child. Establishing these links can be very demanding for you and the parents. Recognizing this and talking out any concerns in a relaxed low-key manner will prove useful.

### Initial Interview

The initial interview between parents and center staff may be at the center or at the child's home, if it is certain that the parents feel comfortable about this. Whatever the setting this initial interview needs to be as relaxed as possible, ensuring that parents feel confident enough to ask questions. A relaxed communicative situation will depend on a physical space where parents and the staff member are sitting in comfortable chairs without a desk or table separating them. Some offices within centers are quiet while others are busy, noisy areas. The interview will be more productive if a quiet comfortable location is provided.

There are important written records to be collected (refer to written records section), and useful material (handbook and newsletter) for parents to receive. This collection and dissemination of information needs to be secondary to the personal face-to-face contact which you and the parent are sharing. This interview affords an important opportunity to begin to establish a relationship with the parent. If the parent has the child with them, play materials and a safe space to play are important. There are alternatives for the child. Parents from the committee at one center organized for another parent to be with the child, who could see into the room where the parent and staff member were talking. This allowed the parent a chance to talk without having to attend to the toddler and to meet some other people at the center. This type of sensitive contribution will come from a center where staff and parents share a cooperative relationship.

## Home Visits

Home visits can provide an important bridge between the child care center and the home situation. They should be offered as an optional opportunity, which parents will use if they feel comfortable about staff. The visit can be short and low-key but is most exciting for the toddler. If the child becomes overly excited the visit may be cut short and then repeated at a later date. This type of visit is instrumental in establishing a coop-

erative working relationship with the family, when it reflects a level of parental acceptance of staff. It is vital that the family is inviting you into the home and welcomes your visit. The imposition of a visit on an unsure family would damage your working relationship with the family rather than extend parent-staff links.

## Acknowledging Parents' Arrivals and Departures

Daily interactions with the parents during arrival and departure times reflect how parents and staff are linking together. Stonehouse (n.d., No. 6) has developed a set of guidelines to assist staff to focus on some of the key issues involved in these important routine contacts. Welcoming families and consistently acknowledging their arrival and departure will need written support. This parent-staff daily record is described in the section on written records which follows, and ensures that all staff involved with the toddler during the day know about special messages from the parent or can leave information for the parent at departure time.

## Provide Information about the Program

Parents of young children are keen to know about the contents of their toddler's day. It is vital to share this material either during the arrival or departure time. Newsletters and notice boards can be used for interesting items to read or photos related to the center's program. Small discussion groups can also assist parents to understand special features of the program and interests of the group. This opportunity also allows parents to share perceptions of their child's day with other parents and staff.

## ASSESSMENT AND PLANS FOR FAMILY INVOLVEMENT

Some features of this step will be occurring as part of the establishment of good relationships, and the collection of information will continue during future steps. The distinctive aspect of this step is that previous parents' needs are not assumed to represent those of the present families attending the center. Working through the following points helps to ensure against stereotyping families, and enables each family to express their needs. Nedler and McAfee (1979) have outlined five significant features for staff to consider in the classroom setting. They emphasize the importance of planning appropriately to meet particular parents' needs.

### Surveying Parent Interests

During the initial interview parents can be given a form which is designed to find out how they would like to be involved, both during the center's operating hours as well as outside them. The form might establish what roles they would be interested in fulfilling.

Small group discussions where parents can talk together about how they would like to be involved and what they would like the center to offer can be

beneficial. This information can be circulated to other parents to encourage their ideas. Large group meetings can provide information about parent needs, but they need to be skillfully chaired and a method for allowing all parents an opportunity to contribute must be ensured.

### Individual Suggestions

Individual daily contacts can provide an indication of parent needs and interests. Information needs to be recorded, noted and shared with the parent to ensure that the parent's meaning has been understood clearly. A permanent suggestion box located in a central place in the center provides an opportunity for individual suggestions throughout the year.

### Analyzing and Planning

Survey forms need to be carefully examined and general results presented to families as a special report. Particular parents' interests or ways in which parents would like to be involved need to be followed up quickly. Survey results and points from discussions need to be used as a basis for staff and center management committees to plan future events.

Two examples from the analysis of parents' interests in joining the daily program follow. The first is a mother who was particularly interested in gardening. She noticed that the playground needed some additional shrubs, and she offered to buy and plant four small shrubs with the children. She reorganized her work times so that she could spend time one morning participating in this way. Both children and staff enjoyed the experience and viewed the growing plants with special interest.

The other example involves a father who was a professional musician who worked at night playing classical guitar. He offered to play acoustic guitar once a week during morning tea. This was an open relaxed time when food was available to the children, so the father played the guitar as soft background music. His daughter was very excited to have her father joining the program, and children and staff were exposed to beautiful classical guitar music. These are only two examples of a number of contributions which can occur through following up on parents' interests and having established a good working relationship between staff and parents.

## PROVISION FOR PARENTS' INTERESTS AND NEEDS

There are many considerations to be noted when providing pertinent options for parent involvement. These considerations can be clustered into the three general areas of group size, content and timing.

### Group Size—Large and Small

Some parents will prefer to be involved in small groups or as individuals, while others will enjoy large scale events. Other families may choose to use a combination of both large and small groups. Parents should have the choice.

### Timing—Regular and Special Times

Events provided at regular weekly or monthly times can meet various needs. Parents at one center wanted the opportunity for regular social contact with other parents, so they suggested a weekly drop-in coffee time. This was held at 4:00 on a Wednesday in the parent-staff room; a simple, enjoyable regular event used by different parents and staff each week.

Special events suggested by parents which reflect general community interest can also be successful. One such event, again suggested and organized by parents, created interest and involvement from both families and local com-munity groups. Parents were interested in the different local school options available in the area, including primary, independent and alternative schools. Representatives from each of the schools were invited to join a panel to explain their program and then respond to questions. The meeting commenced with an introduction in which center staff explained the program at the day care center, and one of the parents chaired the event. This meeting created a lot of local interest. It was well attended and received local press coverage. It was a special unique event which came from the parents and brought parents and staff together, as well as strengthening links with the community.

### Content

Parent observation and participation in the toddlers' daily events at the center is not viewed as an option for involvement. The approach taken is that it is a basic tenet, a necessary part of full time day care for young children. This is part of the open door policy which provides a foundation for effective parent/staff relationships.

There are a number of ways that parents can be involved in a center, and all should be valued equally. They include the following:

1. Management of center
2. Program planning
3. Program participation
4. Parent discussion groups
5. Educational lectures
6. Workshops
7. Social functions
8. Fundraising
9. Local community meetings
10. Local excursion support
11. Written communication.

Families will have some social and some educational needs. A child care center can often provide a personal link between people who live in the same street and may not know one another.

134

To meet one another in a social situation at the child care center can enhance this link and help to reduce the sense of isolation which many families experience.

Staff at child care centers can pass on valuable information about children's development and learning, directly or through setting up a parent library.

Certain locational considerations are important when planning events to be held within child care settings. Providing a supportive, attractive environment will enhance the event. A parent discussion is one simple example. Providing enough comfortable chairs arranged in one circle will be an important factor in facilitating real discussion. The physical setting needs to be welcoming, attractive and not too cluttered. Equipment (for example, cups, plates, writing materials) should be accessible to parents. This minimizes parents' sense of being outsiders in a place where staff and a small number of very involved parents are the only ones who know where things are.

## COOPERATION

The previous process steps will not occur in the neat packages suggested here. However they will combine to provide this last cooperative phase of parent/ staff relationships. Parents and staff can now share and contribute to one another in rewarding enriching ways. It is useful to recall Margaret Henry's (1984) model which outlines the roles parents can fulfil in the child care setting. She writes about these roles having an important function in the cooperation stage as parents act as decision makers, fosterers of their own child's development, informed consumers, resource people for children and for adults, and as learners.

### Share Information about the Children

A cooperative relationship will enable parents and staff to share vital information about the toddler in a constructive manner. This may occur on a daily basis or during shared parent discussion. A general sharing of information about the toddler's special interests will also be of interest to parents. The communication is two-way and may be staff- or parent-initiated.

### Share Resources

These resources may be from parents to staff or from staff to parents. They may appear in various forms and can include the following: equipment, materials, developmental information, popular press items, new books, films and television programs. The resources will generally have some direct relevance to young children, but some families may share in other ways. For example, a parent who is particularly skilled in the sewing area may add to the children's home corner items. This parent may be willing to share these skills with other parents and staff at the center and provide workshops or sewing classes one night a week at the center.

### Special Staff Support and Extended Information

When parents feel comfortable and confident about staff, they may enquire about specialized support. They may ask for clarification of some aspect of the development of their toddler. This concern may need referral to professionals connected with but outside the center. This additional support and information will not be a threat if parents and staff are experiencing a cooperative relationship characteristic of this phase.

### Parent Involvement in the Program and Program Planning

Parents may choose to become involved in the program in a variety of ways, as outlined in the previous step. In this final stage benefits for all concerned

135

can be identified. Parents will not feel constrained and unsure, and staff will feel supported. Parents will often reorganize their working day to build in time to join in the program. Parents may choose to join in daily events, bring in something special to share, help with excursions outside the center, or invite the children to visit their home or work place.

Parents may be interested in planning together with staff for their child or joining with other parents and staff to discuss some general areas of interest within the program. Some centers where shared program planning meetings have occurred have resulted in parents rearranging their work schedules so that they could take part. Parents may volunteer to write notes from the meeting about the plans to share with parents who cannot attend. The meetings may involve different parents from time to time. Meetings can be informal, not adhering to a rigid format, and parents will attend as they are interested.

The cooperative step in the process enables a mutually supportive relationship to flourish between child care staff and families. It is beneficial for the child, for the parents and for the staff; without this cooperation individuals become isolated and remote, and the task of providing care of high quality for the toddler becomes unattainable.

## Parent Involvement Options

### 1. Management of the Center

Some child care centers are parent-run cooperatives established through joint parent and community efforts. These centers naturally necessitate high levels of parent involvement. Other centers may not be structured such that parent involvement is an automatic part of the management and decision-making process. Parents need to be provided with options for real involvement in decisions which will affect the center's future and day-to-day functioning. It will be beneficial for staff to assist parents to become part of this process.

### 2. Program Planning

Plans for individual children and for the group generally will become more effective when parents are involved. Talking to families about the way staff plan for their toddler and encouraging their involvement will lead to effective, worthwhile plans. Not all parents may choose to be directly involved; however they are entitled to the option.

### 3. Program Participation

Parents who wish to be involved in particular program experiences will find it helpful to have some guidelines about the type of program offered for toddlers. This form of participation may involve the parents in a more active role than the perhaps more relaxed interactions occurring when parents choose spontaneously to join their toddler at the center for part of the day. Program participation might link with plans that staff and the parents have been coordinating together, or it might relate to a regular program event such as music, story reading, or cooking. Some parents enjoy working with staff in this direct manner, and it is rewarding for the toddler involved, for the staff, and for the other children.

### 4. Parent Discussion Groups

Smaller discussion opportunities will mostly occur within the center. Parents should be involved in the selection of discussion topics and times. Parents will also be able to select the group size, although more than fifteen people in one group can inhibit relaxed open discussion, so that encouragement for less than fifteen would probably be useful. Starting the discussion in a relaxed welcoming hospitable manner, such as by offering tea or coffee and introducing parents who may not know one another, are important staff roles. These roles will need to be initiated by staff but parents may very well take them on themselves as the year progresses.

### 5. Education Lectures

Interesting speakers sharing information on topics of particular concern to families will often attract good attendance. These meetings need to be well advertised. Noting them in the newsletter, on the notice board and through individual contact will help to ensure that everyone knows about the event. Working parents are busy people with many commitments, and it is important that they all receive information about planned meetings well in advance.

### 6. Workshops

Puppetry, dance, music and nutrition are only four from a long list of workshop topics which may interest parents.

These are enjoyable opportunities where both children and parents can be actively involved. The time, location and topic must come from the parents. A photographic record of these events can allow parents who are unable to attend to share in some aspects of the event.

### 7. Social Functions

Center social events can encompass an enormous range of enjoyable occasions. As with other parent options for involvement, they will only be attended if they reflect parents' choices and interests. Some events may include the whole family; consequently plans must take into account the toddlers needs, as they become overwhelmed in a large scale event in a strange setting. A family picnic within the center grounds during the weekend for children in a particular group can prove quite successful. Staff will need to provide the link between families who may not know one another, although they may be living in the same street with toddlers attending the same child care center.

### 8. Fund Raising

Parent organization of and involvement in fund raising is often equated with successful parent participation. This is only one facet of parent involvement and needs to be considered in this way. Parents may need to support centers in this way and some parents may choose to be involved. However, it is advisable to be realistic about the amount of fund raising that the families at a center can support. Continual links between social and fund raising events can ultimately discourage parent participation.

### 9. Local Community Meetings

The center can provide a venue for meetings which may also interest the local community. Educational lectures selected by parents may also be of interest to other families in the area and will enable a pooling of resources. The opening up of the center to the local community helps to establish a supportive community network that will benefit the center and the families. Local community meetings will need to be well organized and may require the support of an outside chairperson. These meetings may also attract media coverage, and this can promote community understanding about the important service which day care programs provide.

### 10. Local Excursion Support

Parents may alter their work program to join the group for a local excursion, or they may provide the venue, if parents invite children to visit their work place or home. This is exciting for the child involved. If the location is near the center, the outing will not prove too demanding for the toddlers. It is important to talk with parents who will be involved beforehand so that everyone is clear on the actual timetable and the aims and objectives of the excursion.

### 11. Written Communication

Parents may be interested in becoming involved in the center's written communications. They may decide to contribute to the newsletter preparation, notice board or the handbook. They may contribute special expertise with art work, layout, printing or writing. Staff and parents will need to communicate carefully to ensure the success of this type of cooperative effort.

## WRITTEN RECORDS

Written records are particularly important when families are placing young children in full time care situations. It will be necessary to record the name, address and care requested on an initial form when a child is placed on the waiting list. When a child first commences at the center, it will be necessary to collect information about the parents and the child. There are a number of sample forms outlined in various texts, and there are a range of different forms being used currently at centers. The most comprehensive, up-to-date examples are provided by Sebastian (1986). They are as follows:

- Personal Information Record Form (p.246)
- Children's Personal History (pp.247, 248)
- Quick Reference Index Card (p. 249)
- Authorization to Collect Your Child (p.251)
- Accident Record Form (p. 253).

Two additional records which will assist effective parent/staff communications are a parent/staff daily record and a parent/staff interaction chart.

## Parent/Staff Daily Record

This form provides a daily record of the toddler's day. It is compiled by the parents and the staff, who note any special or unusual items that should be communicated to all involved with the two-year-old on that day. O'Brien et al., (1979) and Willis and Ricciuti (1975) also provide sample forms for this purpose. The Parent/Staff Daily Record form (see Figure 2) draws on these sources.

This is a sample form, and it will be more effective for staff to work with parents to create a suitable daily form which contains enough information but is not time consuming to complete. A checklist system where the answer which applies is ticked may be more useful in some centers. It must be stressed that written exchange of information must be viewed as a supplement to, not a substitute for, face-to-face verbal communication.

## Parent/Staff Interaction Chart

This chart (see Figure 3) provides an ongoing record of parent contacts, allowing staff to review links with all families. Obviously, it is not a chart to be displayed, but a way for staff to ensure regular communication.

# Figure 2

## PARENT/STAFF DAILY RECORD

Child's name: _____ Date: _____

Child's previous night      — Sleep?    _____

                              — Food?    _____

                              — Other?    _____

Child's breakfast — Time    _____ Amount _____

Any special messages today?   _____

_____

Today your child really enjoyed the _____

_____

_____

Your child ate _____

Your child slept _____

Toilet information _____

Medicine _____ Given at _____ By _____

Other messages:

# Figure 3

## PARENT/STAFF INTERACTION CHART

| FAMILY | MONTH | FEBRUARY | | | MARCH | | | |
|--------|-------|--------|--------|--------|--------|--------|--------|--------|
| NAME | Week 1 | Week 2 | Week 3 | Week 4 | Week 1 | Week 2 | Week 3 | Week 4 |
| Smith | MFFF | Away | (TV) MMM | FM | | | | |
| Vallejos | MMMM | (Music) | (GP) | (Prog) | | | | |
| | MMM | MFMF | | MFM | | | | |
| Richardson | F | — | Interview | MFM | | | | |

M   =   Mother
F    =   Father
GP  =   Grandparents
M or F indicates a brief conversation with the mother or the father.
A word in brackets e.g. (TV) indicates the topic for a more involved discussion.
All staff involved should contribute to chart.

## WRITTEN COMMUNICATION

Written communication is a particularly important part of programs for parents of under threes. Parents need to be able to take home written communication from the center and look at it when they are ready. The written communication will be more effective if it reflects the approach of respect and acceptance which has been discussed. The center's written communications may take different forms, and it is useful to note particular points about each type.

### Parent Handbook

A parent handbook provides general information about the center's operation, about staff, about policies, and about center philosophy. Sebastian (1986) provides useful information about this document. Presentation and organization need to be considered. There may be parents with expertise in the area of publications printing or graphics who can advise on layout and booklet organization.

### Newsletters

A welcoming friendly newsletter reaches out to families in a special way, connecting them with other people within the child care setting. The newsletter provides day-to-day organizational information. The number of newsletters needed per year will depend on particular family and staff needs. It is useful to set a regular time for families to expect the newsletter, and an effective method of distribution is vital. Newsletters can inform and act as an important network between staff, families and the wider community. Parents of two year olds are anxious to know of day-to-day happenings and proposed events, as it enables them to be part of their toddler's day. Staff changes for under threes are very important, and again the newsletter can ensure efficient dissemination of this information. It is helpful to display the current newsletter and keep a file of the year's letters for visitors and family friends. The collection of material, drawing up and printing of the newsletter can be a shared staff-parent experience and tends to be more effective when parents are involved.

### Notice Boards

Notice boards need to be centrally located with permanent pinning space. This notice board can become a daily meeting point and can communicate in an instantaneous way. It is important for notice boards to be organized in an attractive logical manner and to be changed regularly. A notice board which stays the same week after week slowly dies. Parents will stop looking at it, and it serves no purpose. Parents and staff can be involved in contributing to notice board displays, and a small section for general interest items such as newspaper articles and brochures reinforces the parent-staff partnership approach. It is important to find out how staff and parents would like to use the notice board. For children involved in under threes' programs clever use of polaroid photos and small items about daily events can act as a principal link between toddlers and parents. Some centers have devoted a permanent section of the main notice board to an introduction to the center. This contains a photograph of each staff member, their name and their position. Knowing who works where is important for families and visitors to the center.

## ORIENTATION PROGRAM FOR NEW FAMILIES

Toddlers need time to find out about new surroundings, and they will be more settled if their parents are with them when they explore their new day care center. Different centers have developed different systems for accommodating these needs. One orientation program which has proved successful operates from the Munro Centre, a parent-run cooperative for under threes at Queensland University. The parents and staff felt that the child's orientation to the program was so important that a condition of accepting a place at the center was acceptance of their particular orientation program. This system involves six to eight visits to the center by the infant or toddler and their family, before the child commences. The family is linked with one particular staff member after their initial interview, and this staff member will help the family find out more about the center during these visits. These times are organized to fit with the parents' work schedule, and if it is not possible for the parent to attend, then another person who is close to the child, for example a grandparent, may attend. The system has been working well now for four years. Staff and families feel it supports the parent, staff and the child.

Christine Cataldo (1983) has drawn attention to the crucial role which parents have in child care centers:

"Parents are mediators of how experiences affect their child. Particularly at the infant and toddler level, interactions between children and their mothers and fathers may be seen as the focal point of the education program." (p. 9)

Parents must feel part of the center to be able to fulfil their role as mediators of their toddlers' experience. It is the job of center staff to take the lead. Staff and parents will then support and strengthen one another, and the benefits are both tangible and rewarding.

### REFERENCES

Cataldo, C. (1983). *Infant Toddler Programs.* Reading Mass; Addison-Wesley Publishing Company.

Henry, M. (1984). Expanding Caregiver Perspectives on Parent Involvement. In *Handbook for Day Care.* Canberra: Australian Early Childhood Association Inc.

Nedler, S. and McAfee, O. (1979). *Working With Parents: Guidelines for Early Childhood and Elementary Teachers.* Belmont, California: Wadsworth Publishing Company.

O'Brien, M. et al., (1979). *The Toddler Centre. A Practical Guide to Day Care for One- and Two-Years Olds.* Baltimore: University Park Baltimore Press.

Sebastian, P. (1986). *Handle with Care—A Guide to Early Childhood Administration.* Melbourne: A.E. Press.

Stonehouse, A.W. (n.d.) *People Growing: Issues in Day Care.* Numbers 5, 6, 7,8. Melbourne: Lady Gowrie Child Centre.

*Photographs:* Cynthia a'Beckett

# Chapter 13

# The Context of Care: Staff

## Penny Ryan

*The provision of care of high quality depends ultimately on the quality of the staff who work with children. In turn, the quality of the staff who work in child care is dependent to some extent on the attractiveness of the working conditions. Given that, it is amazing that there is care of high quality in Australia. Ryan's chapter portrays the particular challenges to workers in child care, both in their day-to-day work with children, as well as in the larger arena of unions, career structure, and the society at large.*

*While they fight to ameliorate some of the conditions that hamper the provision of care of high quality, it is important that people working at all levels in children's services not be self-serving and not appear to be. They must have clear links in their own minds between improved status and conditions for themselves and a better experience for children. If they do not, and if they do not educate the community to recognize programs of high quality and to appreciate their importance, it is all too easy for people outside the profession to* dismiss the protestations as self-serving efforts to improve their own lot. Ryan elucidates clearly the links between the conditions under which child care workers go about their jobs and the ways these affect the care provided to children.

At any gathering of child care workers, whether the official topic is music programming or children with special needs, the conditions of work in long day care invariably become the subject of lament. This is not because long day care attracts a special group of complaining individuals. The reason for the complaints of child care workers is that they have something to complain about. The staff turnover rate in long day care centers of 48 per cent over a two year period in New South Wales indicates the degree of workers' dissatisfaction with individual centers, if not with the entire industry (Community Child Care, NSW, 1987).

What are working conditions actually like for child care workers in Australia? Child care workers without formal training are paid roughly the equivalent of a cleaner's wage. Staff with a two year Child Care Certificate receive approximately only two thousand dollars more, with no increments; consequently except in the rare case where there is a separate award*, someone with years of experience is entitled to no more than a worker straight out of training. The fact that qualified teachers in child care are better paid serves to highlight the issue of status as reflected by pay levels: teachers' awards are attached to the comparatively prestigious awards of primary and secondary teachers, while the other workers are "just child care workers".

The situation is worse outside the community sector. In centers operating on a profit basis, it is common for workers to be paid less than award wages. Unions spend a great deal of time trying to get already paltry award wages paid.

142

*See appendix

Apart from wages, hours are long, as significant numbers of child care personnel work a 40 hour week, and breaks are short. With some exceptions, there is little provision for preparation time. Time for staff to meet to plan is often beyond the means of a center. Sick leave varies widely, but many workers, including untrained and two year trained staff, are entitled to as few as five days per year. This occurs in an occupation that involves close contact with children with illnesses, and staff often require lengthy periods off work.

There has been much excellent writing about what needs to be done to improve this state of affairs at the level of unionization, lobbying and other public political work, and these issues are discussed later in the chapter. The principal focus in this chapter, however, is on the issues as they affect staff at the center level. In order to understand the factors which inhibit workers from improving the quality of care or from improving their own working conditions, it is critical to look at how working conditions are experienced on a day-today basis. It is possible to identify key factors which, if tackled at a center level, can open doors to significant improvement in services and a substantial increase in the level of industrial awareness among workers.

The rest of this chapter includes an account of the general difficulties created for child care workers by their conditions. Four specific factors that affect workers' functioning are then discussed, followed by some practical strategies for tackling them.

So how can one describe the texture of work in a child care center?

The primary concern of a center may be to look after and educate children, but a large part of every day is spent on additional tasks which add up to a significant part of the work. These include interacting with parents, maintaining other workers, looking after visiting students, supporting management committees*, preparing activities and cleaning them up, ordering supplies, taking care of administrative details, and of course, answering the phone for the one hundredth enquiry that week from a parent looking for care for a toddler.

The needs of a group of children place great physical demands on staff. Chronic back pain is one of the most frequent occupational health injuries of child care workers. The emotional demands are also immense, particularly attempting to give individual attention while work-

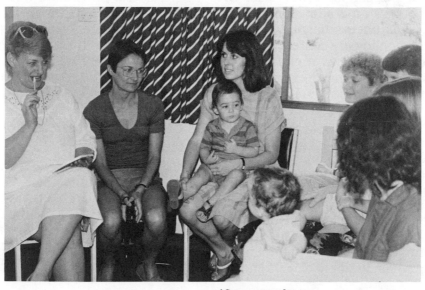

ing with a group of children. The difficulties increase as the needs of individual children vary. These may range from attempting to integrate a child with Down's Syndrome to dealing with the emotional needs of a child who has been sexually abused.

The ratio of adults to children puts increased pressure on staff in centers. Some States and Territories specify inadequate staff:child ratios in their licensing regulations, given the physical and developmental needs of children under three. For example, one center providing care exclusively for children under three had nine babies under the age of nine months with two workers to care for them. These babies could receive little more than inadequate custodial care. Yet even these ratios are undermined by the actual conditions in a real center. In many centers teacher-directors are counted as primary contact staff and included in the overall adult: child ratios, even though a survey of 70 directors conducted by Community Child Care in 1986 found that none spent more than half their time with the children, and many spent no time at all. Further, centers are not provided with funds for relief staff to replace staff at lunch and other breaks and may be required to budget for fewer than the number of sick days allowed for under awards. This occurs despite evidence that staff in child care centers use more than half their sick leave entitlements. The result is that almost every day the staff:child ratios are stretched.

It is no wonder that child care workers feel that their lot is a hard one. Conditions such as these in other industries would surely have prompted widespread industrial action. There are a number of factors which account for the absence of such action in the child care industry, including the isolation of workers into small units; the low level of unionism; the multiplicity of unions covering small numbers of workers; the difficulty in pinpointing the body responsible (Government provides the purse strings but management committees employ); the relative newness of the industry as a place of large-scale employment; and the lack of public support because of the general failure to see much difference between parenting and caring for children in a group.

Whereas other human services, such as hospitals, that provide for the total care of people, provide a wide range of specialist workers, child care workers are required to act as maintenance personnel, counsellors to children and parents, teachers, environmental planners, preventative health and diagnostic workers, cleaners, clerical workers and nutritionists. Elsewhere, a worker seeking to fulfil any one of these roles would at least be free of the demand to be fulfilling others at the same time.

As Marcy Whitebook (1984) points out:

> Working with children demands constant attention. Children cannot be placed "on hold" while adults attend to their personal needs. Consequently, staff frequently work full days without regularly scheduled breaks, even when entitled to them by law. (p. 77)

It is useful to think in terms of four primary obstacles to staff working together to improve the current nature of child care: low self-esteem; difficulty of doing the job well; isolation both within and between centers; and unresolved differences in background and training.

## 1. Child Care Workers' Low Self Esteem

The reality of what working with young children in a group actually requires of adults does not match the way this work is generally seen. The child care industry has found it difficult to explain to the community at large that child care work requires different skills and training from those required of parents. This difficulty has been reflected in low wages and poor conditions of work. Research indicates that child care workers know the nature of the demands of providing optimum learning environments for young children—that to do it well requires a combination of knowledge, intelligence, flexibility, creativity and caring on the part of adults. As well, the provision of quality early childhood programs is essential for the society as a whole, and the payoffs are well documented (High/Scope, 1982).

The lack of acknowledgement from the surrounding society that child care work is complex and demanding leads child care workers to internalize this view. Many workers report being asked at a party what they do for a living, and when they reply, "I'm a child care worker", they are often met with a blank stare, a quick change of topic or a comment such as, "That must be nice, getting to play all day".

A poor self concept about the worthwhileness of one's work is in direct conflict with the goals held for children in care. Early childhood theories promote the view that it is essential to children's development that a concept of their own self worth be nurtured. The attempt of an adult to nurture the self worth of children while being told by society that to work with children is demeaning is akin to a chain smoker running a quit-smoking clinic!

Workers report feeling unappreciated and unacknowledged. Often, in an attempt to direct some of this feeling to an outside cause, parents and other workers come in for blame. Staff complain bitterly about parents who "just use us and never seem to notice when we do good things with their children".

The low self esteem of child care workers is part of a cycle low self esteem contributes to workers' sense of powerlessness to alter events and makes political or industrial organization more difficult. The lack of willingness to take industrial action is seen by at least one union as a significant factor in why in 1987 many New South Wales child care workers did not have the benefit of the 38 hour week, the only award out of 35 covered by the Miscellaneous Workers' Union* that does not enjoy these conditions. Consequently, as conditions remain worse than those experienced in other industries, or even in comparison to pre-schools within the same industry, workers find it harder to believe that their work is indeed essential to the society.

## 2. The Difficulty of Doing the Job Well

From talking with many hundreds of child care students and workers over the past six years it has become clear to the author that when child care workers begin their work they do so with a commitment to do their best for young children. The demands already outlined—physical, intellectual and emo-

*See appendix                                    145

tional—begin to challenge this expectation from the first day in an actual center.

Young children also enter care with sets of expectations. In general they look to adults to play in the sandpit or help them with a puzzle, to protect them from hurt, to notice any difficulties in their lives, to delight and enjoy them, to put band-aids on imagined bruises and real ones, to cuddle and hold them close for lengthy periods of time while they cry or feel fragile, to teach them about the world, to talk to and listen to them, and to be more or less endlessly available! The same conditions that hinder caregivers require the children to make some hard adjustments as well.

What are staff to make of their original goals and expectations of working with young children when confronted with the realities of day care? Many leave, while others struggle on, attempting to keep sight of their original goals. Many of those who stay feel at some level that it is their personal failure, while others make condemnatory remarks about the worthwhileness of day care for young children: "A nine hour day in this center is too long for children." Many workers complain about parents in ways such as, "Parents just dump their children here", or, as the author heard recently, "The center shouldn't open 52 weeks a year; if it did parents would never take their children on holidays." These comments reflect a despair about the quality of care they feel able to provide. If centers were joyful experiences for children, the level of concern about "too much" contact with the center would not be as high.

## 3. Isolation from Peers

The structure of the long day care industry has provided for the establishment of small centers employing between three and twenty workers in one workplace, often located a long distance from a comparable service. The standard forty place centers built over the last five years in New South Wales provide for six primary contact workers and two to three ancillary staff. While some of these centers have been built by Councils that provide advisory resources and assistance to link centers, most have not. For rural centers the nearest child care service of any kind may be 400 kilometers away.

Isolation between centers is further exacerbated by the lack of planned in-service training. While a number of organizations provide some in-service training, it is often costly, frequently oriented to directors only, geographically inaccessible, infrequent and requiring overworked staff to give up more time in attendance. There are only rarely opportunities to meet with other workers with similar training (or lack of training) and learn from each other. Attempts to decrease isolation have met with varied success.

One Sydney Council has spent a great deal of effort and money attempting to resource their centers and decrease isolation. They have introduced employing two teachers in recognition of the lack of time teacher-directors have to work face to face with children; they have set up a regional in-service training network and provide regular courses. Directors meet monthly for half a day; all staff are employed one week prior to opening; staff are encouraged to visit other centers; two administrative and resource workers are employed full time by Council (one early childhood trained with many years experience in long day care). Interestingly, this Council's child care staff turnover rate of 25 per cent is much lower than the State average of 48 per cent.

Despite the relative success of this Council's attempt to deal with staff's isolation problems, many remain that reflect the structural conditions of the industry and workers' internalization of those structures. While directors meet regularly, other staff members have little or no opportunity to meet with other center staff. While center staff are encouraged to visit other centers to look at different ways of approaching organization, few actually do. This is largely because of the constant under-staffing: workers feel guilty if they create even greater stress on co-workers by "unnecessary" departures. There are also reasons for reluctance to take up this opportunity that relate to the internal structures of centers.

Isolation not only only exists from center to center but within centers as well. The pressure to perform the primary goal of the center of looking after and educating children while at the same time being responsible for the maintenance, administration, cleaning, and community liaison work, means that there is no legitimate time set aside in the day for contact between adults. Breaks and lunch times are rotated to be taken individually or at best in pairs. Where breaks are taken these amount to two ten-minute breaks and a half hour lunch break in an eight hour day. While newer centers have staff rooms, many do not, and in these centers staff take fewer breaks. These breaks may be the only opportunity within work hours for staff to have contact with each other without children around. The need to communicate about current concerns in each other's non-work lives, backgrounds or experiences that explain current behavior are largely unfulfilled, producing in many workers a sense of working in total isolation. While school teachers work largely in isolation when in the classroom, breaks and lunch times provide opportunities to meet with the other staff.

If the opportunity to communicate about major general concerns of staff remains unmet, the opportunity to communicate about the planning and implementation of work within the cen-

ter is even harder. Currently, unlike conditions in preschool or schools, no preparation/planning time exists within some industrial awards*, nor is funding specifically provided for this purpose. In many centers planning of activities is done in workers' heads individually on the way to work, or in pairs during so-called breaks. One worker at a large inner city center catering for seventy children describes this 'planning process:

"I would get up at 6.00 am and get Maya's breakfast. In between snatches of conversation with Maya about her homework, arrangements for the afternoon and how she couldn't change her clothes again this morning, I'd start to think about what I could plan for the day. I'd get to work at 7.30 along with two other workers, open up the center, get a few quick activities set up, start greeting parents and children, and put on a load of washing. By 8.30 I'd have attempted to comfort 10 children who didn't speak any English as they lost sight of their parents for the day, and I'd realize that the outdoor area was not set up. Only myself and one other worker liked thinking about the outdoor area activities, and while it wasn't really my task if I was on early shift, inevitably I would be the one to set up. In fact whatever the shift I was on, this would occur. There was never any time to talk to other workers about why they didn't take it on; it was just left to me. So I'd go to the storage shed, which didn't have shelves, and start to dig down to get out the water table, which of course was piled high with equipment. Through all this at least two children who were particularly unsettled would be clinging to me. I'd then quickly plan in my morning tea break other activities for the next hour, and check them out briefly with another worker before setting them up. Some of us worked easily together, others didn't. There was no time to discuss ideas for activities beyond the next hour, no time to think or plan for individual children. The worst thing for me was the discovery accidentally from another worker after three weeks that the five Vietnamese children in my group (all non-English speaking and first time in day care) were even more bewildered and upset, because in Vietnamese culture children sit on seats, not on the floor, and many of my activities had required them to be on the floor".

Not only is there a lack of planning time to address the needs of children, there is also little or no time for staff meetings to address the overall needs of the center. Many centers hold staff meetings irregularly or at rest times when children are supposedly asleep. For centers with 0-5 year old children the chance that all children will be asleep at the same time is remote, and for centers attempting to individualize the program to allow children to sleep when they need it, direct conflict of interest between adults' and childrens' needs occurs.

Because of the lack of time to pass on basic information about children, parents or the center's functions, when staff meetings are held they tend to be dominated by the Director's need to give information to the rest of the staff. While a staff meeting's primary purpose should be to give staff the opportunity to reflect on the recent workings of the center and to look at areas of consolidation or change for the future, pulling all staff into a functioning team, they often become little more than a listing of basic information and desperate pleas for participation by Directors.

Overall, staff work in many centers observing each other rather than interacting with each other to tackle the needs that exist. It is no wonder that, as one child care worker who has since left to work as a teller in a bank, put it: "Sometimes it felt as if I worked in a factory. We weren't supposed to be talking to each other, we were meant to be with the children. The only time that we got to sit and relax was when the kids were asleep or outside. But even then we were meant to be doing all the other things that were needed, like varnishing the blocks or cleaning the store room. It got to be such a desperate need (to talk to another worker) that we'd hover in the kitchen just to exchange comments about what we'd done the night before. The pressure just isn't there in the bank."

## 4. The Difference Between Workers' Training, Backgrounds and Goals

Workers enter centers with very different backgrounds, training and goals. While there exists a body of early childhood theory that is reflected in the various State and Territory regulations, advisory services, training colleges and overall practices of services, an enormous gap exists between the notion of quality and the practice of quality by workers. This gap has been widely observed and is the subject of many reports, including one by the editor of this book. Many of the industry constraints that make it difficult for workers to implement ideal early childhood theory in the everyday care of young children have been outlined above. As well as the constraints already listed, the differences that exist between individual workers and the lack of time to examine or resolve those differences further restrict the practice of quality care.

A typical child care center has at least five workers with different training working together, and a further number without training. The focus in nurses' training on health and safety, for instance, is very different from that of teachers. When workers received training will also affect the body of theory they may refer to when practising early childhood education. There have been major changes to courses for Child Care Certificate holders and teachers over the past five years. The on-the-job training that workers build from experience in children's services or as parents further creates differences in practice between center staff.

However, probably of equal importance to training and experience in the industry are the influence of workers' own experience of childhood. Child care centers have staff from an enormous variety of backgrounds, including socioeconomic class, culture, and sometimes gender. Unlike other workplaces where strict demarcations are evident between the actual work, in child care all staff do essentially the same tasks, with the exception of administration and co-ordination. While socio-economic class differences may have led to the opportunity to train or not train, or to undertake a specific type of training, when placed in the center, all workers are employed to do much the same work (Whitebook, et a/., 1982). The children and families using the center are also often mixed in terms of wealth, occupation and culture.

As a result of backgrounds and values in their own families, staff will often find themselves in conflict with each other on child rearing practices, with the "theory" of early childhood or with the families of children in their care. The values individual workers received in their own families as to their attitudes to men and women, how affection and discipline were given, attitudes toward families that were "different" from their own (in such things as wealth, cultural background, physical characteristics), or the importance of education, will often result in a conflict between "practice" and "theory". For instance, hitting children as a form of discipline is outlawed by State/Territory regulations and condemned by early childhood theorists, and alternatives to it are taught by all training institutions. While there is no

doubt that increased stress and exhaustion contribute to the incidence of physical punishment of children in centers, differences in practice between workers experiencing the same level of stress can be attributed in large part to differences in values they received in their own childhood.

Given such differences between workers and the lack of legitimate time to discuss or resolve these differences, how do center staff work together as a team? In many centers, the differences result in open conflict between workers, often resulting in a worker leaving the center. In others, centers develop rigid routines in working with children that minimize the need to notice differences. An interesting observation of research in this area is made in an article on "The Adult World of Day Care" by Willa Pettygrove and James Greenman (1984). They report:

In spite of what appeared to be close communication between teachers and aides, persons working in the same classroom reported significant differences in beliefs regarding children, child rearing and education, but none of the teachers and aides were aware that such differences existed.

Communication was limited and was concentrated on co-ordination of the program routine. Deeper analysis of program goals and children's needs tended to be overlooked. Neugebauer (1975) found that in only 15 per cent of centers studied were staff members in full agreement on the major areas of programme emphasis. Staff had never discussed curriculum objectives. . . Teachers have a much firmer idea of what to do than of the goals and choices that underlie curriculum.

A nearly universal desire in day care centers is to achieve a smooth, stable routine that minimizes the chance of confusion and disorder. . . The emphasis on routine and activities rather than on goals and outcomes also reduces the need to face areas of potential disagreement. (p. 96)

Thus the attempts to change a center's program and to improve the quality of adult/child interaction comes up against both structural constraints and difficulties deriving from individual differences. Until time is made available and staff are encouraged to examine differences, it will be hard for significant improvements in the quality of care to be made.

So much for the bleakness of the present situation. Of course, there are countless attempts at every conceivable level to improve these conditions. Formally and informally, as individuals or groups, through unions and lobbying campaigns, people tackle these issues constantly. The rest of this chapter is a compilation of practical strategies which hopefully will contribute to this aspect of the movement to create excellent early childhood services in Australia.

## INCREASING SELF ESTEEM OF CHILD CARE WORKERS

In order to fight for changes to their working conditions, child care workers need to be convinced of their own worth. This can start at the work place, and can take just one worker to model her attitude to have far reaching effects on other workers at the center. How does one model self esteem as a child care worker?

Firstly, a staff member promotes feelings of self worth by appreciating herself and other workers, commenting when another worker does something well, pointing out what one appreciates about their work, their friendship or them as human beings.

Secondly, workers can challenge expressions of powerlessness or self put-down. "What can you expect, we're just child care workers" can be challenged by "We can expect a lot." Working in an atmosphere where (at least) staff know

that they are appreciated and respected for the work they do makes it possible to expect that others should view the work in the same light. While much of this can be done daily on an informal basis, an occasional structured staff development meeting should also tackle this issue.

## ALLOCATING TIME FOR WORKERS TO SPEND WITHOUT CHILDREN

### Award Breaks*

While it is understandable that workers do not take their award breaks, it is in the short and long term detrimental to themselves and the children in their care if they do not. It is impossible to do the work of a child care worker for eight hours, to give good attention to children's needs, without a break. By joint agreement staff need to be firm and insist that for the good of children in their care and for themselves they will take breaks. This also means paying attention to the environment in which they are taking breaks. For centers without a staff room a temporary measure might be to walk out of the building, to enable the worker to notice a world exists outside the needs of young children!

For centers with staff rooms, staff need to create good non-child oriented environments. Many staff rooms become storage areas for equipment, preparation areas for the next lot of activities, and many are built with a viewing window to playrooms with the expectation that staff will be on duty even when on breaks. Staff rooms need comfortable, back-supporting furniture, pleasant restful colors and pictures on the wall, magazines, coffee and tea making facilities, storage for workers' belongings, and plants. Some of the improvements will require an increase in funds and action at a different level.

150

*See appendix

## Non-contact Time

By structuring the work differently it is possible to make clear what tasks need to be done, provide workers with work away from direct contact with children, vary the work for all and make best use of the broad skills of all workers.

Some large centers, built on a traditional pre-school model, have highly structured role divisions. Trained workers are allocated particular rooms, while untrained workers spend a bulk of their time doing cleaning, preparation of art materials, and preparation of food, rather than interacting with children. The effect of this structure is to put large amounts of stress on the workers solely responsible for children for eight continuous hours (with them having fewer breaks unless children are forced to sleep) and to under-utilize the skills of the untrained staff. In other centers with more fluid job descriptions, lack of organization still leaves some workers without consistent variation in work.

By making a list of the work to be done in the center (everything from house-

keeping tasks to administration to programming) and identifying the time needed to do the task, and by whom the task should be done, it is possible to develop a list of jobs for everyone in the center. Some jobs will be taken by specific workers. For example, the director and book-keeper may be the only ones who do fee relief for confidentiality purposes, or the cook will be the principal preparer of food for lunch. However the list should contain many jobs that give caregiving staff time away from direct responsibility for children. Such a list may look like this:

| Daily | Weekly | Fortnightly | Monthly |
|-------|--------|-------------|---------|
| Set up outdoor activities | Tidy storage | Order supplies | Revamp storage |
| Laundry | Water indoor plants | | |
| Prepare morning tea | | | |
| Water garden (hot weather) | | | |
| Bank fees | | | |

A daily or weekly chart then sets out 15 minute to half hour periods where each worker undertakes the tasks involved, without direct responsibility for children. This system will often free up some of the administrative/co-ordination time of directors to allow them more time to spend in direct contact with children. It also allows other staff to see some of the work involved in the director's role and decreases resentment of the director's absences from the playroom.

## BREAKING DOWN ISOLATION

### Budget for Staff Development

Include in the budget adequate estimates for every member of staff (including relief staff) to have access to some formal in-service sessions during the year. This should include the costs of courses.

In-service courses may be available through varying institutions, but where they are not centers may have to link with those closest geographically to organize local in-service committees to sponsor courses needed.

## Exchanging Staff

The exchange of staff between centers, particularly those offering similar services but having differences in methods of implementation, is reportedly a highly effective method for staff to make contact with other viewpoints, methods of operating and other workers in the industry.

## Peer Support Groups

Regular meetings of peer support groups assist in tackling the issues of isolation from other workers from similar skill areas and open up broader views than are often expressed within a single work place. Peer support groups have been established effectively among directors, Child Care Certificate workers and nurses in differing regions. These small groups of around five staff from different centers meet for a few hours per month. The primary purpose of the meeting is to give everyone the opportunity to meet, talk to and be listened to by others sharing similar experiences in an informal setting. The groups vary in format but generally everyone gets roughly equal time to talk. The author was a member of one directors' support group which met for one year for one evening per month. There were five directors from geographically distant centers (one member used to drive fifty kilometers to attend). Discussion centered on aspects of work, each meeting looking forward to the next instalment on how particular problems had progressed. The format varied, but a recurrent theme was to answer loosely the following questions during each person's turn: "What have been my achievements at work so far? What is the current situation facing me?" "What are my goals for the next month?"

## Decreasing Isolation Within the Center—Staff Meetings

A focal point for decreasing staff's sense of isolation while at the same time making the work easier, is the role of the staff meeting in a center. Ideally, staff meetings should be held either in work time with competent relief staff being totally responsible for the children and regular staff out of earshot, or, more feasible at present, outside work time with compensation of paid overtime or time-in-lieu provisions. Staff meetings should be at least two hours every two weeks, if not weekly.

Current federal funding guidelines allow inclusion of payment for participation in staff meetings in the budget. However, to get staff to agree to meet outside work hours, even with compensation, will be hard if staff meetings do not meet individual members' needs.

Having got agreement to at least meet once outside work hours, what can be done to make the meeting worthwhile for all participants? Firstly, remember and state clearly the goal of staff meetings. Staff meetings are the time when all staff have the opportunity to reflect on how the center has been working and their own contribution to the work, to plan the next period. Staff meetings should provide all staff the opportunity to be heard, for everyone to be treated with respect, and all opinions encouraged. Secondly, for meetings to work there needs to be an agenda, decisions recorded and a chair. While this seems to be stating the obvious, many meetings fail because no attention is given to the process of the meeting. Most commonly directors are assumed to be chairing the meeting simply because of their position, not because of their displayed ability to do so.

Agendas should not be set by the director in isolation. Staff can be asked in the week prior to the meeting about any issue they want to see discussed at the staff meeting. Staff may be reluctant to add anything before being convinced that their contribution is actually wanted. The agenda will after a short while be no difficulty, and can be formulated by a piece of paper being left on the staff room notice board or given to a staff member as a responsibility or partially set by the previous meeting.

An exercise book for recording minutes and decisions is a useful way of keeping track of what has been agreed to, and importantly, who agreed to do it. Decisions need to be read back to the meeting, particularly when there have been conflicting viewpoints, to check that they are indeed decisions. Rotating the responsibility for taking the minutes reduces the arduousness of the task, so long as everyone is clear how to go about recording decisions.

In small groups, it will often feel unnecessary and imposing to have a chair. However with a chair (even an unacknowledged one) the meeting will go much better. Reluctance to have a formal chairperson is often based on fear of meeting procedures. In small groups formal meeting procedure is frequently unnecessary and inappropriate. Instead the chair's job is to keep people's attention on the issue being discussed, and to keep an eye on the time. The chair can set the tone for the meeting by reaching out to staff who usually do not speak and interrupting those that dominate the meeting. This can be done more easily than supposed. Directors, who are frequently put in the position of "running" the staff meeting, often desperately look to members to participate. A typical center staff meeting in the author's experience has a director listing information interspersed with an occasional "Would someone like to comment on that?" or "Do you agree?" or "Will we do this?", at which point one or two staff will talk animatedly while the rest will sit quietly with expressions ranging from indifference to hostility on their faces. A decision will be made, only to find to the director's frustration that it is at best half-heartedly implemented or at worst reversed in practice.

Decisions made without real discussion, contribution and commitment by members simply will not work well. Why do some staff remain silent or contribute only a small amount? Generally people remain silent because they do not feel safe venturing an opinion. Silence brings a common assumption that people do not have an opinion, but this is a false assumption. People may not have sufficient information to commit themselves to a view, but they do have the basis of a view, namely their own experience and intelligence. Lack of feeling safe may stem from many things operating in the individual's life and in the group. These may range from "If I say something Joan will jump on me and I don't want to have an argument with her", or "I'm not sure that I agree with Sophia but I don't know enough to say why", or "They'll think I'm stupid", or "They know more than I do because..." or "If I say something about this I'll get stuck with doing it", or "It doesn't matter what I say—they will just do what they want".

Faced with these difficulties, how does a chair achieve the goal of the staff meeting and ensure a tone of respect and encouragement of expression of opinion?

1. State the goals of a staff meeting and the rules (mainly that all opinions are wanted, and everyone is to be treated with respect). Get clear agreement when the meeting will start and end, and stick to it.

2. Have a flexible rule when discussing an issue, which is that "No one speaks twice before everyone speaks once", or "No one speaks three times before everyone speaks twice." While this may be treated flexibly it is a good rule for the chair to remember to help her notice that Sophia has said nothing while Jan has talked at length. At this point, the

chair says as Jan opens her mouth, "Oh, Jan could you wait, others haven't spoken yet." Chair turns to Sophia and says (with interest), "What would you like to say?"

3. Ensure that everyone is listened to, prevent direct interruptions or second conversations occurring at the same time, or members looking with glazed eyes somewhere else. This can be done by modelling real interest, by looking and listening with real attention to the person talking.

4. Prevent "put down", implied or direct. Occasionally a clear attempt will be made to undermine the validity of an individual's argument, by saying something like, "That's a really stupid thing to say" (meaning, "You're really stupid for saying it", rather than "I don't agree because..."). More frequently, put-downs will take the form of "Any good child care worker would know/ agree/ think...", or "As anyone who knows anything about the early childhood theory would think/do..." Sometimes put-downs will involve the chair in direct intervention: "Joan is not stupid, you just disagree—What was your point?" Sometimes explaining in general terms that put-downs decrease safety and giving some examples will help change behavior. Mostly modelling treating individuals with respect but still being able to disagree with their views will assist in achieving safety of the group. Being a chair does not prevent you from having a turn to speak or venture an opinion—but if you are heatedly involved in the discussion you may need someone else to act as chair while you speak!

5. Finally, a chair needs to radiate confidence and positive expectations to the meeting. Starting the meeting by saying, "Let's get on with it or we'll be here for hours," or "I'd rather be home," will not achieve a meeting where all staff get a chance to think well together. If the chair starts the meeting with the expectation that it is interesting, that at least she/he wants to hear what everyone thinks, and communicates this, the meeting will achieve more.

## Handling Conflict

Where possible, the best place to handle conflict will often be in the staff meeting, not in the corridor or playroom as workers interact with the children or parents. If staff meetings have achieved a level of safety that enables people to talk and be listened to with respect, they become a safer forum to discuss issues of conflict.

If the issue is one that has already built up a lot of heat take care about plunging straight into it. Propose to the group that everyone gets a chance to speak once on the issue, then all break into pairs to take turns to be listened to and talk without interruption before returning to continue debating the issue.

Breaking into pairs will provide the opportunity for some of the steam to come off before debating the issue in the general staff meeting. It also allows people to actually identify what they think about the issue without committing themselves within the bigger group. Resume the debate and attempt to identify whether there is more information that is needed, or whether it is important that a decision be reached at this meeting.

If a conflict has continued for a period of time and seems to be making no progress, it is often better to make a decision. In some cases this may be by abiding by the majority view, or in some cases it may be that the director or management structure imposes a particular decision. (For example, a center recently developed a set of guidelines for disciplining children. The majority of staff wanted to include permission to hit children as a last resort. The director and a minority of staff members were opposed to this, and the director was also aware of Government's regulations which prevented hitting children. The director therefore did override the majority view on this issue.)

Where a controversial decision is taken that is not supported by all the staff, it may be necessary to introduce a review period for the decision to be reassessed. An example of this was a center where the director initiated a change in program from an age segregated program to family grouping. After many discussions with staff and parents, and sending staff on information-gathering trips to other centers practising family grouping, the majority of staff supported trying a family grouping program. A minority were opposed. The change in program was begun, but a review period of three months was agreed to, so that an evaluation of how it was working could happen. At the end of the three months it was reviewed and several adaptations were made. All staff except one (who left) are now adamant that this program has been beneficial to the center as a whole. Having the review period allowed for unsure and opposing staff to feel that the decision was not irreversible if their fears proved correct.

## EXPLORING DIFFERENCES IN BACKGROUNDS AND TRAINING

As has been pointed out, without confronting differences between staff in attitudes regarding the basic practices of early childhood, centers will rely more and more on rigid routines or staff will leave the center. The continued failure to discuss attitudes and debate policies is reflected in the substantial failure of many centers to adopt truly multicultural, non-sexist, or disability-integrated programs. Poor structures relating to staffing affect the quality of the program for children.

To deal effectively with such differ-ences and to allow debates around programs and policies for centers to flourish, substantial changes to the funding of services will have to occur. Staff need access to time to talk out these issues, and access to continued training and resources. In the short term, what can be done at a center level?

At a staff development day or at a regular staff meeting, set aside time to learn about each other's histories. At the beginning of a center's operation, or as new workers are introduced, or as the center progresses, it is important to spend a bit of time reviewing workers' attitudes and what experiences have shaped attitudes. Questions to have each staff member answer (maybe to be done in small groups, each person talking five to ten minutes) will vary depending on the issue confronting the center at the time. Some common areas of differences where it would be useful for workers to review their own histories and to hear of others' experiences are:

How did your family express affection? How were you disciplined?

What messages did you get about the differences between boys and girls, men and women?

How did your family regard people who were richer or poorer?

What value did they place on education, holidays, money?

What place did religion have in your early life?

What were the strengths of growing up in the culture that you grew up in?

What aspects of your own childhood would you change for your own children?

Of course many of these histories can be learned in more informal ways, such as by meeting regularly for a staff dinner, but very often such social events will allow you to know about each other's current lives, not understand pasts.

## CHANGE AT THE INDUSTRY LEVEL—A COMMON CHILDREN'S SERVICES AWARD

While at present child care workers remain unorganized, employed by many different employers and covered by many different unions (eight in New South Wales alone), there nevertheless remains the need for a long term goal for the improvement of working conditions. It is possible that overall changes to the union movement through the creation of "industry unions" and amalgamations may eventuate in one union creating a Federal Award* to cover all child care workers. Such a move would have advantages in strengthening child care workers' organizing power, particularly with the Federal Government. Instead of management committees* being the legal employers while the Federal Government holds the power over funding and these employment conditions, it may be possible to negotiate more directly with the real employers. One award would have the advantage of reorganizing the conditions of a single workplace for all workers and create common conditions and assist in career structures within services.

What needs to be in a children's services award*? At meetings of child care workers some demands are commonly made. These include a 38 hour working week, six weeks holiday, a non-primary contact director or co-ordinator, two hours preparation and programming time per week for all primary contact staff plus a weekly two hour staff meeting; study leave and extended sick leave to 22 days per year. The achievement of such an award will not be easy, particularly in the current economic climate. However, the increased unionization of workers, moves in Australia's industrial organization, and the staffing crisis in centers may be an effective push to improve conditions. Currently the West Australian Consent Award between a few centers and the Miscellaneous Workers' Union provides some of the above conditions and may be a model for a national award.

Ultimately, many of the difficulties facing centers for staff and children can only be confronted by industrial and political action. Such action need not only be thought of in terms of traditional means such as strikes. Parents can be major allies in helping to fight for improvement in conditions for workers out of concern for their children. The use of the media to highlight conditions, rotating closures of centers, taking children to the workplace and pressure from parents' own unions may all be useful measures in bringing about improvements. However, unless child care workers themselves take the initiative and express their commitment to quality care for children by recognizing that their own conditions must change, it will be hard to achieve the necessary improvements.

Simply exhorting staff to join unions has not as yet brought about a readiness for political action. Somehow the consistent complaints of workers about their situation must move beyond a need to reiterate the difficulties to take broader action. As a beginning step, the tackling of these difficulties at a center level is a powerful move. By addressing what can change now in a work place, staff gain self esteem, a sense of their own power and an understanding of what the larger difficulties and constraints are.

Deborah Brennan and Carol O'Donnell point out in their book *Caring for Australia's Children* (1986):

Despite the setbacks, child care in the 1980's is an established area of public policy, an entrenched political issue and a focus of organized activity by many groups. Constant pressure will need to be maintained, however, to secure the gains that have been

*See appendix

made and to move closer towards a national commitment to caring for Australia's children. (p. 151)

## REFERENCES

Brennan, D. and 0'Donnell, C. (1986). *Caring for Australia's Children*. Sydney: Allen & Unwin.

Brennan, D. (1984) *Working Conditions and Quality Child Care*. Unpublished manuscript.

Community Child Care Co-operative (1987). *Impact of Funding Changes on Long Day Care in New South Wales*. Sydney: Community Child Care Co-operative.

High/Scope Educational Research Project, Center for the Study of Public Policies for Young Children (1982). *The Cost Effectiveness of High Quality Early Childhood Programs*. Ypsilanti, Michigan: High/Scope.

Pettygrove, W.B. and Greenman, J.T. (1984). The Adult World of Day Care. In J.T. Greenman, and R.W. Fuqua (Eds.). *Making Day Care Better*. New York: Teachers' College Press.

Whitebook, M., Howes, C., Friedman, J., and Darrah, R. (1982). Caring for the Caregivers: Staff Burn-out in Child Care. In L. Katz (Ed.). *Current Topics in Early Childhood Education*, Vol. 3. Norwood, N.J.: Ablex.

Whitebook, M. (1984). Caring for Children as Work. In J.T. Greenman and R.W. Fuqua (Eds.). *Making Day Care Better*. New York: Teachers' College Press.

*Photographs:* Lady Gowrie Child Centres, Perth and Adelaide

157

# Chapter 14

# Staff Burnout— The Ultimate Reward?

## Margaret Clyde

*The particular stresses on caregivers of toddlers are focused on in the following chapter. Clyde argues that while they are subject to all the problems that face child care workers in general, those people who work with one to three year olds are in some ways in more demanding and difficult circumstances. This thought-provoking chapter should encourage early childhood personnel to look critically at themselves and their work situation.*

Infant/toddler caregiving is the scarcest commodity in the world of child care provision in any community...The quality infant/toddler caregiver is a special kind of nurturing person, with keen observation skills; flexible, creative, comforting with a calm style that radiates secure commitment to the infant/ toddler's well-being. (Honig, 1985, p. 2)

Job satisfaction is one of the most widely researched topics in psychology. Over 4,000 articles have been written on the subject... Only moderate attention has been paid to the topic as it relates to teacher education, and the unique concerns of early childhood educators at the pre-school level remain largely unexplored... The factors that influence work attitudes take on an urgency when we read statistics indicating that staff turnover in childcare centers averages 30% a year. (Jorde-Bloom, 1986, pp. 167-168)

Researchers have identified a large number of potential stressors for people who work in caregiving roles, including nurses, teachers, social workers and child care workers. General considerations relevant to toddler caregivers include the volatile state of child care services in this country; the community's questioning of the role of child care workers; changing child care patterns, including the need for more care provision for infants and toddlers outside the home; and the undefined role of the toddler caregiver, who assumes crucial but not total responsibility for the development and welfare of a toddler at a critical time in the child's life.

This chapter will look at these problems in more detail, including environmental variables (the organization of child care, the physical setting, the ambiguity surrounding the caregiver's role and worker relationships), and personal variables such as the personality of caregivers and their knowledge, skills and attitudes relating to their exacting role as toddler caregivers.

A decade ago it was unusual for a child care center to accommodate children under the age of two years. There were fewer working parents with very young children who looked for child care outside their own home or the home of a family member, friend or neighbor. This view was reinforced by caregivers themselves, who suggested that it was somehow "better" for the babies and toddlers to be at home, while wondering how such young children could be incorporated into existing child care programs for the over twos. It would be true to admit that there are many parents and caregivers and other "experts" who still agree with this view, but it must be recognized that infant/toddler child care is the fastest growing component of the child care market place (Wittmer, 1985). In fact, child care programs which do not offer places for infants and toddlers suffer a competitive disadvantage.

The other side of the coin however is that parents and caregivers, while accepting the notion of group toddler care in a center, have a long way to go to achieve consensus on the role of the caregiver in helping toddlers develop self-help skills such as toileting, feeding and dressing, and in assisting toddlers to learn more about their physical and social environment. As new research is disseminated to parents and caregivers alike it becomes increasingly obvious that the very young child is more dependent than the older child on the caregiver, more vulnerable to adversity and "less able to cope actively with discomfort or stress from without or within" (Ad Hoc Day Care Coalition, 1985, p. 1).

The potential for serious developmental damage to young children who do not receive adequate, individualized care in the earliest years of life is obvious; it follows then that in addition to the need for physically healthy environments, infants and toddlers require social interactions with adults who are not only patient and warm, but who are also capable of responding to each child's individual personality. The toddler's needs can best be met by a special relationship with a person who "nourishes, protects and is harmoniously available on a regular, predictable basis" (Honig, 1985, p. 3). It would be no doubt alarming to tally the numbers of centers which make few provisions for adults and toddlers to form special relationships of attachment and friendship, or which do not recognize this as a critical part of the daily program. The nurturing role is acknowledged but not encouraged as a professional role. This lack of clear definition has made the role of the toddler caregiver more demanding, more stressful and more ambiguous. When combined with the continual physical demands made upon the caregiver of toddlers, it is not hard to believe that the ultimate reward of the toddler caregiver is burnout and loss of self esteem.

## The Child Care Worker's Day

The caregiver walks a very delicate line between balancing the needs of the parents and the needs of the child on many occasions. Many parents who place their toddlers in care do so not from choice but from necessity; they may have earned the criticism of spouse, family members and work peers by doing so and feel guilty or frustrated that they cannot spend more time with their toddler at such a critical stage of their child's development. When parents call at the center they are often tired, cranky, pushed for time or feeling guilty about the situation. The situation is brimming full of potential anxiety; the caregiver has the job of trying to balance the parent's need to leave the center quickly and the toddler's need to finish a block building, or the task of explaining why

159

the toddler had a sleep during the day, contrary to the parent's strict instructions. These interactions appear at first glance to be fleeting and minor, but they help to develop the basic relationship between the parent and the center worker and point up the important issues of control and power. Who is in charge, the parent or the caregiver? Very quickly an adversarial situation can develop between staff and parents and result in stress for those involved.

Feelings on these issues may see-saw rest during the toddler's time at the center? What amount of control do they want their toddler to exhibit about such matters and their interactions with adults? The questions are many, but they serve to point up two issues: the crucial role of child care at the toddler stage of development and the potential for a stress-related relationship between parent and caregiver until a compatible relationship has been reached.

When the child has settled at the center for the day, the potential for stress-

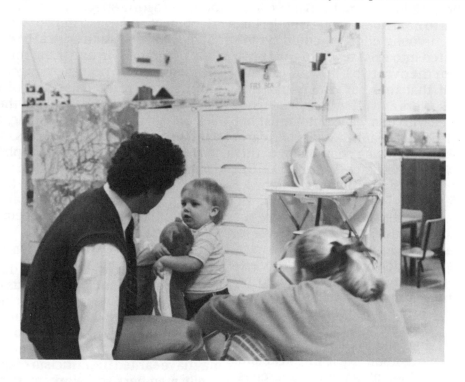

but they cannot be avoided; they have to be discussed honestly and openly in order to bring a measure of comfort and clarity to the parent/worker partnership. However, the stress of such continual interaction over a prolonged period of time must take its toll on the caregiver. Yet every critical issue must be discussed and clarified on an individual basis with every parent. Is the child to be fed on demand or on schedule? What procedures have been initiated for toilet training? What is their feeling about a sleep or related experiences does not decrease. The tedious, repetitive tasks take over; how to get through the midday meal with the demands of many toddlers all being met simultaneously; helping them to cope with delays in serving the meal; helping sleepy toddlers to be prepared for a rest or toileted; helping toddlers to settle down in a group situation with many backs to be rubbed and many sleep songs sung. The toddler caregiver could be forgiven for slipping into "automatic gear" and failing to remember to ensure that all routine times are a rich source of language and learning for the young child or that modelling empathy and kindness in a systematic way in order to promote interpersonal caring is an integral part of the job.

Finally, when the tired caregiver has waved goodbye to the last toddler, the task of planning experiences can take place. The caregiver has to think about every child, the needs of each individual child, and the ways in which the caregiver can meet the needs of each child and family. Such a process takes time and reveals the complexities occasioned by trying to meet individual needs in the context of a large organization.

## The Individual and the System

In group care it is common knowledge that an intense involvement with an individual child readily creates a demand by other children for equal time (Ainsworth, 1985). The result may well be a "rivalrous frown" by co-workers together with a possible warning against over-involvement or at least a curt reminder that not every staff member can engage in such an intense reaction. Similarly the caregiver's impulse to deal with children according to the situation rather than the center's rules can easily be interpreted as operating without standards or denying support to fellow caregivers. This is particularly obvious when a caregiver's action suggests that the center's rules of toileting, feeding, outdoor play, or other aspects of care are viewed as inflexible or not totally applicable at a given time. On other occasions the caregiver will realize that the individual needs of the toddler negate the application of common rules. These complexities, and many more which occur on a daily and often hourly basis, serve to point up the interactional conflict between the role of the individual caregiver and the processes and systems of the large child care center. A

child care worker within an organizational context must always exist in a "dual world of two contradictory systems" (Ainsworth, 1985, p. 27).

## Stress and Imbalance

Stress, which is popularly believed to lead to job discouragement, burnout and high staff turnover in child care settings in particular, is caused by an imbalance between the caregiver's skills, attributes and abilities, and the task required of caregivers (Hosking & Reid, 1985). This imbalance normally relates to a situation in which the demands of the job are too great or the demands of the job are too boring and repetitive; that is, jobs in which such small demands are made upon the worker that their needs for stimulation and meaning are not met. Both these situations could in fact prevail in the contemporary child care setting.

It is no wonder that burnout is a rather common occurrence in child care workers. Ainsworth argues that burnout, rapid staff turnover, a high degree of personal frustration, and perplexing differences in job expectations can all be traced to these contradictory work situations. While these complications emerge for all persons who work in human services, the repercussions could be of more concern in the case of the toddler caregiver, for it is common knowledge that "the care and training of children is directly related to the sense of well-being experienced by their caregivers" (Ainsworth, 1985, p. 23).

One of the paradoxes of occupational stress is that although the community recognizes that stress can occur as a result of discrepancies between occupational demands on the one hand and the worker's capacities, needs and expectations on the other, the community has failed to recognize that the nearer the person approaches to being able to meet the demands of the job, the greater the stress; in other words, the frustration of continually trying to meet the demands and not quite getting there is greater than job demands which are obviously too numerous or difficult (Hosking & Reid, 1985). This could be the case with child care workers, whose job has great potential for doubts, indecision and frustrations. Feelings of doubt about the role of caregiver, lack of feedback and communication about the job being done, as well as concerns about the adequacy of training and preparation for the role, all contribute to the frustration.

## Participation and Communication

There is a great deal of evidence to show that when people are given the opportunity to participate in decision making about important aspects of their work they are more satisfied and experience less stress. On the other hand, people who feel powerless to make any changes, either because of the way in which decisions are made within the center or because of the application of bureaucratic rules and regulations, often feel a sense of hopelessness and frustration at not being able to attain their objectives.

Similarly, lack of communication, or poor communication between staff, especially those working in the same room, is a common source of stress for caregivers. In addition there is overwhelming evidence demonstrating the link between stress and lack of support and feedback. Neugebauer (1985) has produced a Director Evaluation checklist in which he looks at four different leadership traits. These include the leader's desire or otherwise to control the caregiver's behavior through such strategies as rules, notices, threats and disciplinary action,lines of communication, offering and taking of advice from staff and the provision or non-provision of feedback. Clearly Neugebauer has a

particular leadership style in mind to minimize stress among staff:

A director's decision-making style has been found to be strongly related to the tone of interpersonal relations in the center. Centers in which directors encouraged staff participation in decision-making exhibited significantly higher levels of staff motivation, mutual support and trust, communication and clarity of objectives than did centers with authoritarian directors. (Neugebauer, 1985, p. 20)

## Lack of Clarity about Role

In addition to the need for communication in all directions in a child care center, the toddler caregiver has a further potential source of stress, namely role ambiguity.

Many people who work with toddlers take on the role without a clear understanding of the characteristics and foibles of toddlers:

Toddlers are active explorers. They eagerly try new things and use materials in different ways. Toddlers want to be independent and they have a strong sense of ownership. (Gonzalez-Mena, 1986, p. 47)

Many parents and caregivers have experiences of toddlerhood as a time when the young child, having developed surprising powers of mobility, proceeds to explore the total environment as speedily and thoroughly as possible, and at the same time moves sometimes awkwardly towards a level of autonomy that a mature adult would be proud of. In this exhausting and stressful process meals can become chaotic because toddlers play with their food, toilet training often is perceived as a struggle of wills, while adult-planned and directed experiences get disrupted as toddlers "do their own thing"; toys are pulled off the shelves, puzzles are strewn on the floor, water and sand become media for body painting, and group activities end in torment and a clash of wills. It is no wonder then that an untrained or poorly prepared caregiver would find this situation stressful.

The problem is exacerbated by the fact that many caregivers feel pressured into demonstrating that these same toddlers are "learning something". The uninitiated caregiver may feel compelled to establish learning activities of dubious value to the child in order to demonstrate that the adult is playing a part in the toddler's learning processes.

The unfortunate part of this all too common situation is that trained, confident, supported caregivers know that such activities are only valuable if they assist development, by encouraging the use of the senses in "hands-on" experiences, by developing self-help skills and feelings of independence and trust.

Adults who recognize the special needs of toddlers, such as sensorimotor learning and the development of autonomy, don't just tolerate this age group—they genuinely like toddlers. (Gonzalez-Mena, 1986, p. 49)

## Stress—Environmental and Personal

One of the more interesting and intriguing aspects of stress and burnout is the knowledge that caregivers and others react to potentially stressful situations differently; one caregiver's stress is a welcome challenge to another. In addition the complexity of stress is frequently overlooked in that it would be fair to suggest that anyone in a center suffering from stress and burnout would probably admit that it involved a multiplicity of problems at home and at work over a period of time, combined with the personality of that particular caregiver.

Just at the causes of stress are varied, so are the physical and psychological symptoms; they may include poor physical health in general, high blood pressure, increased irritability, frequent headaches and increased anxiety and depression, all resulting in increased absenteeism from the center.

Many books and articles on the subject of stress have suggested "remedies" including regular exercise, meditation, time management, suitable diversions and assertiveness training. While some or any of these remedies might bring temporary relief to the stressed caregiver, they fail to address the real causes of stress, which will continue to cause, sustain or add to the stress. Many of the causes are environmental and can only be alleviated by changes to the physical setting of the center or toddler's room; (for example, the number of children in the group, noise level, light, color, format of the room); organizational structures, including time for planning and understanding of routine procedures, resources, support services, policies, clear delineation of the caregiver's role and relationship with parents and other caregivers and the amount of time to be spent in face to face interactions with toddlers; and the quality of the interpersonal relationships between the caregiver and director and other caregivers. The "pressure cooker" nature of a child care center does not encourage the kind of colleagiality and peer support which is needed in such a complex and consuming role (Jorde-Bloom, 1986).

Many of the causes of stress are personal and relate to the individual personalities involved and the concern by many caregivers that they have been trained and prepared inadequately for the demanding role of toddler caregiver. Job satisfaction is also closely related to the stage of career development reached by individual caregivers. Katz (1972) has described a series of stages relating to the professional development of early childhood educators, moving from the initial "survival stage" to the "mastery level". She has suggested that anxieties and concerns are different at each stage, thereby exposing caregivers to different kinds of vulnerability and stress at various stages, due to the different expectations associated with each stage of professional development.

## Knowledge—A Stress Reducer

While caregivers may argue that any, or indeed all of the factors listed above as stress inducing are out of their control, the final area is not; this includes the development of knowledge about toddlers and parents, skills in working with toddlers and parents, and attitudes about their role as caregivers.

Knowledge is perhaps the most obvious stress reducer: knowledge of the physical, social, emotional and cognitive development of the first three years of life; knowledge of the importance of the environment that fosters all these aspects of development, including a language-rich environment, and knowledge about parenting roles. Stress reducing skills include the ability to form genuinely affectionate attachments with toddlers and the ability to care for each toddler as an individual without being perceived as "playing favorites", thereby usurping the role of other caregivers or more importantly, the primary caregiving role of the parents; to have sufficient health, energy and resourcefulness to enjoy and guide the "abundant energy of infants and toddlers" (Ad Hoc Day Care Coalition, 1985, p. 15).

## Cognitive Appraisal

A third area which has attracted increasing attention lately as a source of caregiver stress has been labeled "cognitive appraisal". Cognitive appraisal attempts to explain why people with similar abilities and training react in different ways to the same responsibilities or overall work load. Cognitive appraisal is the person's perception of the environment as being potentially beneficial, potentially harmful or irrelevant.

According to this theory, people who suffer more stress may have a false perception or false understanding of a situation, and this makes these people more vulnerable. Smith (1981) has suggested that early childhood workers appear to be susceptible to many of the major vulnerabilities which contribute to stress and depression. They include an exaggerated need for approval, an unhealthy demand for perfection, a feeling of entitlement ("I deserve it"), feelings of achievement as a measure of work, and a lack of feeling of autonomy ("I am a victim"). While these comments may appear harsh on the first reading, they do bear a further look. Early childhood workers have a conspicuous ability to observe and interpret children's behavior in order to plan programs but, as Smith states, "We do like to be in charge, to be the center of things and think everyone should like us too; we have to feel in control and feel seriously threatened whenever we sense a loss of control" (Smith, 1981, p. 2).

People who operate in this way tend to distort readily; they may jump to conclusions, to magnify the situation and engage in emotional reasoning ("I feel that way so it must be so"), to engage in personalization ("It's all my fault"), and to label or mislabel situations. Unfortunately these cognitive distortions affect perceptions of reality and seriously affect the ability to cope.

Piaget has suggested that people who engage in this form of behavior are similar to people who operate at the pre-operational stage of cognitive development, using perceptions rather than the more sophisticated conceptions, and who cannot "decenter" or see another position or relate two positions simultaneously to the same situation ("the beads are either brown or wooden—they can't be both"). To take this analogy further, Piaget would suggest that just as cognitively people have to move from percepts to concepts, so emotionally they have to move from "desire" to "will"; to move effectively from the pre-operational to a more concrete form of coping which includes both positive and supportive strategies. Smith has the last word on this contentious, but possibly appropriate topic:

> We can invoke will over desire in stressful situations—we can change our mind to include perspectives bigger than our own. Understanding a stressful situation is a developmental process involving identification of variables, seeing relationships, and doing mental operations with those relationships. (Smith, 1981, p. 6)

This cognitive appraisal approach may prove to be a useful supplement for toddler caregivers in their determination to overcome the environmental and personal variables inherent in their role.

## REFERENCES

Ad Hoc Day Care Coalition, Washington, (1985). *The Crisis in Infant and Toddler Child Care.* ERIC Document ED 264009. Also available from the National Association for the Education for Young Children, Washington, D.C.

Ainsworth, F. (1985). *Group Care Practice.* London: Tavistock.

Gonzalez-Mena, J. (1986). Toddlers: What to Expect. *Young Children*, Vol. 42, No 1, November, 47-51.

Honig, A.S. (1985). Issues in the Provision of Quality infant/Toddler Care. Paper presented at the Resources for Child Care Management Conference, New Jersey. ERIC Document 255322.

Hosking, J. & Reid, M. (1985). Teacher Stress: an Organisational Perspective. *The Educational Administrator*, No. 25, Summer, 3-27.

Jorde-Bloom, P. (1986). Teacher Job Satisfaction: A Framework for Analysis. *Early Childhood Research Quarterly*, Vol. 1, No. 2, June, 167-183.

Katz, L.G. (1972). Developmental Stages of Pre-school Teachers. *Elementary School Journal*, Vol. 1, 50-54.

Neugebauer, R. (1985). Are you an Effective Leader? *Child Care Information Exchange*, Number 46, November, 18-26.

Smith, D.0. (1981). A Cognitive Approach to Stress Reduction in Early Childhood Professionals. Paper presented at USC Piaget Conference, 1981, Los Angeles. ERIC Document 225 677.

Wittmer, D. (1985). The Infant/Toddler Boom. *Caring for Infants and Toddlers*, vol. 1, No. 1, Fall, 1-2.

*Photograph:* Cynthia a'Beckett

# Chapter 15

# A Brief Word About Occasional Care

## Anne Stonehouse

*Virtually everything written in the previous chapters applies to the care of toddlers regardless of whether they attend a center on a full-time, part-time, or occasional basis. However, there are some issues that relate specifically to occasional care that are covered briefly in the following chapter. There is a great need for resources to assist people to offer occasional care of high quality to this age group.*

Increasingly parents are seeking regular part-time (one or two sessions of a couple hours duration) or occasional care for their toddlers. This type of care, which will be referred to as occasional care, is accommodated in different ways. In some centers, a certain number of spaces in a "long day care" program are reserved for occasional care. Some centers have a separate group for occasional care children of all ages. Occasional care centers exist in some communities, and many children are provided occasional care in family day care homes. Practitioners and academics, as well as policy makers, appear to be divided about which is the best arrangement. Looking at it from the perspective of toddlers' needs, one can identify some strengths and challenges in each of the above arrangements.

Unfortunately, occasional care suffers still from being thought of as "just child minding", in large part because children spend relatively small amounts of time there. However, it must be said that exactly the same criteria for assessing the quality of a program should be applied to occasional and long day care. In brief, this means that occasional care should afford toddlers the following:

1. Warm, caring adults known to the child.

2. A predictable physical and social environment that the child becomes familiar with.

3. A small group of children, to allow for some moments of peace and quiet, and to enable the child to make sense of the situation.

4. Developmentally appropriate and interesting activities and experiences.

5. Assistance with separating and settling in.

The biggest challenge of occasional care for toddlers comes from their particular need for security, and the possible difficulties they may have in feeling happy in care because of infrequent attendance. The implications for programs are that children should have the opportunity to form relationships with staff who get to know them and whom they get to know. In some occasional care there seems to be a philosophy that because there is a large turnover in children, it does not matter if there is in staff also. Precisely the opposite is the case.

Secondly, the staff:child ratio should be higher in occasional care, to enable staff to have time to help children settle in.

Thirdly, programming for children in occasional care makes it difficult to provide continuity, as the presence of particular children or even the age composition of the group may not be known beforehand. There may be greater need than in long day care to plan experiences and activities that are appropriate for very diverse ages.

The above-mentioned conditions can be met both when toddlers are mixed in for occasional care with a group of full-time children in care and when they are separate. However, each of these arrangements has its own distinct advantages. These are outlined below.

When occasional care spaces are mixed into a group of children in full-time care, one major advantage to the occasional care children is that they come into a predictable, stable group. A new child coming into this group would be with settled children who are familiar with the routines of the program. Staff would not be faced with a group of children unfamiliar with the center, each other, and the adults. Disadvantages would be that programming for both groups (the regular children and the occasional children) might be difficult, particularly if the numbers of "regular and full-time" and those who came occasionally are very unbalanced. Some staff feel that the disruptions to the program when some children are coming and going while others are more permanent or full time are too great and preclude offering a good experience to either category of children. Obviously, the staff:child ratio would have to be increased in a group where there are children who come occasionally, as these toddlers would have special needs. Otherwise, all children could be disadvantaged.

Offering occasional care completely separately has the advantage of providing some focus for planning. It may be easier to control group size to take into account the presence of new children who may need extra attention. The disadvantage is of course that the group composition is never stable and is somewhat unpredictable in size and age range. There may be several children settling in at the same time, and with toddlers, distress creates distress.

Although family day care is beyond the scope of this book, it is worth noting that the provision of occasional care for toddlers in a family day care setting alleviates many of the problems alluded to above and can meet the necessary conditions cited above for quality occasional care for this age group.

# Conclusion

Some readers will have found that much of the information contained in the preceding pages is familiar to them, and that it reflects what they are already doing with toddlers. If so, that is excellent, and it is hoped that by recognizing their own beliefs and practices, they feel renewed, supported, and inspired to continue to seek better ways to care for this age group. There is a great need for those people who care for under three year olds to support one another, to encourage good practices, and to demonstrate to their colleagues as well as to the wider community the complexity and creativity of their work.

Caring for babies and toddlers still suffers from the image in some places that "anyone can do it". While evidence mounts up about the importance of the very early years of life, caregivers of under three year olds often suffer from being afforded lower status than their colleagues who work with three to five year olds. Pre-service training courses tend to focus more heavily on the over three year olds, at least in part because in general more people teaching in those courses have had experience with the older age group. There are fewer programs of high quality for toddlers than for over threes. Consequently, this situation does not enable many students to see and learn from exciting, rich, appropriate programs for this age group. As a result, a number of child care workers express a preference for the older children, and so it goes.

It is this author's firm conviction that caring well for one to three year olds is more challenging, demanding, and complex than is doing an excellent job with over threes. It is the author's hope that the preceding pages confirm this conviction and engender in workers and potential workers an enthusiasm and excitement for working with toddlers.

# Appendix

# Explanation of Terms

**Industrial awards** are agreements between unions and employers which are registered in industrial courts. Once registered, the agreement is legally binding on both the union and the employers named in the award. Because Australia has a Federal system of government, it has both State and Federal levels of government. The industrial system also has these two tiers, with State and Federal industrial courts. Awards which are registered in the Federal industrial court are referred to as **Federal awards.**

Usually awards come about through the efforts of a union to obtain desired pay and working conditions for members. Sometimes unions and employers reach agreements on the terms of an award through negotiations outside the industrial court. When this occurs the award is registered as a *consent award*. Frequently, agreement on all the terms sought by the union cannot be reached through negotiations alone. Disputes are given to the industrial court to decide. Awards in which some or all of the terms have been settled in this way are registered as *arbitrated awards*. Although unions create awards to protect their own members, all workers mentioned in the award, whether union members or not, are included in the award coverage.

The sorts of things that can be included in awards, besides rates of pay, are agreements about meal and coffee breaks (**award breaks**), sick leave, maternity leave, standard working hours, and the like. Industry specific conditions can also be included. In child care awards, a set amount of preparation time when workers are free to leave the classroom might be such a condition which could be specified in an award.

At present, unions tend to have coverage of workers on the basis of skills, rather than the workplace. So, in child care, one union might cover teachers, another union might cover nurses, and a third union might cover most of the rest of the workers in a center. Each of these groups would come under a different award. Nurses working in child care, for example, might have the same award as nurses working in doctors offices and in private hospitals. Early childhood educators, whose teacher training would enable them to work in the younger end of elementary school as well as in preschool (3-4 year olds) and child care programs (where they usually work with 3-4 year olds), would often have the same award as teachers in elementary and high schools. Staff specifically trained to work in child care usually have two years of technical training, and are most commonly covered by Federal awards.

### Management Committees

Child care services sponsored by community groups usually have **management committees** whose task is to oversee the management of the program. These committees are normally made up of members of the sponsoring organization, who take up the positions on the committee in a volunteer capacity.

Management committees work in different ways, but most often take responsibility for policy development, financial management, and hiring of the center director. In many community based child care programs, the parents using the service form all or part of the management committee.

**The Miscellaneous Workers' Union (FMWU)** usually covers untrained child care assistants and cooks, cleaners and gardeners who may work in child care centers. Frequently, no union covers administrative staff within a center. Each State and Territory has a different set of industrial awards, so it is not possible to make general statements about child care awards in Australia. The range of awards which cover workers in children's services are referred to collectively as **children's services awards.**

172

# Other Redleaf Press Publications

*Basic Guide to Family Day Care Record Keeping* — Clear instructions on keeping necessary family day care business records.

*Calendar-Keeper* — Activities, family day care record keeping, recipes and more. Updated annually. Most popular publication in the field.

*Child Care Resource & Referral Counselors & Trainers Manual* — Both a ready reference for the busy phone counselor and a training guide for resource and referral agencies.

*Developing Roots & Wings: A Trainer's Guide to Affirming Culture In Early Childhood Programs* — The training guide for Roots & Wings, with 11 complete sessions and over 170 training activities.

*The Dynamic Infant* — Combines an overview of child development with innovative movement and sensory experiences for infants and toddlers.

*Family Day Caring magazine* — The best source of information on every aspect of home-based child care.

*Family Day Care Tax Workbook* — Updated every year, latest step-by-step information on forms, depreciation, etc.

*Kids Encyclopedia of Things to Make and Do* — Nearly 2,000 art and craft projects for children aged 4-10.

*The (No Leftovers!) Child Care Cookbook* — Over 80 child-tested recipes and 20 menus suitable for family child care providers and center programs. CACFP creditable.

*Pathways to Play* — Help children improve their play skills with a skill checklist and planned activities.

*Practical Solutions to Practically Every Problem: The Early Childhood Teacher's Manual* — Easy-to-use handbook covers the gamut of problems early childhood teachers encounter, and offers effective solutions.

*Roots & Wings: Affirming Culture in Early Childhood Programs* — A new approach to multicultural education that helps shape positive attitudes toward cultural differences.

*Sharing in the Caring* — Packets with family day care parent brochure, contracts and hints.

*Staff Orientation in Early Childhood Programs* — Complete manual for orienting new staff on all program areas.

*Survival Kit for Early Childhood Directors* — Solutions, implementation steps and results to handling difficulties with children, staff, parents.

*Teachables from Trashables* — Step-by-step guide to making over 50 fun toys from recycled household junk.

*Teachables II* — Similar to *Teachables From Trashables*; with another 75-plus toys.

*Those Mean Nasty Dirty Downright Disgusting but… Invisible Germs* — A delightful story that reinforces for children the benefits of frequent hand washing.

## CALL FOR CATALOG OR ORDERING INFORMATION
## 1-800-423-8309